HAPPY NORDIC KNITS

MODERN STRANDED-COLORWORK DESIGNS FROM THE HEART OF SCANDINAVIA

Une Cecilie Oksvold

QUARRY

Quarto.com

© 2025 Quarto Publishing Group USA Inc.
Text © 2025 Une Cecilie Oksvold. Published in agreement with NORTHERN STORIES. (All rights reserved)

First Published in 2025 by Quarry Books, an imprint of
The Quarto Group, 100 Cummings Center, Suite 265-D,
Beverly, MA 01915, USA.
T (978) 282-9590 F (978) 283-2742

EEA Representation, WTS Tax d.o.o.,
Žanova ulica 3, 4000 Kranj, Slovenia.
www.wts-tax.si

All rights reserved. No part of this book may be reproduced in any form without written permission of the copyright owners. All images in this book have been reproduced with the knowledge and prior consent of the artists concerned, and no responsibility is accepted by producer, publisher, or printer for any infringement of copyright or otherwise, arising from the contents of this publication. Every effort has been made to ensure that credits accurately comply with information supplied. We apologize for any inaccuracies that may have occurred and will resolve inaccurate or missing information in a subsequent reprinting of the book.

Quarry Books titles are also available at discount for retail, wholesale, promotional, and bulk purchase. For details, contact the Special Sales Manager by email at specialsales@quarto.com or by mail at The Quarto Group, Attn: Special Sales Manager, 100 Cummings Center, Suite 265-D, Beverly, MA 01915, USA.

10 9 8 7 6 5 4 3 2 1

ISBN: 978-0-7603-9681-0

Digital edition published in 2025
eISBN: 978-0-7603-9682-7

Library of Congress Cataloging-in-Publication Data available

Design: Kelley Galbreath
Layout and cover: Hanne Løvdal/Lovedales Studio
Photographer: Harald Wanvik

Printed in Guangdong, China TT 052025

*For Grandma Margot,
Grandma Randi, and
Great-grandma Hallfrid*

Creating something by myself using my own hands brings me so much joy. And knitting with colorful yarns always brightens my mood on dark days.

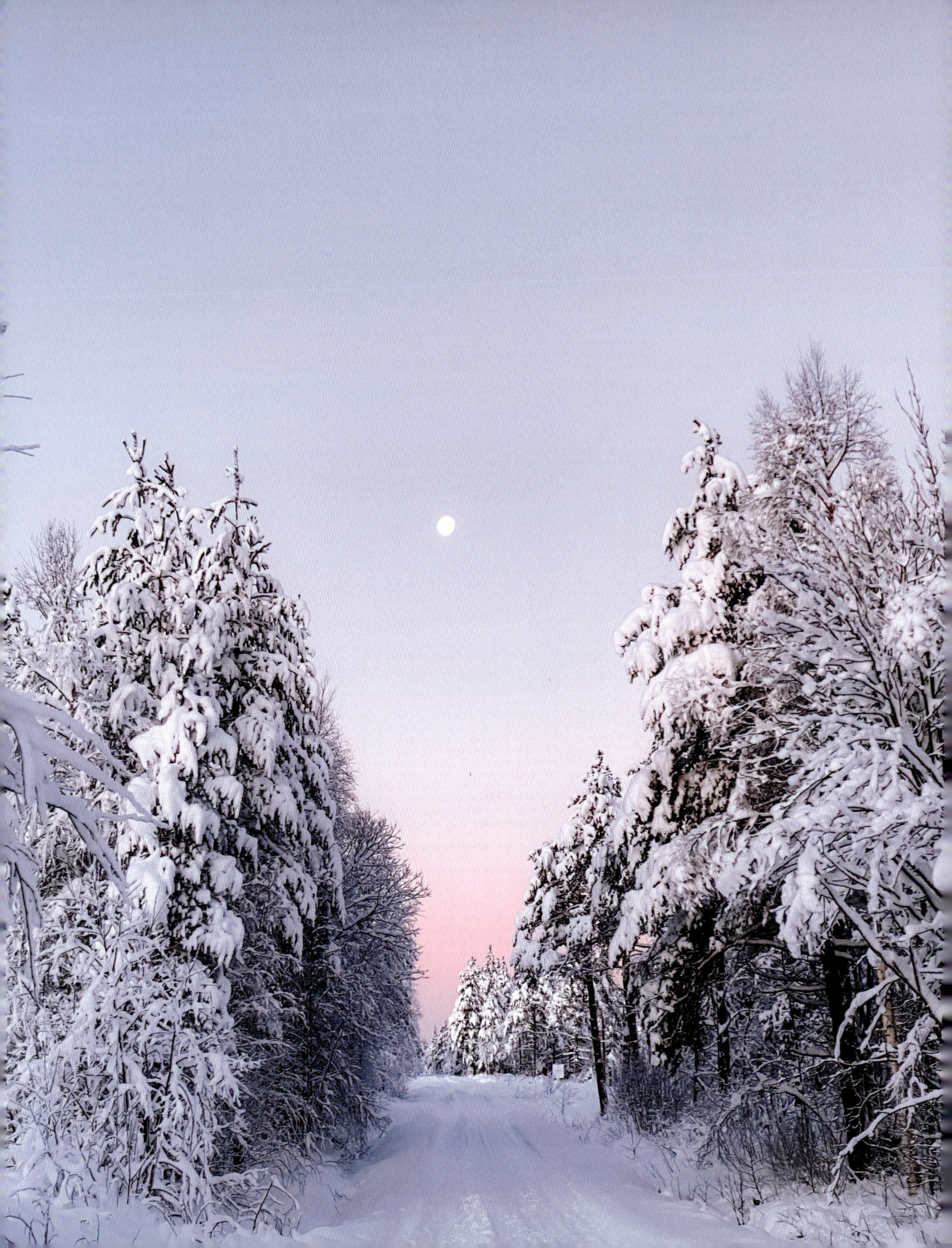

CONTENTS

Introduction: Hi! 7
A Creative Boost Against Mentally Cloudy Days 8
How to Use This Book 11

Patterns 13

Yrjar Sweater 15
Blossom Sweater 23
Frostbite Sweater 31
Frostbite Mittens 41
Sleeping Bag Slippers 44
Lucie Oversized Sweater 48
Mountain Sweater 59
Mountain Mittens 69
Maddis Sweater 74
Bitter Cold Balaclava 84
Bitter Cold Neck Warmer 92
Bitter Cold Headband 94
Bitter Cold Mittens 96
Lofoten Folk Sweater 99
Lofoten Folk Sitting Pad 110
Leif Sweater 113
Une Sweater 123
Reading Socks 131

Zero-Waste Projects 135

Worsted-Weight Scrap Sweater 138
Bulky-Weight Scrap Sweater 145
Huv Hat 151
Felted Insoles 155
Neck Warmer 159

Techniques 163

Gauge 164
Colorwork Tips 167
Stitches 169
Decreasing Technique 173
Bind-Off Technique 173
Assembling 174
Size Guide 176
Felting Guide 179
Washing and Maintenance 182

Afterword 187
Acknowledgments 188
Index 191

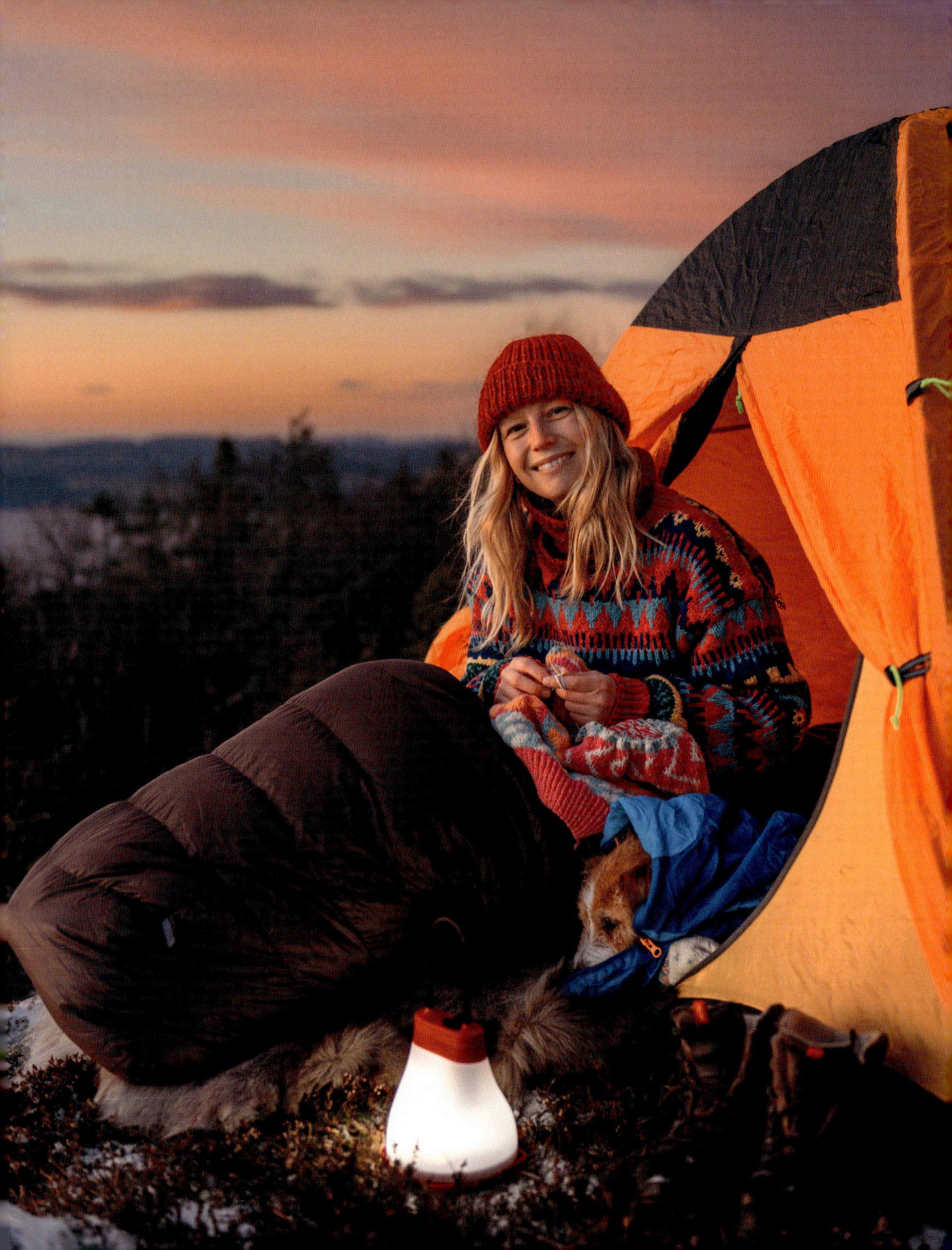

Hi!

My name is Une Cecilie. Since 2016 I have worked to make the outdoor lifestyle more popular and to tell people how therapeutic it can be for our mental health to live outside. I call myself an outdoor-living newbie who got a prescription for nature. I give talks and lectures, manage social media, and write books on the subject. I adore short weekend trips and love adventures nearby. And when I am on one of my adventures, I prefer wearing colorful knits made in delicious, warm Norwegian wool.

I wrote the books *Friluftsfersking* (*Outdoor-Living Newbie*) and *Turdagboka* (*Diary from a Trip*) to inspire and help other people get out there and live the outdoor life. It's an obvious next step to follow up with a book filled with warm, colorful outdoor clothing to help you truly enjoy being outdoors and exploring nature, no matter the weather.

If you would like to follow along and learn more about my universe, I share my own mental health and outdoor-living journey along with my knitting tips and tricks on Instagram @unececilie. And on www.unececilie.no you can find my e-books, lecture, and patterns.

Did you know that colors can give us feelings of calm, pride, joy, relief, hope, and love?

A Creative Boost Against Mentally Cloudy Days

Ever since I was a little girl, I have carried two things with me. One is anxiety. The other is creativity and the joy of making something from nothing using just a couple of sticks and a skein of yarn. I was only six when I had my first anxiety attack. To my despair, this unwelcome guest would visit me night after night throughout my childhood. I was so afraid of the horrible feeling that would come and take over. Sweat would bead on my forehead, even though I was cold and had chills all over my body. My stomach burned, I couldn't breathe, and I struggled to keep the nausea at bay. The fear that anxiety could strike at any moment was so strong, I became very attached to my mom and dad. I was afraid to do much outside the house, and I was always on guard, prepared for another panic attack. When, at eight, I learned to knit, it gave me a creative boost and a wonderful sense of accomplishment. It became a form of therapy that I could engage in safely without having to leave the four walls of my home.

At 24, I discovered the mental break nature can give and I became an outdoor-living newbie. As the outdoors became a sanctuary for me, my knitting habits changed. I suddenly needed more warm, functional, and practical outdoor clothing. With a lot of help from my sister and knitting teacher Stine, we created some of the absolute favorites in my outdoor-living wardrobe. In writing this book, I have received invaluable assistance from her as a technical designer, turning my creative designs into reality. Without her, this book wouldn't have come to life. Go and check out @stineoksvold on Instagram for knitting courses, patterns, and lots of creative inspiration.

I have continued to carry both my mental baggage and the joy of knitting into adulthood. During the toughest times, there is almost nothing that feels as good as coming inside from a hike in the woods, curling up under a warm blanket, and picking up the knitting needles. Creating something entirely my own with my own hands brings me so much joy, and knitting with colors always lifts my spirits on mentally cloudy days.

In this book I want to share my joy with you, so you also can find a sanctuary in your creative corner when you need it. I have chosen to openly share my life and my journey throughout the designs and the patterns, both because it feels natural to do so and because I hope that you, too, will find hope and inspiration in my story.

Most of all, I hope that the garments in this book will accompany you on new adventures into nature and help create memories for life!

Happy knitting-joy hugs,

Une Cecilie

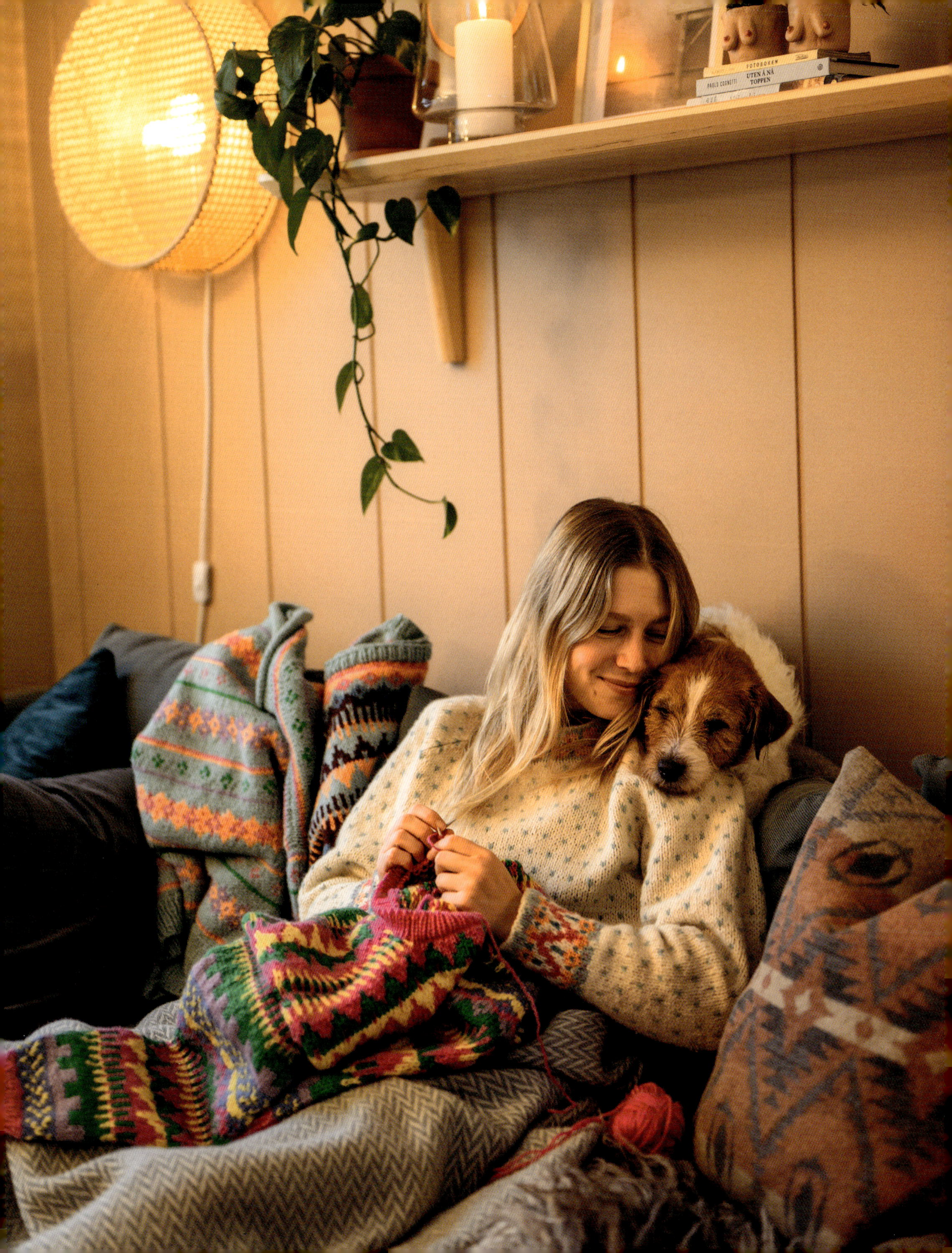
FOTOBOKEN
PAOLO COGNETTI
UTEN Å NÅ TOPPEN

The patterns
in this book feature yarns
made in Norway. Substitute
yarns as needed from your stash
or local yarn store, just take care
to check your gauge.

To convert measurements
from imperial to metric,
multiply by 2.54.

How to Use This Book

This book is divided into three parts: the first is patterns for colorful outdoor clothes, the second features zero-waste projects, and the third is a handy glossary of techniques.

For the pattern section with colorful outdoor garments and accessories, I have created designs inspired by my life and my story. These garments represent everything I have been through and are the result of a lot of personal growth, learning, and intense experiences. I have used different types of yarn and techniques in these designs, resulting in garments suitable to be worn on the coldest winter days and others ready for the rest of the year.

Many of my designs feature allover patterns and have a quite bold look, while others are calmer and more muted. The garments use a variety of techniques, so even beginning knitters can make several of the designs without complicated and advanced finishing.

The names of the designs reflect the stories behind them. Several of the patterns are named for something or someone that has been important in my life—be it a person, a place, or a cabin. Before each pattern, you'll get a glimpse into the story behind the design. I hope these stories bring you both inspiration and joy, just like the knitting itself.

In the second section of the book, I have gathered projects that help you use up your colorful leftover yarns. Zero-waste projects use up all the yarn remnants we are often left with after finishing larger knitting projects. Projects for yarn remnants aren't just useful, they are a creative puzzle to solve when you need to use what you have on hand. Only your imagination sets the limits!

The technical glossary in the last section provides you with the information you need to achieve the best possible garment. This section works as a reference guide to use throughout your knitting journey. If you're a beginner, I recommend reviewing the section on knitting gauge before starting with the patterns. You will also find useful information on how to care for your garments so they last as long as possible. There's even a dedicated felting guide, which is incredibly useful if you plan to make one of the felted outdoor accessories in the book.

Some of the projects are traditional, others more creative, and I love every one of them. Enjoy!

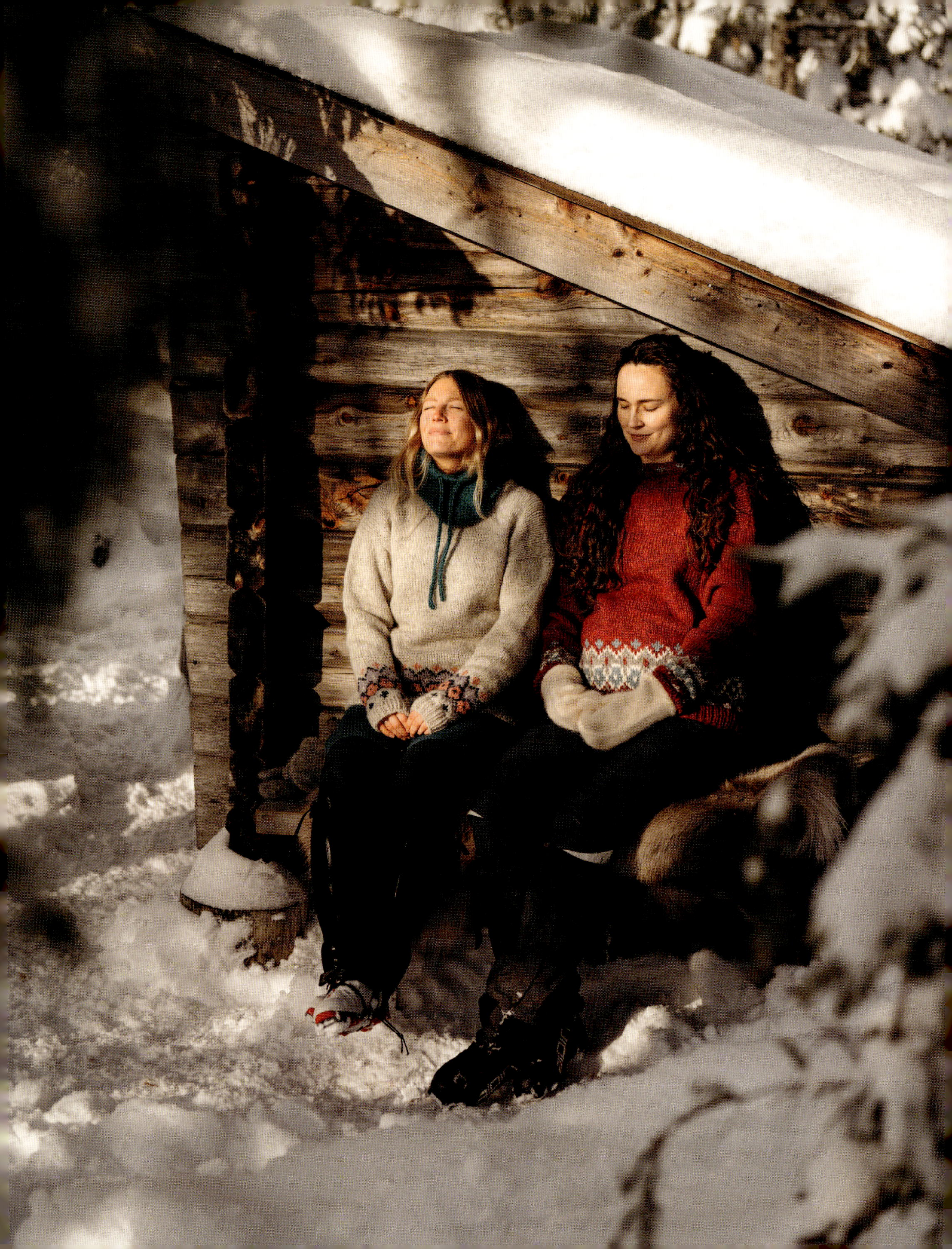

PATTERNS

These designs were inspired by different parts of my life and my journey. My goal has always been to break taboos and show that life is more than the perfect pictures that most people share. Life can take many unexpected turns. Sometimes it hits us hard. And that is how it's supposed to be. Because if everything was picture perfect, we would never grow, learn, or enhance our experiences as individuals.

Those who have followed me for some time on social media or read my book *Friluftsfersking* (*Outdoor-Living Newbie*), know that I have been open and sometimes brutally honest about how the mind can darken, the body can give up, and life can feel impossible.

But it's not impossible.

I am living proof of that. Even in my darkest moments, there have been small glimmers of light that have pulled me forward. In these designs, I've tried to capture the essence of those glimpses—moments large and small that have brought me joy, a sense of accomplishment, hope, and meaning. Some come from a cherished memory, others from life-changing experiences.

I hope some of them touch your heart.

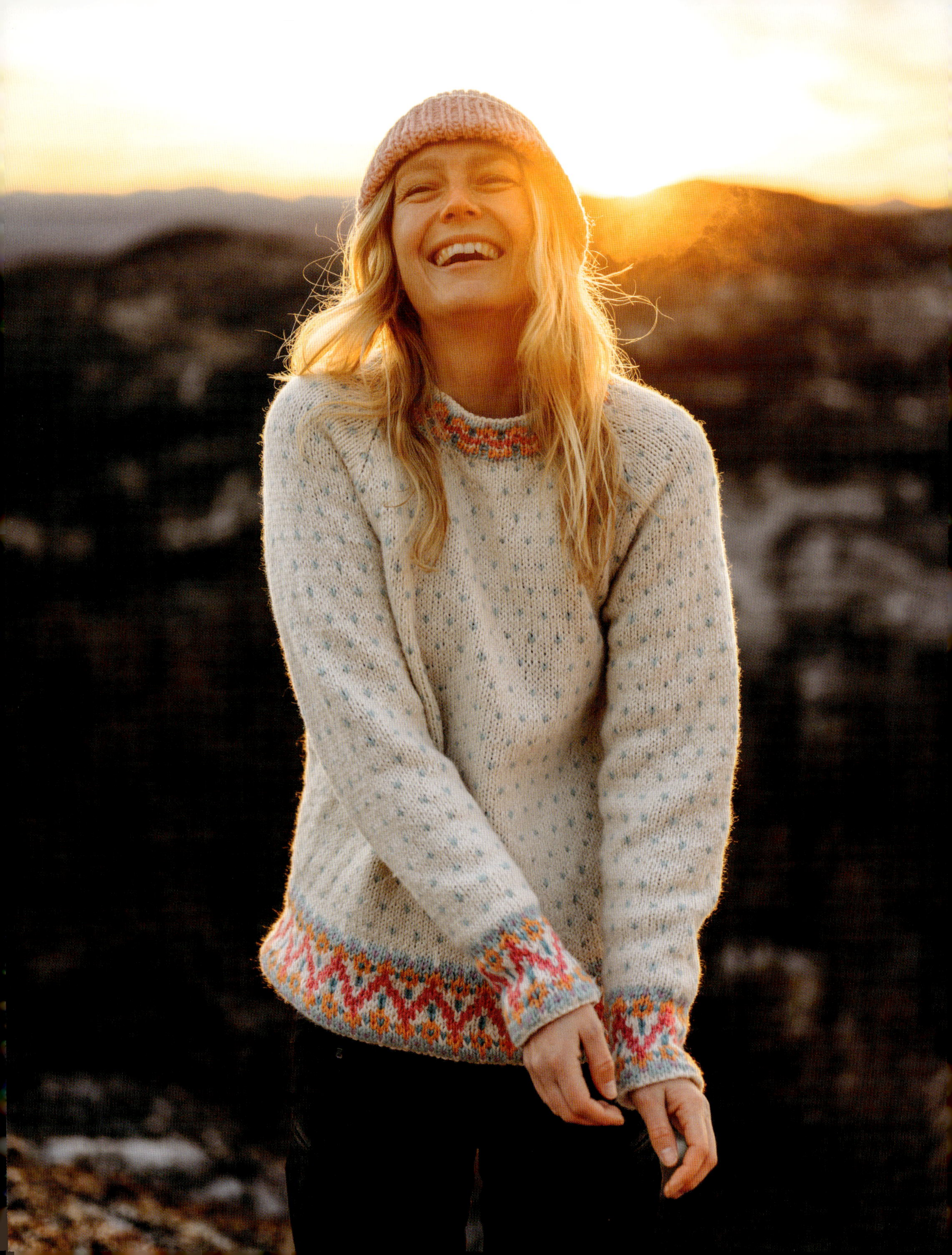

Yrjar Sweater

Ever since I was a small child, anxiety has been a constant part of my life. Thirty years ago, when I was growing up, people didn't talk much about mental health. We didn't know that my struggles with fear, nausea, and panic were related to a diagnosis. When I was six years old, my parents took me to a doctor who ordered a lot of tests that showed that I was completely healthy. So I was sent home, believing that this was just how life was supposed to be—filled with fear and unease. I thought everyone else felt the same way and that it was completely normal. I didn't know any better.

Not until I was depressed and entered the healthcare system again at 19 did I find out what was behind my limitations in life. I was diagnosed with generalized anxiety disorder and recurrent depression.

When I first shared my story about having anxiety since childhood, many people were surprised. They hadn't seen it in me and couldn't understand it. Some thought something must have happened at home, that I had an unstable upbringing. But that's miles from the truth. My childhood was warm, safe, and truly exceptional.

I grew up in the safest little street in Brekstad in the early 1990s, where we kids could run between houses and play freely together in complete safety. It was almost like we had our own little *The Children of Noisy Village* universe. There were no mobile phones, no social media. Just play, mischief, laughter, and, of course, some arguments now and then. We were a big group of adults and kids who had so much fun together. We played, grilled, had games and competitions, built bonfires by the river, and listened to very loud Norwegian rock music.

Every now and then, we'd also go on a holiday ski trip to the mountains, and there would be idyllic vibes, sunshine, and hot dogs cooked over the bonfire. At that time, outdoor life wasn't my biggest passion. Actually, I didn't like it at all. But there was still something about the atmosphere at Yrjarhytta, as the area is called, that made the experience enjoyable, despite wet clothes and my lack of skiing experience.

When I think back on that time, I feel the deep sense of security I had with my parents and the certainty that I belonged in the group, a wonderful mix of children and adults.

The Yrjar Sweater is inspired by this period of my life. By my mom sitting in the sun with sunglasses that were far too small, trying to keep the fire going. By my dad building ski ramps with the other dads. And by the sweaters they wore back then. It's almost as if I can still smell the bonfire and see the happy faces of the adults as we kids tumbled down the hill in soaking wet clothes. It is a fantastic childhood memory.

In Yrjar, only a small amount of yarn is required for most of the pattern colors. The actual yarn amount is specified, allowing you to use yarn left over from other projects.

Sizes
XXS, XS (S, M, L, XL) (2X, 3X, 4X, 5X)

Garment Measurements
This sweater is designed to have approximately 6" (15 cm) of positive ease.
Bust: 36½, 38½ (40¼, 43¾, 45¾, 47¼) (48¾, 52¼, 56, 61½)"
Total length: 22½, 23 (23½, 24¾, 25½, 26½) (27¼, 27½, 28, 28¼)" or desired length
Sleeve length: 19, 19 (19¾, 20, 20½, 21¼) (21¾, 21¾, 22, 22)" or desired length

Yarn
Hillesvåg Luna (100 % Norwegian wool: 220 yd [200 m]/100 g) or
Rauma Fivel (100% Norwegian wool: 110 yd [100 m]/50 g) or
Hillesvåg Varde (100% Norwegian wool: 220 yd [200 m]/100 g)

Actual Yarn Amounts
Color 1: 350, 365 (390, 415, 435, 450) (470, 510, 540, 590) g
Color 2: 40, 42 (44, 48, 50, 52) (54, 58, 61, 66) g
Color 3: 22, 23 (24, 26, 27, 28) (29, 31, 33, 36) g
Color 4: 21, 22 (23, 24, 26, 27) (28, 30, 32, 35) g
Color 5: 6, 6 (7, 7, 8, 8) (8, 9, 9, 10) g
Color 6: 3, 3 (4, 4, 4, 4) (4, 5, 5, 5) g

Needles
US size 7: 16" and 32" circulars and set of double-pointed needles.
Adjust needle size as necessary to obtain gauge.

Gauge
18 stitches × 24 rows in stockinette st = 4 × 4"

Tip: If you knit more loosely or tightly over the colorwork section, you'll need to adjust your needle size to ensure it doesn't become too loose or too tight.

How to Knit this Sweater

You will knit the body and the sleeves in the round from the bottom up to the armholes. You'll join these pieces and decrease for the raglan yoke up to the collar.

Body

Knit the folded hem as follows: Cast on 168, 176 (184, 200, 208, 216) (224, 240, 256, 280) stitches on US size 7 circular needle with color 1, place marker to mark the start of the round, and knit in stockinette stitch for 20 rounds. Purl 1 round.

Knit the pattern following Chart 1 as follows: Beginning with stitch 8, 6 (4, 8, 6, 4) (2, 6, 2, 4) of each chart round, knit to stitch 8, then repeat stitches 1-8 to last 7, 5 (3, 7, 5, 3) (1, 5, 1, 3) stitches, then work stitches 1-7, 5 (3, 7, 5, 3) (1, 5, 1, 3).

Knit the chart from round 1 to 30. Then repeat rounds 21 to 30 until the piece measures 15¾, 16¼ (16½, 17¼, 17¼, 17¾) (18, 18, 17¾, 17¾)" or to the desired length from the purl round. Note which round of chart was worked last.

On the next round, bind off for the armholes as follows: Bind off the first 4, 4 (5, 5, 6, 6) (7, 8, 9, 9) stitches of the round. Knit the next 75, 79 (81, 89, 91, 95) (97, 103, 109, 121) stitches in established pattern for front. Bind off the next 8, 8 (10, 10, 12, 12) (14, 16, 18, 18) stitches. Continue in established pattern until 4, 4 (5, 5, 6, 6) (7, 8, 9, 9) stitches remain on the round, then bind these off. Set the work aside and knit the sleeves separately.

Sleeves

Knit a folded hem as follows: Cast on 41, 43 (43, 45, 47, 49) (51, 53, 55, 57) stitches on US size 7 double-pointed needles and knit in stockinette stitch for 4 rounds. On the next round, decrease 2 stitches as follows: Knit the first stitch, knit 2 together, knit until 3 stitches remain, knit 2 stitches together through back loop, knit the last stitch. Continue decreasing this way every 5th round 3 more times. You now have 33, 35 (35, 37, 39, 41) (43, 45, 47, 49) stitches on the needle and have knitted a total of 20 rounds. Purl 1 round.

Knit the pattern following Chart 1 as follows: Beginning with stitch 1, 8 (8, 7, 6, 5) (4, 3, 2, 1) of each chart round, knit to stitch 8, then repeat stitches 1-8 to last 0, 7 (7, 6, 5, 4) (3, 2, 1, 0) stitches, then work stitches 0, 1-7 (1-7, 1-6, 1-5, 1-4) (1-3, 1-2, 1, 0). Knit the chart from round 1 to 30. Then repeat rounds 21 to 30.

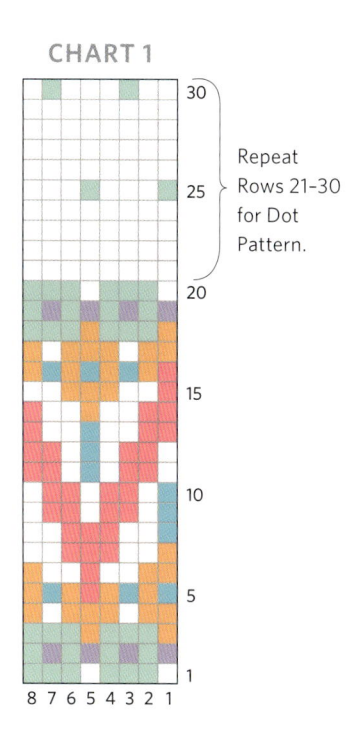

At the same time, on round 5 of the chart, increase 2 stitches as follows: Knit the first stitch, pick up the strand between stitches front to back with the left needle, and knit it through the back loop. Knit the pattern until 1 stitch remains, pick up the strand between stitches from back to front with the left needle and knit it. The increased stitches are knitted as an extension of the pattern. Repeat the increase in the same way on rounds 10, 15, and 20 of the chart. You now have 41, 43 (43, 45, 47, 49) (51, 53, 55, 57) stitches on the needle.

CHART 1

Repeat Rows 21-30 for Dot Pattern.

From here, continue increasing every 1, 1 (1, ¾, ¾, ¾) (¾, ¾, ¾, ¾)" until you have 65, 67 (71, 77, 81, 83) (87, 93, 99, 105) stitches on the needle. Continue knitting in pattern until the sleeve measures 19, 19 (19¾, 20, 20½, 21¼) (21¾, 21¾, 22, 22)" or your desired length, ending with same round of chart as for body.

Bind off for the armhole as follows: Bind off the first 4, 4 (5, 5, 6, 6) (7, 8, 9, 9) stitches of the round. Knit until 4, 4 (5, 5, 6, 6) (7, 8, 9, 9) stitches remain on the round and bind these off. You now have 57, 59 (61, 67, 69, 71) (73, 77, 81, 87) stitches remaining on the needle.

Knit 1 more sleeve in the same way.

Raglan

You will now knit the stitches from the body and sleeves onto the same needle, while placing 4 markers for the raglan as follows: Working next round of chart pattern, knit all the stitches from one sleeve onto the needle. Place a marker. Continuing in chart pattern, knit all the stitches from the front of the body to the armhole. Place a marker. Knit all the stitches from the second sleeve onto the needle. Place a marker. Knit all the stitches from the back of the body to the end. Place a marker for the beginning of the round. You now have a total of 266, 278 (286, 314, 322, 334) (342, 362, 382, 418) stitches on the needles.

Color 1: Luna, unbleached white 400

Color 2: Luna, mint green 444

Color 3: Luna, light orange 428

Color 4: Luna, rose 447

Color 5: Luna, light teal 435

Color 6: Fivel, lavender 05

CHART 2

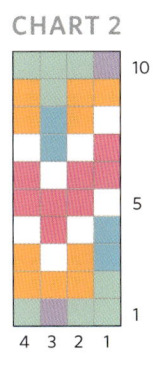

On the next round, you will decrease for the raglan as follows: Knit the first 2 stitches of the round together with color 1. Knit until 2 stitches before the next marker. Then, do a SSK (slip, slip, knit) with color 1 (see page 173). Knit the 2 stitches after the marker together with color 1. Repeat this raglan decrease in the same way at the next 2 markers, doing a SSK before the marker and knitting 2 stitches together after the marker. All decreases are done using color 1. Continue knitting until 2 stitches remain at the end of the round and do a SSK with color 1.

You have now decreased by 8 stitches and have 258, 270 (278, 306, 314, 326) (334, 354, 374, 410) stitches left. Knit the next round without decreasing.

Continue doing the raglan decreases in this way on every other round until you have decreased a total of 16, 16 (17, 19, 21, 22) (23, 25, 27, 28) times.

You will now have 138, 150 (150, 162, 154, 158) (158, 162, 166, 194) stitches left on the needle.

On the next round, you will bind off the 25, 25 (27, 27, 29, 29) (31, 31, 33, 33) stitches at center front as follows: Knit the first 34, 38 (37, 41, 37, 38) (38, 38, 38, 47) stitches in established pattern. Bind off the next 25, 25 (27, 27, 29, 29) (31, 31, 33, 33) stitches. Knit to the end of the round. Cut the yarn. You now have 113, 125 (123, 135, 125, 129) (127, 131, 133, 161) stitches remaining on the needle.

Continue knitting stockinette stitch back and forth in established chart pattern, while shaping front neck at both sides. Continue raglan decreases as usual on every other row. Start at the right front with the right side of the sweater facing. Bind off the first 3 stitches on the needle. Knit to the end of the row. Turn, and bind off the first 3 stitches on the needle. Purl to the end of the row. Continue knitting back and forth in the same way, binding off 2 stitches at the beginning of the following 2 rows, then binding off 1 stitch at the beginning of the following 4 rows. End with a purl row, so that the next row is on the right side. You have now decreased 7 stitches on each side and have 71, 79 (79, 89, 81, 83) (83, 85, 87, 115) stitches remaining on the needle.

Neckline

Knit all the stitches on the needle with color 1. Continuing around the neckline, pick up and knit 1 stitch for each bound-off stitch to the start of the round. Cut the yarn and move the start of the round to the middle of the back of the sweater. Place a marker. You now have 110, 118 (120, 130, 124, 126) (128, 130, 134, 162) stitches on the needle.

On the next round, decrease 34, 42 (40, 50, 40, 42) (40, 42, 42, 70) stitches evenly as follows:

XXS:
Knit 2, knit 2 together, knit 2, knit 2 together.
Knit 1, knit 2 together. Repeat from * to * 7 times.
Knit 2, knit 2 together, knit 2, knit 2 together.
Knit 1, knit 2 together. Repeat from * to * 6 times.
Knit 2, knit 2 together, knit 2, knit 2 together.
Knit 1, knit 2 together. Repeat from * to * 7 times.
Knit 2, knit 2 together, knit 2, knit 2 together.
Knit 1, knit 2 together. Repeat from * to * 6 times.

XS:
Knit 2 together, knit 2 together.
Knit 1, knit 2 together. Repeat from * to * 8 times.
Knit 2 together, knit 2 together.
Knit 1, knit 2 together. Repeat from * to * 9 times.
Knit 2 together, knit 2 together.
Knit 1, knit 2 together. Repeat from * to * 8 times.
Knit 2 together, knit 2 together.
Knit 1, knit 2 together. Repeat from * to * 9 times.

S:
Knit 1, knit 2 together. Repeat from * to * 40 times.

M:
Knit 1, knit 2 together. Repeat from * to * 5 times.
Knit 1, knit 2 together, knit 2 together. Repeat from * to * 20 times.

Knit 1, knit 2 together. Repeat from * to * 5 times.

L:
Knit 2, knit 2 together, knit 2, knit 2 together.
Knit 1, knit 2 together. Repeat from * to * 36 times.
Knit 2, knit 2 together, knit 2, knit 2 together.

XL:
Knit 1, knit 2 together. Repeat from * to * 42 times.

2XL:
Knit 2, knit 2 together. Repeat from * to * 4 times.
Knit 1, knit 2 together. Repeat from * to * 16 times.
Knit 2, knit 2 together. Repeat from * to * 4 times.
Knit 1, knit 2 together. Repeat from * to * 16 times.

3XL:
Knit 2, knit 2 together, knit 2, knit 2 together.
Knit 1, knit 2 together. Repeat from * to * 38 times.
Knit 2, knit 2 together, knit 2, knit 2 together.

4XL:
Knit 2, knit 2 together, knit 2, knit 2 together.
Knit 1, knit 2 together. Repeat from * to * 8 times.
Knit 2, knit 2 together, knit 2, knit 2 together.
Knit 1, knit 2 together. Repeat from * to * 9 times.

Knit 2, knit 2 together, knit 2, knit 2 together.
Knit 2 together, knit 2 together.
Knit 1, knit 2 together, knit 2 together, knit 2 together. Repeat from * to * 11 times.
Knit 2 together, knit 2 together.
Knit 1, knit 2 together, knit 2 together, knit 2 together. Repeat from * to * 11 times.

5XL:
Knit 2 together, knit 2 together.
Knit 1, knit 2 together, knit 2 together, knit 2 together. Repeat from * to * 11 times.
Knit 2 together, knit 2 together.
Knit 1, knit 2 together, knit 2 together, knit 2 together. Repeat from * to * 11 times.

You now have 76, 76 (80, 80, 84, 84) (88, 88, 92, 92) stitches on the needle. Knit the pattern following Chart 2. Work rounds 1–10 of chart.

Continuing with color 1 only, knit 1 round, then purl 1 round. Knit 10 rounds. Bind off all stitches.

Finishing
Sew the underarm seams. Fold the hems at the body, sleeves, and neckline to the wrong side and stitch them in place with loose stitches. Weave in all loose ends. Block or steam the sweater for a neater finish.

Color 1: Luna, light orange 428
Color 2: Varde, burgundy 2104
Color 3: Luna, mint green 444
Color 4: Luna, petrol 443
Color 5: Luna, rose 447
Color 6: Luna, unbleached white 400

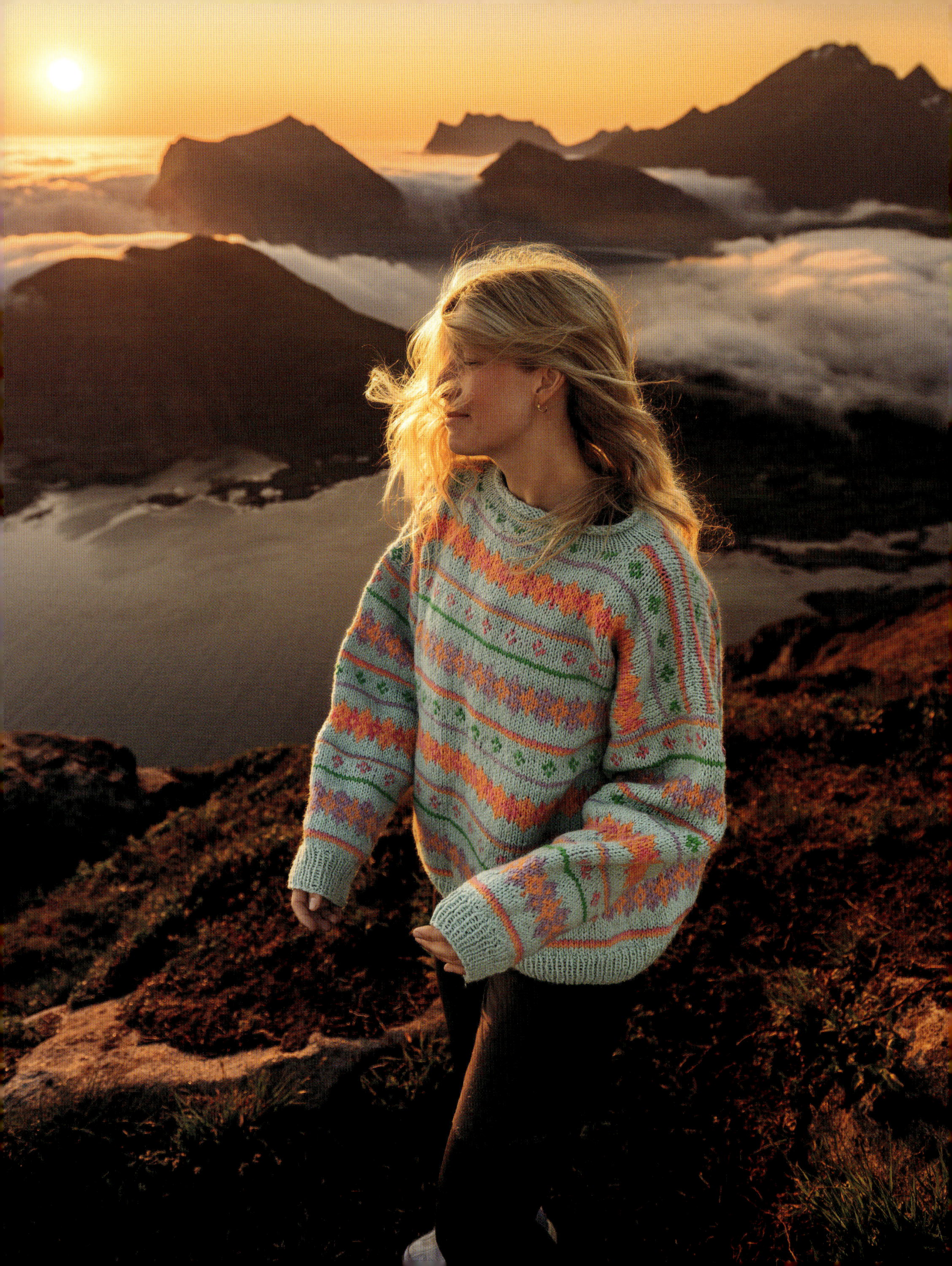

Blossom Sweater

After I was diagnosed with anxiety disorder at the age of nineteen, I had mixed feelings of anger and hope. I was angry because I wished I had known about it earlier, so I could have tackled my challenges sooner. I felt hope, because I now knew what I needed to work on. I started to believe that there were still opportunities out there for me.

I set to work and did everything I could to get better. For a couple of years, I saw a psychologist, which led to a two-week stay in a psychiatric ward.

In that place, I was just one of many. I felt that my problems were being minimized, and that I was a burden to the staff. They rushed around me, eager to get me well as quickly as possible so they could send me back out. It was disheartening. I felt neither seen nor heard in the psychiatric system. Eventually, I realized that this wasn't the right solution for me. Gradually, I turned more towards alternative methods, like healing through holistic therapy, acupuncture, meditation, osteopathy, and tapping. But after countless hours of treatments that didn't lead anywhere, I ended up broke, tired, and frustrated. A student in my early twenties, I couldn't afford to continue expensive treatments. At the same time, I was young and had the romantic idea that, in a few years, I would outgrow these challenges. Perhaps the mental gray clouds were part of growing up and would eventually lift as I got older?

For a while, I stopped all treatments. I ignored the painful feelings I carried and tried to push my problems aside. Even with this poor coping strategy, good things came out of this period. I got my best friend on four legs, Juster, and I met my partner, Harald. But despite all the good things happening, I couldn't keep the darkness inside me at bay. By the spring of 2016, I hit rock bottom, deeper than I ever thought possible.

The bathroom mat became my lifeline as I lay clutching it after yet another panic attack. It was light teal and was soaked with my tears while I lay trembling on the bathroom floor. And so it went, every single afternoon.

I realized it was time to seek help, even though I felt that nothing could pull me out of this darkness. After all, I had tried everything without any luck. Fortunately, I chose to call the doctor's office on a cold April morning when the trees outside the window looked as bare and lifeless as I felt. Gray, naked, and devoid of life. I got an appointment that same day with a doctor I had never met before. At that point, it didn't matter to me who it was as long as someone could be there to catch me in what felt like a free fall off a cliff. Little did I know that this someone would change my life forever.

I entered the doctor's office in a cold sweat, scared and despairing. I was met there by a doctor who, for the first time, saw me truly as I was. The doctor saw something in me that no one else had, and he helped me in an entirely different way. Instead of referring me to therapy or offering me medications to dull the pain, he took the time to talk with me. We had regular meetings every single week, where I sat and cried while he philosophized about life. With a warmth and compassion I had rarely experienced, he asked all the right questions. It was as if he understood exactly how I felt. He read me like an open book and gave me the context I had been missing. Amidst the tears, I tried to grasp everything he was saying, but in the beginning it was difficult. My head felt like it was stuffed with cotton wool, and everything inside was chaos. Until one day, early in May 2016, when he asked me:

But Une, why don't you just take your dog up to the hills, set up a tent, and light a fire?

I thought his suggestion was ridiculous. Other than a few idyllic moments at Yrjarhytta as a child, I strongly disliked outdoor life. I associated it with being wet, cold, tired, and hungry, failing at every part of it. But at the same time, I felt a kind of curiosity stir inside me. I had tried everything else. It couldn't hurt to give this a try, could it?

The next day, I took the tram from downtown to Bymarka in Trondheim. When the tram reached its final stop at Lian, Juster and I hesitantly stepped off. I stood there, wondering what to do, and eventually decided to walk to the water's edge. We sat down and stared out at the lake, which was still covered in ice. Juster became completely quiet, something he rarely was. I tilted my head back and looked up at the sky, which was covered in small, white clouds. Out of nowhere, I felt chills spread throughout my entire body. Soon, the chills were replaced by a warm, euphoric sensation that exploded inside me, filling me with a wonderful warmth and calm. The warmth eventually took up all the space, and the painful knot that had been in my stomach for so many years gave way to a joy that grew bigger and bigger inside me. In that moment, everything felt so incredibly right. Like I had finally come home. Home to the place I had been searching for my whole life. I felt tears roll down my cheeks, but this time, they were tears of joy. For the first time in as long as I could remember, the anxiety released its grip on me. Nature itself had set me free. In that moment, I became a lovestruck, outdoor-living newbie, with nature as my mental sanctuary.

Blossom is inspired by a moment at Lian in May 2016, by the small flowers that come to life in the spring, and by the sanctuary that awakened within me.

Sizes
XXS, XS (S, M, L, XL) (2X, 3X, 4X, 5X)

Garment Measurements
This sweater is designed to have 6–8" of positive ease.
Bust: 38¼, 40½ (43¼, 46, 48½, 52½) (55, 57¾, 60¼, 63)"
Total length: 22½, 22¾ (24, 24¾, 25½, 26½) (27¼, 27½, 28, 28¼)" or desired length
Sleeve length: 17, 17 (17¾, 18, 18½, 19¼) (19¾, 19¾, 20, 20)" or desired length
Note: *The shoulder sits a bit down on the arm and adds to the sleeve length.*

Yarn
Hillesvåg Luna (100 % Norwegian wool: 220 yd [200 m]/100 g) or
Rauma Fivel (100% Norwegian wool: 110 yd [100 m]/50 g)

Actual Yarn Amounts
Color 1: 400, 400 (400, 400, 500, 500) (500, 500, 500, 600) g
Color 2: 100, 100 (100, 100, 100, 200) (200, 200, 200, 200) g
Color 3: 100, 100 (100, 100, 100, 100) (100, 150, 150, 150) g
Color 4: 100 g all sizes
Color 5: 50 g all sizes

Needles
US size 3: 32" circular and set of double-pointed needles
US size 7: 16" and 32" circulars and set of double-pointed needles
Adjust needle sizes as necessary to obtain gauge.

Gauge
18 stitches × 24 rows in stockinette = 4 × 4"

Color 1: Luna, mint green 444
Color 2: Luna, light orange 428
Color 3: Fivel, lavender 05
Color 4: Luna, rose 447
Color 5: Fivel, emerald green 10

How to Knit This Sweater

You will knit the body, yoke, and sleeves from the bottom up to the total length. You will cut steeks for the armholes and sew in the sleeves. You'll knit the neckline last.

Body

Cast on 174, 186 (198, 210, 222, 240) (252, 264, 276, 288) stitches on US size 3 circular needles with color 1. Place a marker to mark the beginning of the round. Work in knit 1, purl 1 ribbing in the round for 2½".

Switch to longer US size 7 needles and knit 1 round with color 1.

Knit the pattern following chart as follows: Beginning with stitch 2, 5 (2, 5, 2, 4) (1, 4, 1, 4) of each chart round, knit to stitch 6, then repeat stitches 1-6 to last 1, 4 (1, 4, 1, 3) (0, 3, 0, 3) stitches, then work stitches 1, 1-4 (1, 1-4, 1, 1-3) (0, 1-3, 0, 1-3).

Repeat rounds 1-54 of chart until the piece measures 11¾, 11¾ (12¾, 13½, 13¾, 14¼) (14½, 14½, 14½, 14½)" or to the desired length.

You will now cast on 5 new stitches on each side for the steeks. These are the stitches that will be cut for armholes later, and they are not included in the total stitch count. You will not knit the pattern over these stitches. Place a marker on each side of the steek stitches as follows:

Knit the first 87, 93 (99, 105, 111, 119) (125, 131, 137, 143) stitches in the established pattern. Place a marker. Cast on 5 new stitches using the main color for the pattern row you are knitting. Place a marker. Continue knitting to the end of the round. Place a marker and cast on 5 new stitches at the end of the round. The steek stitches are now marked on each side.

Continue knitting in pattern as before, but knit the steek stitches either in a solid color or by alternating the colors used for that round for each stitch. Continue working in the established pattern until the piece measures 9½, 9¾ (10, 10¼, 10¾, 11) (11¼, 11¾, 11½, 12)" from the beginning of the steek stitches.

On the next round, you will bind off the center 33, 33 (35, 35, 37, 37) (39, 39, 41, 41) stitches of the front neckline as follows:

Knit the first 27, 30 (32, 35, 37, 41) (43, 46, 48, 51) stitches of the round. Bind off the next 33, 33 (35, 35, 37, 37) (39, 39, 41, 41) stitches. Continue knitting to the end of the round as usual. You now have 141, 153 (163, 175, 185, 203) (213, 225, 235, 247) stitches left on the needle. Cut the yarn.

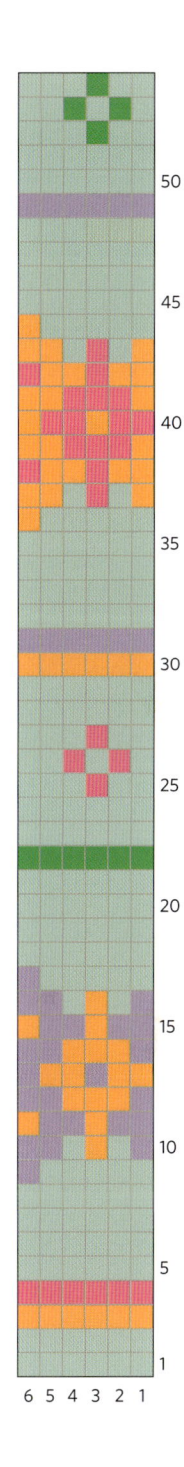

Continue knitting stitch back and forth in established chart pattern, while shaping front neck at both sides as follows: Start at the right front with the right side of the sweater facing. Bind off the first stitch by slipping the first stitch onto the right needle without knitting it. Knit the next stitch, then pass the first stitch over the second stitch and off the needle. Continue working in pattern to the end of the row. Turn the work and bind off the first stitch of the row by slipping the first stitch onto the right needle without knitting it. Purl the next stitch, then pass the first stitch over the second stitch and off the needle. Continue purling in the pattern to the end of the row. Repeat these two rows 1 more time. You have now decreased a total of 4 stitches (2 on each side) and have 137, 149 (159, 171, 181, 199) (209, 221, 231, 243) stitches remaining on the needle.

Knit 2 rows with color 1.

Bind off all stitches.

Sleeves

Cast on 36, 36 (40, 40, 44, 44) (46, 46, 48, 50) stitches on US size 3 double-pointed needles with color 1. Place a marker to mark the beginning of the round. Work in knit 1, purl 1 ribbing in the round for 2".

Switch to US size 7 double-pointed needles and knit 1 round with color 1 while increasing 9 stitches evenly as follows: *Knit 4, 4 (4, 4, 5, 5) (5, 5, 6, 6) stitches, increase 1 stitch, knit 4, 4 (5, 5, 5, 5) (5, 5, 5, 5) stitches, increase 1 stitch*. Repeat from * to * 4 times. End the round by knitting 4, 4 (4, 4, 4, 4) (6, 6, 4, 6) stitches, increase 1 stitch. You now have 45, 45 (49, 49, 53, 53) (55, 55, 57, 59) stitches on the needle.

Knit the pattern following chart as follows: Beginning with stitch 5, 5 (3, 3, 1, 1) (6, 6, 5, 4) of each chart round, knit to stitch 6, then repeat stitches 1–6 to last 4, 4 (2, 2, 0, 0) (5, 5, 4, 3) stitches, then work stitches 1–4, 1–4 (1–2, 1–2, 0, 0) (1–5, 1–5, 1–4, 1–3).

Repeat rounds 1–54 of chart.

At the same time, on round 4 of the chart, increase 2 stitches as follows: Knit the first stitch, pick up the strand between stitches front to back with the left needle, and knit it through the back loop. Knit the pattern until 1 stitch remains, pick up the strand between stitches from back to front with the left needle and knit it. The increased stitches are knitted as an extension of the pattern.

Continue increasing in this manner every ½" until you have 97, 99 (99, 103, 107, 111) (115, 117, 121, 125) stitches on the needle. Continue knitting in pattern until the sleeve measures 17, 17 (17¾, 18, 18½, 19¼) (19¾, 19¾, 20, 20)" or to desired length

Knit 1 round with color 1. Bind off all stitches.

Knit another sleeve in the same way.

Finishing

Sew 2 seams on your sewing machine on each side of the steek stitches and steek the armholes (see page 174). Sew the front shoulder stitches to the back shoulder stitches (see page 169). Sew in the sleeves (see page 175).

Neckline

With shorter US size 7 circular needle and color 1, pick up and knit 70, 70 (74, 74, 76, 76) (78, 78, 80, 80) stitches around the neckline. Knit stockinette stitch in the round for approximately 2½".

Loosely bind off all stitches in knit stitch.

Weave in all loose ends.

Steam or wet block the sweater to finish it.

Color 1: Fivel, emerald green 10
Color 2: Luna, rose 447
Color 3: Fivel, lavender 05
Color 4: Luna, warm yellow 421
Color 5: Luna, orange 422

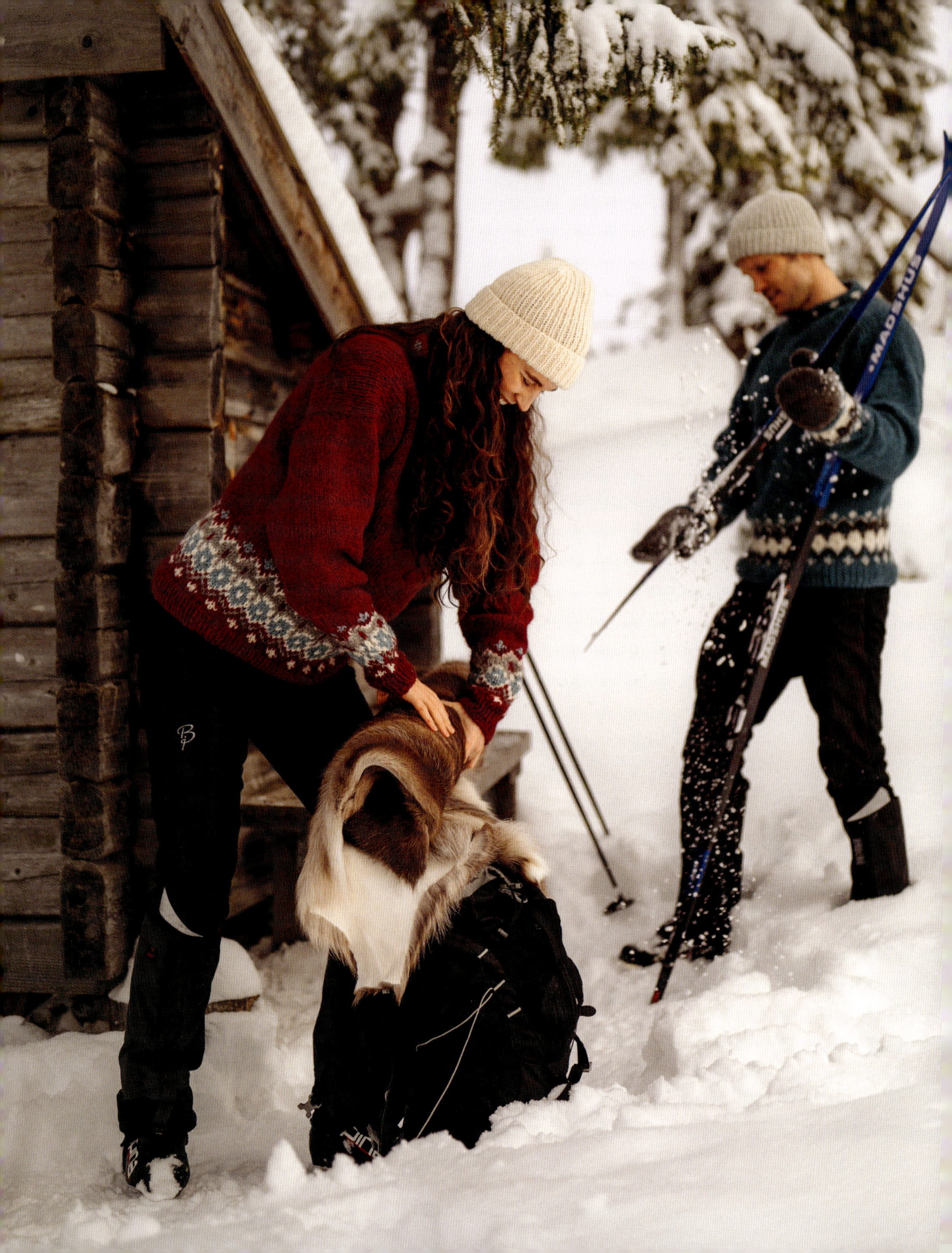
MADSHUS

Frostbite Sweater

After falling head over heels in love with nature, a steep learning curve awaited me as an outdoor newbie. I spent my days wandering the hills, with no other purpose than to be outside. It gave me a sense of calm, presence, joy, and freedom that I had never experienced before. It felt like the missing piece of my life had fallen into place and that this was where I truly belonged. My sanctuary.

But it wasn't always easy being a newbie at outdoor living. I can't count how many times I've gotten lost in the nearby woods, carried way too much gear, forgot gas to cook hot meals, or slept uncomfortably because of a rock under the tent. Yet this journey has been incredibly rewarding, powerful, and meaningful. In all these failed attempts where I lacked knowledge and experience, I learned something new by trial and error. And for someone like me, who is afraid of so much, these are the best opportunities to experience success.

If I didn't do things I was afraid of, I wouldn't do anything at all.

The Frostbite Sweater is inspired by this journey. It's about being scared but still stepping into the unknown in search of success and outdoor experiences. The adventure has involved many campfires that wouldn't light, fear of the dark, wet clothes, and frostbite on my fingers. But at the same time, it has brought countless beautiful sunsets, small, quiet moments alone in the woods with a sense of freedom and peace, and, most importantly, moments of achievement where I've felt totally invincible, strong, and steady within myself. The inner calm that nature gives me is something I truly need when facing the darkness that anxiety can bring. For me, the Frostbite Sweater symbolizes that beyond challenges, we find joy, strength, and fantastic moments we absolutely don't want to miss.

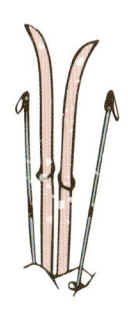

Sizes
XXS, XS (S, M, L, XL) (2X, 3X, 4X, 5X)

Garment Measurements
This sweater is designed to have approximately 4" of positive ease.
Bust: 35½, 37 (39, 40½, 43¾, 45¾) (47¼, 50¾, 55½, 59)"
Total length: 22¾, 23½ (25½, 27½, 28¼, 28¾) (29¼, 29½, 29¾, 30¾)" or desired length
Sleeve length: 17¼, 17¼ (18, 18½, 18¾, 19¾) (20, 20, 20½, 20½)" or desired length
Notice that the shoulder sits a bit down on the arm and is part of the sleeve length.

Yarn
Rauma Vams (100% Norwegian wool: 91 yd [83 m]/50 g) or
Hillesvåg Blåne (100% Norwegian Pelt wool: 125 yd [114 m]/100 g) or
Hillesvåg Troll (100% Norwegian wool: 125 yd [114 m]/100 g)

Actual Yarn Amounts
Color 1: 550, 600 (650, 700, 750, 800) (850, 900, 950, 1000) g
Color 2: 50, 50 (50, 50, 50, 100) (100, 100, 100, 100) g
Color 3: 50, 50 (50, 50, 50, 100) (100, 100, 100, 100) g
Color 4: 50, 50 (50, 50, 50, 100) (100, 100, 100, 100) g

Needles
US size 10: 16" and 32" circular needles and set of double-pointed needles
Adjust needle size as necessary to obtain gauge.

Gauge
14 stitches × 18 rows in stockinette st = 4 × 4"

Tip: If you knit more loosely or tightly over the colorwork section, you'll need to adjust your needle size to ensure it doesn't become too loose or too tight.

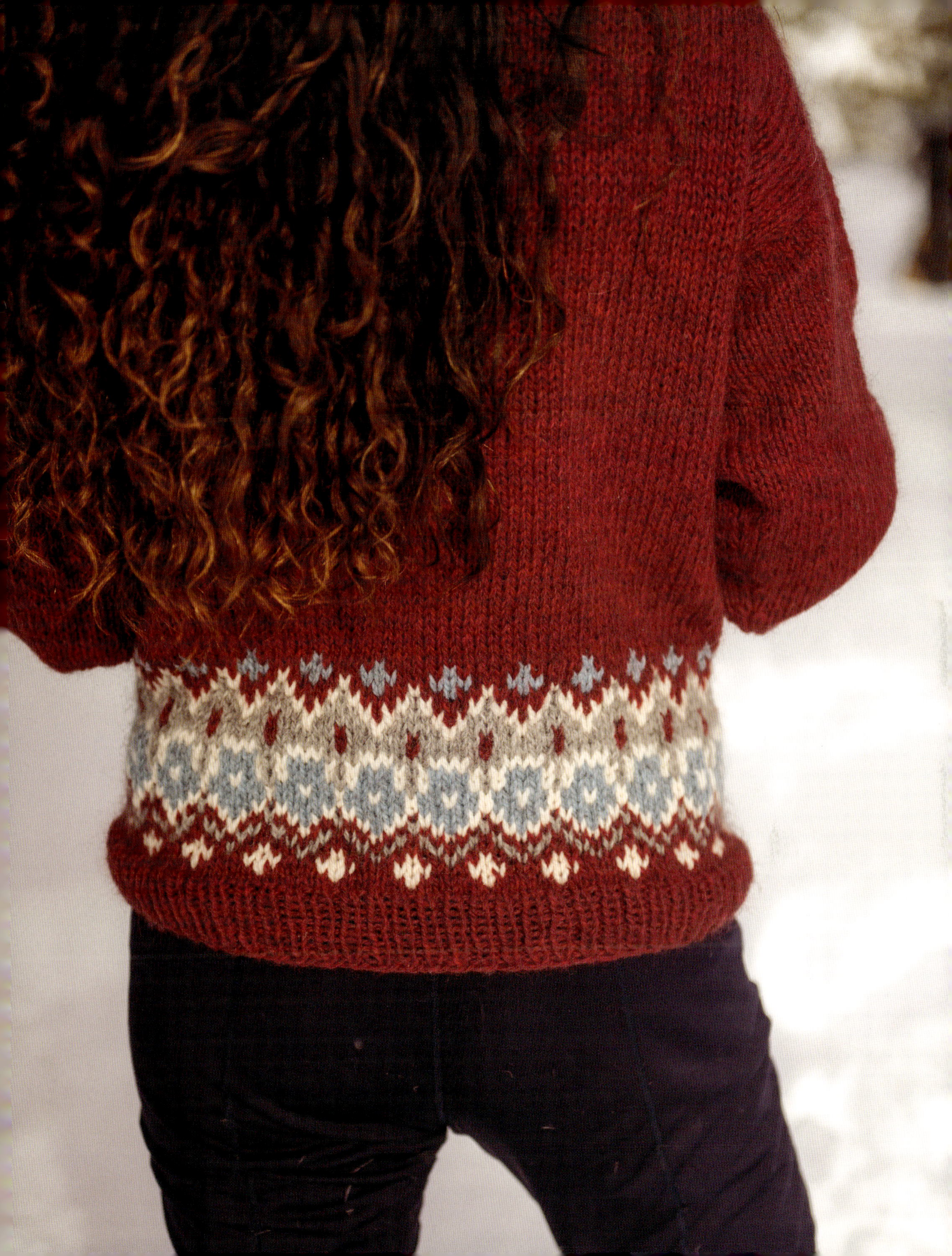

How to Knit This Sweater

You will knit this sweater from the bottom up, dividing the stitches for front and back at the armhole and finishing each part separately. Then, you'll knit the sleeves from the bottom up to the total length before you sew in the sleeves and finish the neckline at the end.

Body

Cast on 126, 132 (138, 144, 156, 162) (168, 180, 198, 210) stitches on US size 10 needles with color 1. Place a marker to mark the beginning of the round. Knit in knit 1, purl 1 ribbing in the round for 2". Knit 1 round with color 1.

CHART 1

Knit the pattern following Chart 1 as follows: Repeat stitches 1–6 for each round. Work rounds 1–20 of chart one time.

Continue with color 1 until the body measures 14½, 15 (16½, 18, 18½, 18½) (18½, 18½, 18½, 19)".

Divide the work into the front and back pieces as follows: Place the first 63, 66 (69, 72, 78, 81) (84, 90, 99, 105) stitches on a scrap of yarn or a stitch holder for the front, and continue with the remaining 63, 66 (69, 72, 78, 81) (84, 90, 99, 105) stitches for the back.

Back Piece

Work the back piece in stockinette stitch back and forth, knitting the first stitch of each row as an edge stitch as follows: From the right side: Slip the first stitch knitwise without knitting it. From the wrong side: Slip the first stitch purlwise without knitting it. When the back piece measures 8¼, 8¾ (9, 9½, 9¾, 10¼) (10½, 11, 11½, 11¾)" from the division, place all stitches on a scrap of yarn or a stitch holder.

Front Piece

Put the stitches for the front piece back on the needles. Work in stockinette stitch, with edge stitches as described for the back, back and forth until the front measures 6¾, 7 (7½, 7¾, 8¼, 8½) (9, 9½, 10, 10¼)" from the division, ending with a purl row.

On the next row, bind off the middle 19, 20 (21, 22, 22, 23) (24, 24, 25, 27) stitches as follows: Knit the first 22, 23 (24, 25, 28, 29) (30, 33, 37, 39) stitches of the row. Bind off the next 19, 20 (21, 22, 22, 23) (24, 24, 25, 27) stitches. Knit the rest of the row. You now have 22, 23 (24, 25, 28, 29) (30, 33, 37, 39) stitches for each front piece.

Place the stitches for the left front on scrap yarn or stitch holder and continue with the stitches for the right front.

Right Front

Continue with a wrong-side row. Purl across the stitches to the neckline. Turn and bind off the first 2 stitches on the needle as follows: Slip 1 stitch knitwise without knitting it, knit the next stitch, lift the slipped stitch over the second stitch and off the needle. Knit the next stitch, lift the first stitch over the second stitch and off the needle. 2 stitches bound off. Knit the rest of the row. Continue back and forth 2 more times, binding off stitches at the neckline as follows: Bind off 2 stitches on the next right-side row, then bind off 1 stitch on the following right-side row.

Color 1: Vams, light gray mélange 03

Color 2: Vams, midnight blue 77

Color 3: Vams, light purple mélange 300

Color 4: Vams, rose 60

Color 1: Blåne, dusty blue 2139

Color 2: Troll, gray 703

Color 3: Troll, graphite 707

Color 4: Troll, white 702

CHART 2

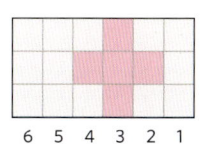

6 5 4 3 2 1

Color 1: Vams, light gray mélange 03

Color 2: Vams, rose 60

You have now bound off a total of 5 stitches and have 17, 18 (19, 20, 23, 24) (25, 28, 32, 34) stitches left. Cut the yarn and place the stitches on a piece of scrap yarn or a stitch holder while you finish the left front.

Left Front
Put the stitches back for the left front back on the needle and continue knitting stockinette stitch back and forth. Start at the armhole edge with a right-side row. Knit across the row. You are now at the neck edge. Turn and bind off the first 2 stitches on the needle as follows: Slip 1 stitch purlwise without knitting it, purl the next stitch, lift the slipped stitch over the second stitch and off the needle. Purl the next stitch, lift the first stitch over the second stitch and off the needle. 2 stitches bound off. Purl across the rest of the row. Continue back and forth 2 more times, binding off stitches at the neckline as follows: Bind off 2 stitches on the next wrong-side row, then bind off 1 stitch on the following wrong-side row. You have now bound off a total of 5 stitches and have 17, 18 (19, 20, 23, 24) (25, 28, 32, 34) stitches remaining. Cut the yarn and place the stitches on a piece of scrap yarn or a stitch holder.

Sleeves
Cast on 24, 24 (26, 26, 28, 28) (30, 30, 32, 34) stitches on double-pointed needles with color 1 Place a marker to mark the beginning of the round. Knit in knit 1, purl 1 ribbing in the round for 2".

Knit one round, at the same time increasing 6, 6 (10, 10, 8, 8) (12, 12, 10, 8) stitches evenly across the round as follows: *Knit 4, 4 (2, 2, 3, 3) (2, 2, 3, 4) stitches, increase 1 stitch, knit 4, 4 (3, 3, 4, 4) (3, 3, 3, 4) stitches, increase 1 stitch.* Repeat from * to * 3, 3 (5, 5, 4, 4) (6, 6, 5, 4) times. Knit 0, 0 (1, 1, 0, 0) (0, 0, 2, 2) stitches. You now have 30, 30 (36, 36, 36, 36) (42, 42, 42, 42) stitches on your needles.

Knit the pattern following Chart 1 as follows: Repeat stitches 1–6 for each round. Work rounds 1–20 of chart one time.

Continue with color 1 while increasing 2 stitches on the next row as follows: Knit the first stitch, pick up the strand between stitches front to back with the left needle, and knit it through the back loop. Knit until 1 stitch remains, pick up the strand between stitches from back to front with the left needle and knit it. Continue to increase in this way every ½" until you have 58, 62 (64, 66, 70, 72) (76, 78, 80, 84) stitches on the needles. Continue without increasing until the sleeve measures 17¼, 17¼ (18, 18½, 19, 19¾) (20, 20, 20½, 20½)" or to your desired length. Bind off all stitches. Work the second sleeve the same way.

Finishing
Graft the front shoulders to the corresponding back shoulder stitches (see page 170). Sew in the sleeves (see page 175).

Neckline
Pick up stitches around the neckline as follows: Place the remaining 29, 30 (31, 32, 32, 33) (34, 34, 35, 37) stitches from the back onto the short circular needle.

Continuing around the front neck, pick up and knit 31, 30 (29, 34, 34, 33) (38, 38, 37, 41) stitches evenly with color 1 so that you have a total of 60, 60 (60, 66, 66, 66) (72, 72, 72, 78) stitches on the needle. Place a marker to mark the beginning of the round. Knit 1 round with color 1.

Knit the pattern following Chart 2 as follows: Repeat stitches 1–6 for each round. Work rounds 1–3 of chart one time.

Continue in stockinette stitches in the round with color 1 until the neckline measures 2½". Bind off loosely. Weave in all loose ends. Steam or wet block the sweater to finish it.

Color 1: Blåne, dark rose 2114

Color 2: Troll, white 702

Color 3: Blåne, nature gray 2115

Color 4: Troll, mélange light teal 7060

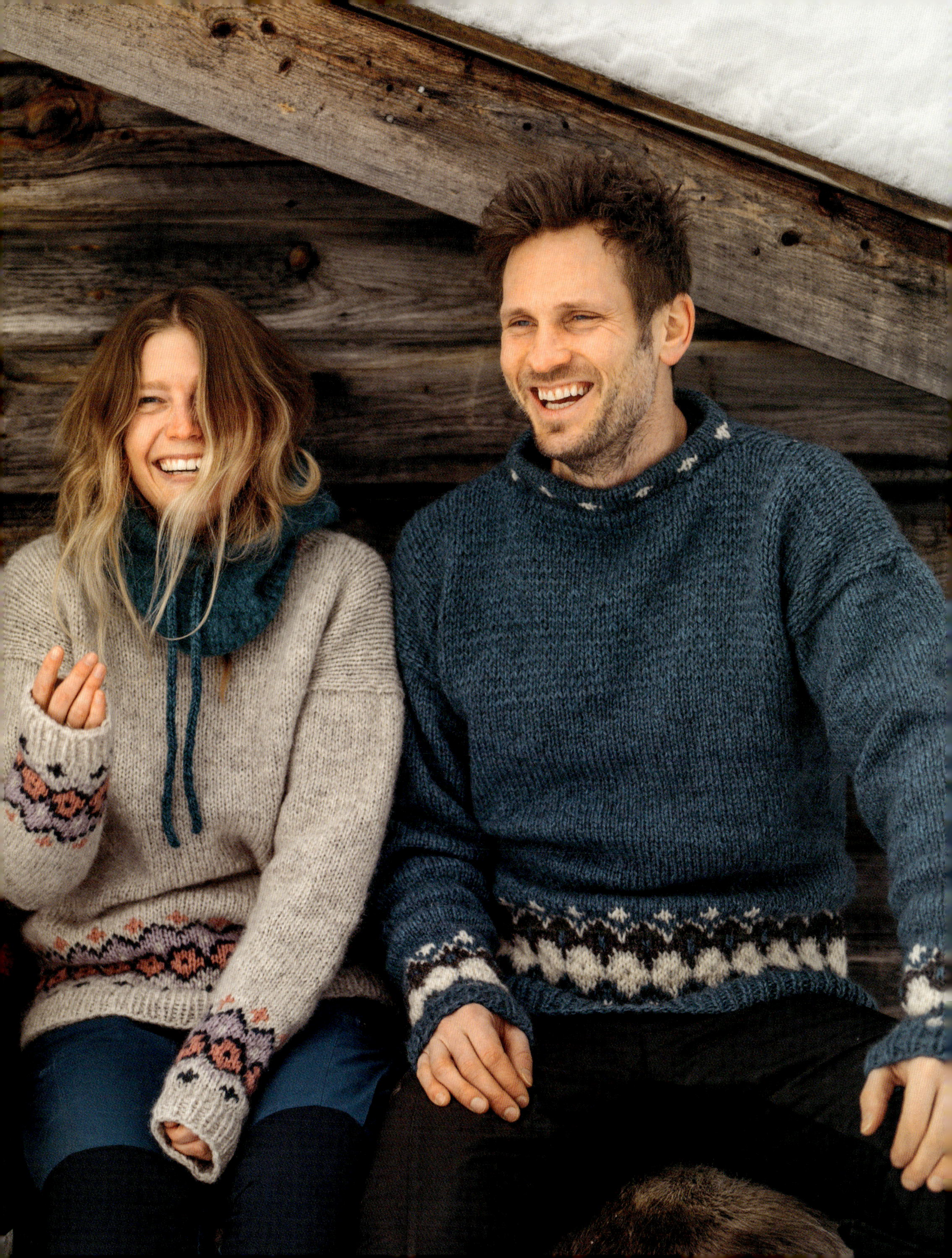

Color 1: Blåne, dark rose 2114
Color 2: Blåne, nature gray 2115
Color 3: Troll, white 702
Color 4: Troll, mélange light teal 7060

Frostbite Mittens

Perfect project for leftover yarn!

Sizes
XS/S (M/L)

Measurements Before Felting
Length (from the cuff to the top of the mitten): 12½ (13⅓)"
Width (below the thumb): 5 (5½)"

Measurements After Felting
Length (from the cuff to the top of the mitten): 8⅔ (9½)"
Width (below the thumb): 4 (4⅓)"

Yarn
Rauma Vams (100% Norwegian wool: 91 yd [83 m]/50 g) or Hillesvåg Blåne (100% Norwegian Pelt wool: 125 yd [114 m]/100 g) or Hillesvåg Troll (100% Norwegian wool: 125 yd [114 m]/100 g)

Actual Yarn Amount
Color 1: 100 (100) g
Color 2: 50 (50) g
Color 3: 50 (50) g
Color 4: 50 (50) g

Needles
US size 10: set of 5 double-pointed needles.
Adjust needle size as necessary to obtain gauge.

Gauge
14 stitches in stockinette stitch before felting = 4"

Tip: If you knit more loosely or tightly over the colorwork section, you'll need to adjust your needle size to ensure it doesn't become too loose or too tight.

How to Knit These Mittens

Right Mitten
Cast on 36 (42) stitches with color 2 on double-pointed needles as follows: Cast on 9 (10) stitches on the first needle, cast on 9 (11) stitches on the next needle. Repeat for the remaining 2 needles. You now have 18 (21) stitches for each side of the mitten.

Work seed stitch for 6 rounds as follows:
Round 1: Knit 1, purl 1 across the round.
Round 2: Purl 1, knit 1 across the round.

Repeat these two rounds two more times.

Knit 8 rounds in stockinette stitch. Knit the pattern following the chart as

Note

The mittens might feel tighter over the patterned section. If this happens, stretch them well while they are still wet to ensure they fit well. Alternatively, you can go up a needle size when working the colorwork section, then go back down to size when knitting stockinette.

follows: Repeat stitches 1–6 for each round. Work rounds 1–14 of chart one time.

Using color 1, knit 1 round decreasing 0 (2) stitches evenly. You now have 36 (40) stitches total. Knit 5 (6) more rounds in stockinette stitch.

On the next round, you'll mark the position of the thumb as follows: Knit the first 6 (7) stitches on needle 1 with a piece of scrap yarn in a contrasting color. Slip the scrap yarn stitches back onto the left needle, knit them with your regular yarn, and knit to the end of the round.

Knit in stockinette stitch until the mitten measures 4¾ (5½)" after the thumb stitches, or to your desired length.

Decrease 8 (10) stitches evenly on the next round as follows: *Knit 2 (2), knit 2 together, knit 3 (2), knit 2 together*. Repeat from * to * 4 (5) times. You now have 28 (30) stitches. Knit 3 rounds without decreasing.

On the next round, decrease 8 stitches evenly as follows: *Knit 1, knit 2 together, knit 2, knit 2 together*. Repeat from * to * 4 times, then knit 0 (2) stitches. You now have 20 (22) stitches on your needles. Knit 3 rounds without decreasing.

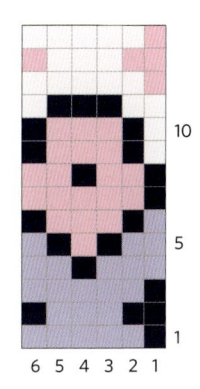

On the next round, decrease 8 stitches evenly as follows: *Knit 1, knit 2 together, knit 2 together*. Repeat from * to * 4 times, then knit 0 (2) stitches. You now have 12 (14) stitches on the needles. Knit 1 round without decreasing.

Decrease 4 (6) stitches evenly as follows:

XS/S:
Knit 1, knit 2 together. Repeat from * to * 4 times.

M/L:
Knit 1, knit 2 together, knit 2 together, knit 2 together. Repeat from * to * 2 times.

You now have 8 stitches. Cut the yarn and pull it through the remaining 8 stitches.

Thumb
Remove the scrap yarn and place the 6 (7) stitches on each side onto double-pointed needles. Pick up 1 additional stitch on each side, so you now have a total of 14 (16) stitches on the needles. Knit in stockinette stitch in the round for 3 (3½)".

On the next round, knit 2 together 7 (8) times. You now have 7 (8) stitches left.

Cut the yarn and pull it through the remaining stitches.

Left Mitten
Knit the same way as the right mitten but mark the position of the thumb as follows: Knit until there are 6 (7) stitches remaining on needle 2. Knit the next 6 (7) stitches with the contrasting scrap yarn. Slip the scrap yarn stitches back onto the left needle and knit them with your regular yarn, and knit to the end of the round. Then, continue the left mitten the same as the right mitten.

Weave in all loose ends. Felt the mittens in a washing machine, a dryer, or by hand. See page 179 for the felting guide.

Color 1: Vams, light gray mélange 03
Color 2: Vams, light purple mélange 300
Color 3: Vams, midnight blue 77
Color 4: Vams, rose 60

Sleeping Bag Slippers

As an outdoor-living newbie with a big fear of both the dark and the unknown, I like to take things step by step at a slow pace. Sleeping outside alone for the first time was a long process for me. I started with day trips into nature, where I packed all the gear I needed and set up camp. I worked on finding peace and enjoyed nestling into the sleeping bag inside the tent, cooking food, and reading books. When the darkness fell, I packed up my things and went home. Eventually, after fourteen months of preparation, I had a wonderful night under the stars—without getting too scared or losing control over things.

As I spent more nights in the tent, I became tempted to challenge myself even more to try new areas of outdoor life, like sleeping in a hammock. It felt scary without a protective shield around me to keep me safe. As someone afraid of the dark, I have a wild imagination that often runs away with me. I was (and still am) often afraid that a scary clown, an axe murderer, or a moose would come and tip over the hammock at night. The first night I slept in a hammock it was about twenty degrees below freezing with completely clear skies. But it felt safe, because if I got too cold or scared, or if a clown appeared, there was an easy escape available with a cabin just a few yards away.

And guess what? It went well! I had a front-row seat to the star show in the sky, my sleeping bag was covered in frost, and I had a wonderful night's sleep. The only thing missing was a little extra warmth on my toes. Despite having a super-warm sleeping bag with a hot water bottle on my stomach, my little feet were freezing.

I've always been someone who feels the cold, and I know there are many who struggle with the same thing. That's why the idea of making a pair of sleeping bag slippers came to me. They're more elaborate than regular slippers for indoor use, so they can keep us warm in the sleeping bag when it's one, ten, or twenty degrees below freezing. These sleeping bag slippers are perfect for that, and I use mine year-round, as the cold-blooded person I am.

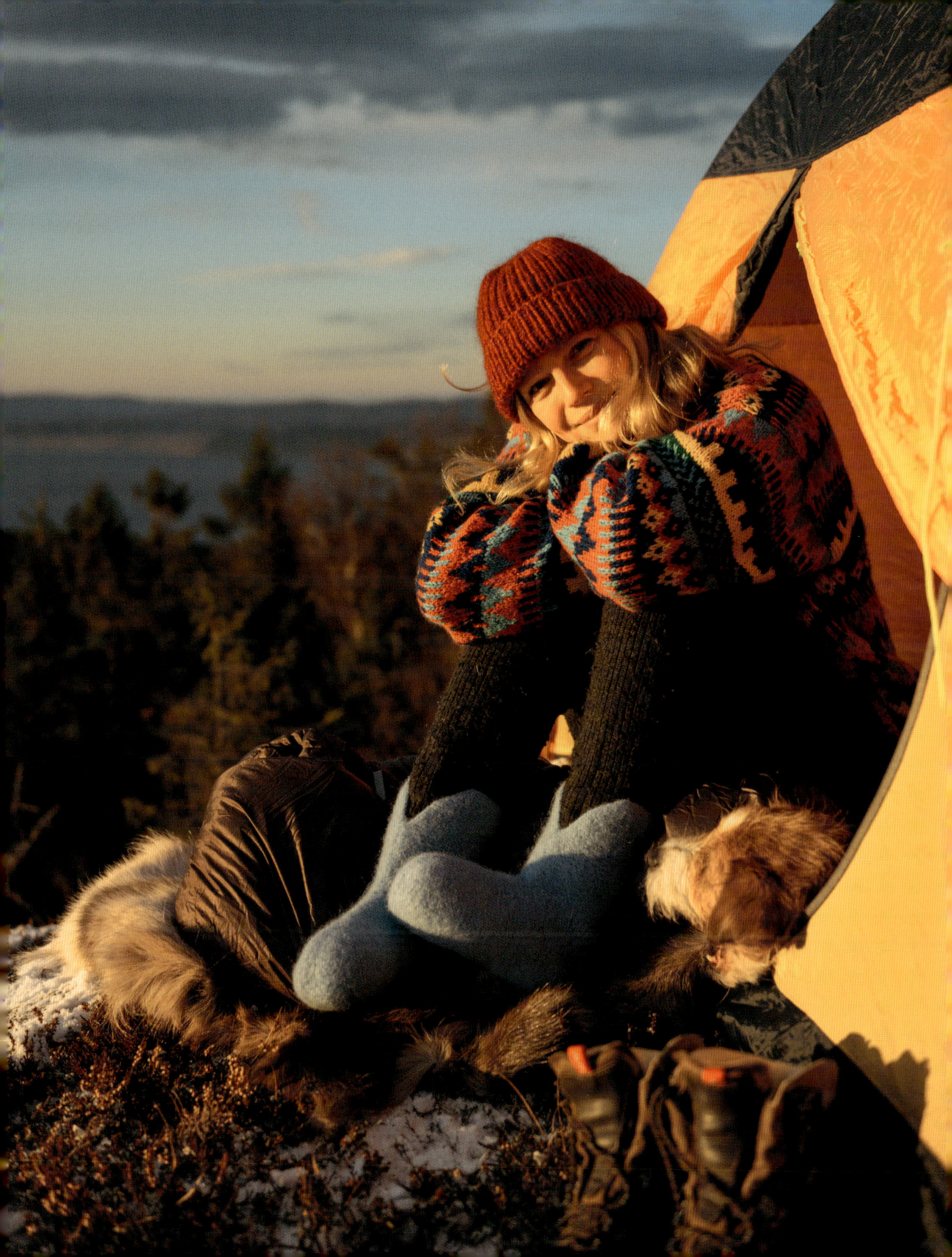

Color:
Vams, light denim blue 50

Sizes
XS/S (M/L)

Measurements
Length of foot before felting: 13 (14½)"
Length of foot after felting: 9¾ (11)"

Yarn
Rauma Vams (100% Norwegian wool: 91 yd [83 m]/50 g)

Yarn Amount
350 g for both sizes

Needles
US size 10: straight or circular needles
Adjust needle size as necessary to obtain gauge.

Gauge
14 stitches in garter stitch = 4"

How to Knit These Slippers

You are going to first knit the foot back and forth in garter stitch from heel to toe. Then, you will sew the foot together and pick up stitches for the ankle. The ankle is knitted back and forth in rows. When complete, the slippers are felted.

Foot

Cast on 46 (50) stitches. Slip the first stitch to the right needle as if to purl without knitting it. Knit across the row. Turn and repeat. You have now knitted one garter stitch ridge.

Continue in this way, back and forth, until you have knitted 22 (24) ridges [44 (48) rows]. On the next row, decrease 1 stitch on each side as follows: Slip the first stitch to the right needle as usual. Knit 2 together. Knit until there are 3 stitches left on the needle, knit 2 together, and knit the last stitch. You now have 44 (48) stitches on the needle. Continue in garter stitch, knitting back and forth and slipping the first stitch of each row, until the piece measures 11¾ (13½)" from the cast-on edge, or the desired length.

Toe

Decrease stitches for the toe as follows: Slip the first stitch to the right needle as usual. Knit 1, knit 2 together. *Knit 2, knit 2 together*. Repeat from * to * 9 (10) more times. You now have 33 (36) stitches on the needle. Knit 2 rows without decreasing.

On the next row, decrease as follows: Slip the first stitch to the right needle as usual. Knit 1, knit 2 together. *Knit 2, knit 2 together*. Repeat from * to * 6 (7) more times, then knit 1 (0). You now have 25 (27) stitches on the needle. Knit 2 rows without decreasing.

On the next row, knit 2 together until there is 1 stitch left. Knit this stitch. Leave about 20" of tail and cut the yarn. Thread the yarn through the remaining 13 (14) stitches and gently pull tight.

Sew the foot together using the 20" tail as follows: Line up the edge stitches from each side and sew using whip stitches with the wrong side facing (see page 169), row by row, up to where you decreased 1 stitch on each side. Sew the back of the slipper together in the same way. Turn the slipper right-side out so the seams are on the inside.

Ankle

Pick up 1 stitch in each edge, stitch around the opening of the slipper as follows: Start at the front seam. Pick up and knit 1 stitch in in the front seam, and 1 stitch in each of the 22 (24) edge stitches to the center back seam of the slipper. Pick up and knit 2 stitches in the back seam and 1 stitch in each of the 22 (24) edge stitches to the front seam. Finish by picking up 1 more stitch in the front center seam. You now have 48 (52) stitches on the needle. Turn.

Knit garter stitch back and forth, slipping the first stitch of each row, until the ankle measures 6 (7)".

On the next row, decrease 1 stitch on each side as follows: Slip the first stitch from the needle as usual, knit 2 together, knit until there are 3 stitches left on the needle, knit 2 together, knit the last stitch.

Turn and knit as usual across the row. Decrease 1 stitch on each side every other row 4 more times. You now have 38 (42) stitches left.

Bind off all stitches. Sew the ankle together on the wrong side, from the bottom of the opening to the row you began decreasing.

Weave in all loose ends. Knit the other slipper the same way. Felt the slippers either in a washing machine, dryer, or by hand. See page 179 for the felting guide. Shape the slippers while they are still wet and let them dry standing up.

Lucie Oversized Sweater

I have been open about my own health, my journey, and my life on social media for many years. But there are some people I haven't shared much about whom I would like to honor in this book: My partner, Harald, and my dear in-laws.

Harald and I met in 2015. He was one of the most fascinating people I had ever met. So calm and grounded, but at the same time incredibly playful, adventurous, and colorful. I still haven't fully grasped how much Harald has taught me in the years we've been together. How much I've grown as a person, for the better, because of him. In addition, I have been incredibly lucky with my in-laws, who welcomed me with open arms and treated me like a part of the family from day one.

After I caught the outdoor bug, it was my in-laws who provided us with outdoor gear they had in storage. Thanks to everything we were able to borrow, we could go on a vacation with a tent, sleeping bags, and all the extras. Since then, camping has become an annual tradition for Harald, Juster, and me. My in-laws also made our first night in a tent possible. It was a fantastic experience, even though we were missing a tent pole and the tent barely managed to stay upright.

Among the things my mother-in-law passed on was a sweater from the 1980s that she knitted herself. It's an absolutely amazing sweater with a classic 1980s look, in many colors and fluffy yarn. I loved that sweater from the moment I saw it.

Ever since I decided to create a knitting book, the idea of designing a garment as a tribute to my in-laws has been growing in my mind. The result is Lucie Oversized Sweater. An oversized, chunky sweater in fluffy yarn, and the only garment in the collection that isn't knitted in 100% wool. It's well worth it for this result, and the sweater is wonderfully warm, whether at a festival, for everyday wear, or out in nature.

The name for the sweater comes from Harald's maternal grandmother, Lucie. She was as lively, caring, and full of life as my mother-in-law. I like to think that's where Harald got his energy and sense of adventure from. I genuinely feel warmth in my heart when I write about these amazing people, and the sweater's design reflects their spark and zest for life.

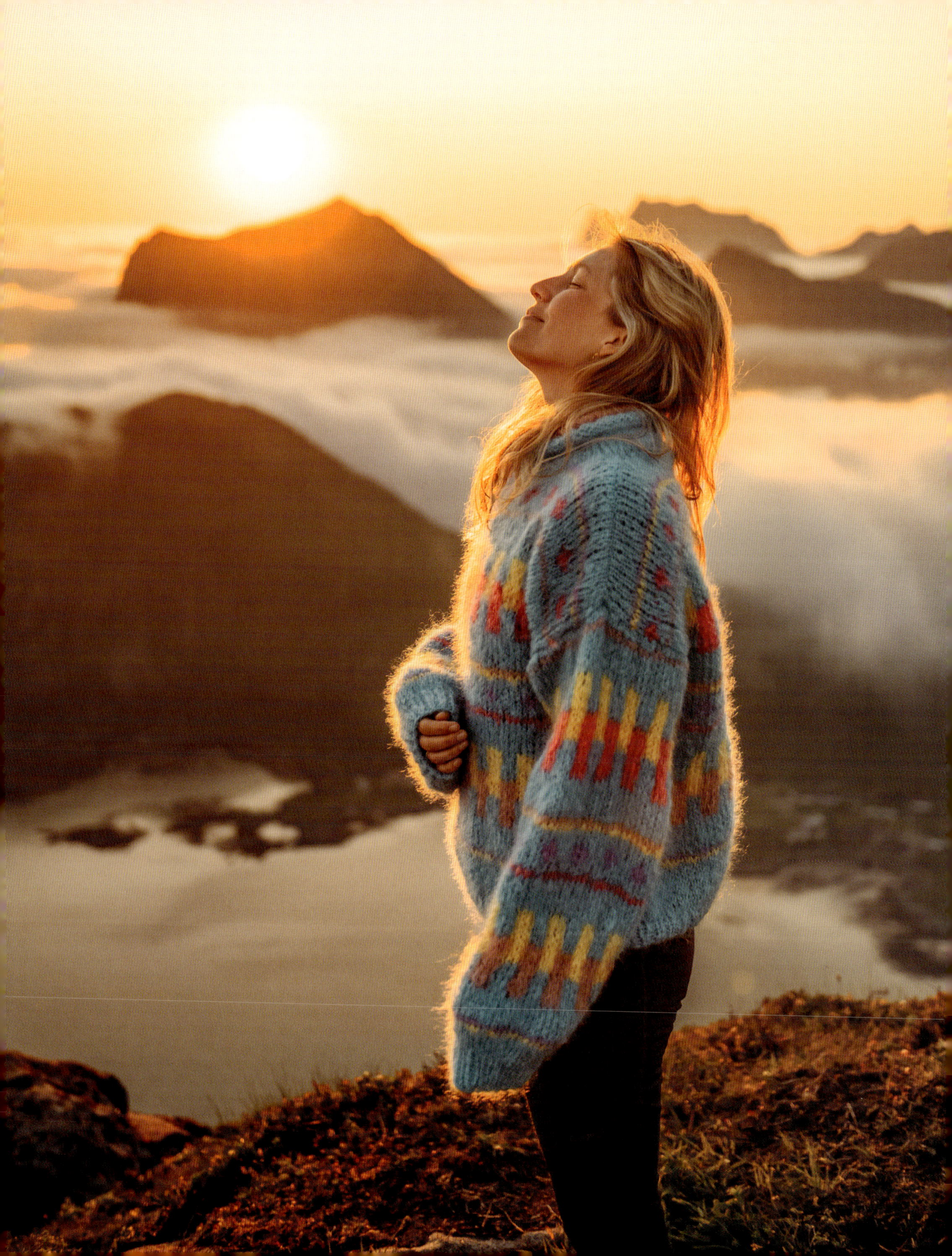

Sizes
XXS, XS (S, M, L, XL) (2X, 3X, 4X, 5X)

Garment Measurements
This sweater is designed to be oversized with approximately 12–14" of positive ease.
Bust: 43¼, 45¼ (47¼, 49¼, 51¼, 53¼) (57, 61, 65, 68¾)"
Total length: 22½, 22¾ (24½, 25½, 26¼, 26¾) (27¼, 27½, 28, 28¼)" or desired length
Sleeve length: 17, 17 (17¾, 18, 18½, 19¼) (19¾, 19¾, 20, 20)" or desired length
Notice that the shoulder sits a bit down on the arm and is part of the sleeve length.

Yarn
Rauma Tjukk Mohair (88% mohair, 7% wool, 5% polyamide: 110 yd [100 m]/50 g)

Actual Yarn Amounts
Color 1: 300, 300 (350, 350, 350, 400) (400, 400, 450, 450) g
Color 2: 100, 100 (100, 100, 100, 100) (100, 100, 100, 150) g
Color 3: 50, 50 (100, 100, 100, 100) (100, 100, 100, 100) g
Color 4: 50, 50 (50, 50, 50, 100) (100, 100, 100, 100) g
Color 5: 50 g for all sizes

Needles
US size 6: 16" and 32" circular needles and set of double-pointed needles
US size 10½: 16" and 32" circular needles
Adjust needle size as necessary to obtain gauge.

Gauge
12 stitches × 16 rows = 4 × 4"

How to Knit This Sweater

You will knit this sweater from the bottom up, dividing the stitches for front and back at the armhole and finishing each part separately. Then, you'll knit the sleeves from the bottom up to the total length before you sew in the sleeves and finish the neckline at the end.

Body

Cast on 106, 110 (116, 120, 124, 130) (140, 148, 158, 168) stitches on US size 6 needles with color 1. Place a marker for the beginning of the round. Work knit 1, purl 1 ribbing in the round for 2".

Change to US size 10½ needles. Knit 1 round with color 1, at the same time increasing 26, 28 (28, 30, 32, 32) (34, 38, 40, 42) stitches evenly as follows:

XXS:
Knit 4, increase 1. Repeat from * to * 26 times. Finish by knitting 2 stitches.

XS:
Knit 3, increase 1. *Knit 4, increase 1*. Repeat from * to * 26 times. Knit 3, increase 1.

S:
Knit 2. *Knit 4, increase 1*. Repeat from * to * 14 times. Knit 2. *Knit 4, increase 1*. Repeat from * to * 14 times.

M:
Knit 4, increase 1. Repeat from * to * 30 times.

L:
Knit 3, increase 1, knit 3, increase 1. *Knit 4, increase 1*. Repeat from * to * 14 times. Knit 3, increase 1, knit 3, increase 1. *Knit 4, increase 1*. Repeat from * to * 14 times.

XL:
Knit 1. *Knit 4, increase 1*. Repeat from * to * 16 times. Knit 1. *Knit 4, increase 1*. Repeat from * to * 16 times.

2XL:
Knit 2. *Knit 4, increase 1*. Repeat from * to * 17 times. Knit 2. *Knit 4, increase 1*. Repeat from * to * 17 times.

3XL:
Knit 3, increase 1, knit 3, increase 1. *Knit 4, increase 1*. Repeat from * to * 17 times. Knit 3, increase 1, knit 3, increase 1. *Knit 4, increase 1*. Repeat from * to * 17 times.

4XL:
Knit 3, increase 1. *Knit 4, increase 1*. Repeat from * to * 19 times. Knit 3, increase 1. *Knit 4, increase 1*. Repeat from * to * 19 times.

XL:
Knit 4, increase 1. Repeat from * to * 42 times.

You now have 132, 138 (144, 150, 156, 162) (174, 186, 198, 210) stitches on your needles. Continue in stockinette stitch in the round if necessary until the work measures 2, 2 (2, 2¾, 3¼, 3½) (3½, 4, 4, 4¼)" from the cast-on edge.

Knit the pattern following the chart (page 52) as follows: Beginning with stitch 6, 4 (3, 1, 6, 4) (1, 4, 1, 4) of each chart round, knit to stitch 6, then repeat stitches 1–6 to last 5, 3 (2, 0, 5, 3) (0, 3, 0, 3) stitches, then work stitches 1–5, 1–3 (1–2, 0, 1–5, 1–3) (0, 1–3, 0, 1–3). Knit rows 1–74 of chart one time.

At the same time, when the piece measures 11¾, 12 (13½, 14¼, 14½, 14½) (14½, 14½, 14½, 14½)" from the cast-on edge or desired length to armholes, divide the body into front and back pieces as follows: Place the first 65, 69 (71, 75, 77, 81) (87, 93, 99, 105) stitches onto a piece of scrap yarn or a stitch holder for the front.

Back Piece

Starting with a wrong-side row and continuing in chart pattern, work back and forth in stockinette stitch over 67, 69 (73, 75, 79, 81) (87,

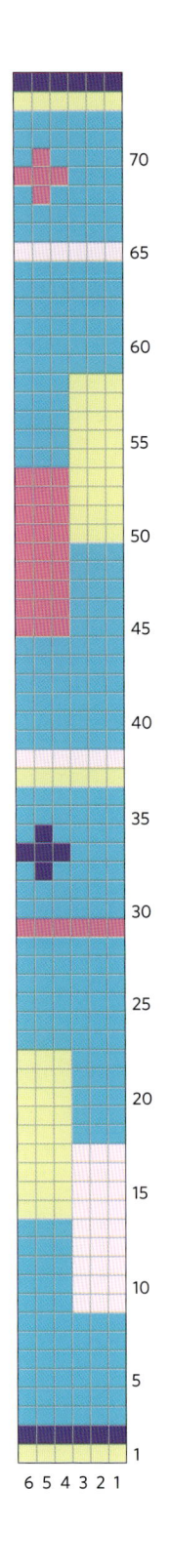

93, 99, 105) stitches for the back. Make edge stitches on each side as follows: On the right side: always slip the first stitch as if to knit, without knitting it. On the wrong side: always slip the first stitch as if to purl, without purling it.

When chart is complete, continue with color 1 only until the back measures 10½, 10¾ (11, 11½, 11¾, 12¼) (12½, 13, 13¼, 13¾)" from where you divided the front and back. Bind off all stitches.

Front Piece

Put the stitches for the front piece back on the needles. Knit the front piece back and forth in the same way as with the back piece until the front measures 9, 9¼ (9½, 10, 10¼, 10½) (10¾, 11¼, 11½, 11¾)" from where you divided the front and back, ending with a wrong-side row. On the next row, bind off the center 17, 19 (19, 19, 21, 21) (23, 25, 25, 27) stitches as follows: Knit the first 24, 25 (26, 28, 28, 30) (32, 34, 37, 39) stitches, bind off the next 17, 19 (19, 19, 21, 21) (23, 25, 25, 27) stitches. Knit the rest of the row. You now have 24, 25 (26, 28, 28, 30) (32, 34, 37, 39) stitches remaining for each side of front.

Place the stitches for the left front (the left side of the sweater) onto a piece of scrap yarn or a stitch holder and continue working on the stitches for the right front.

Right Front

Turn and work 1 wrong-side row. On the right-side row, bind off the first 2 stitches, then knit to the end of the row. Turn and purl back.

Bind off the first stitch at the beginning of the next 2 right-side rows. You have now bound off a total of 4 stitches at the neckline and have 20, 21 (22, 24, 24, 26) (28, 30, 33, 35) stitches remaining. Bind off all stitches on a purl row.

Color 1: Tjukk Mohair, teal 077
Color 2: Tjukk Mohair, lemon yellow 022
Color 3: Tjukk Mohair, rose breeze 184
Color 4: Tjukk Mohair, bright rose 106
Color 5: Tjukk Mohair, purple 110

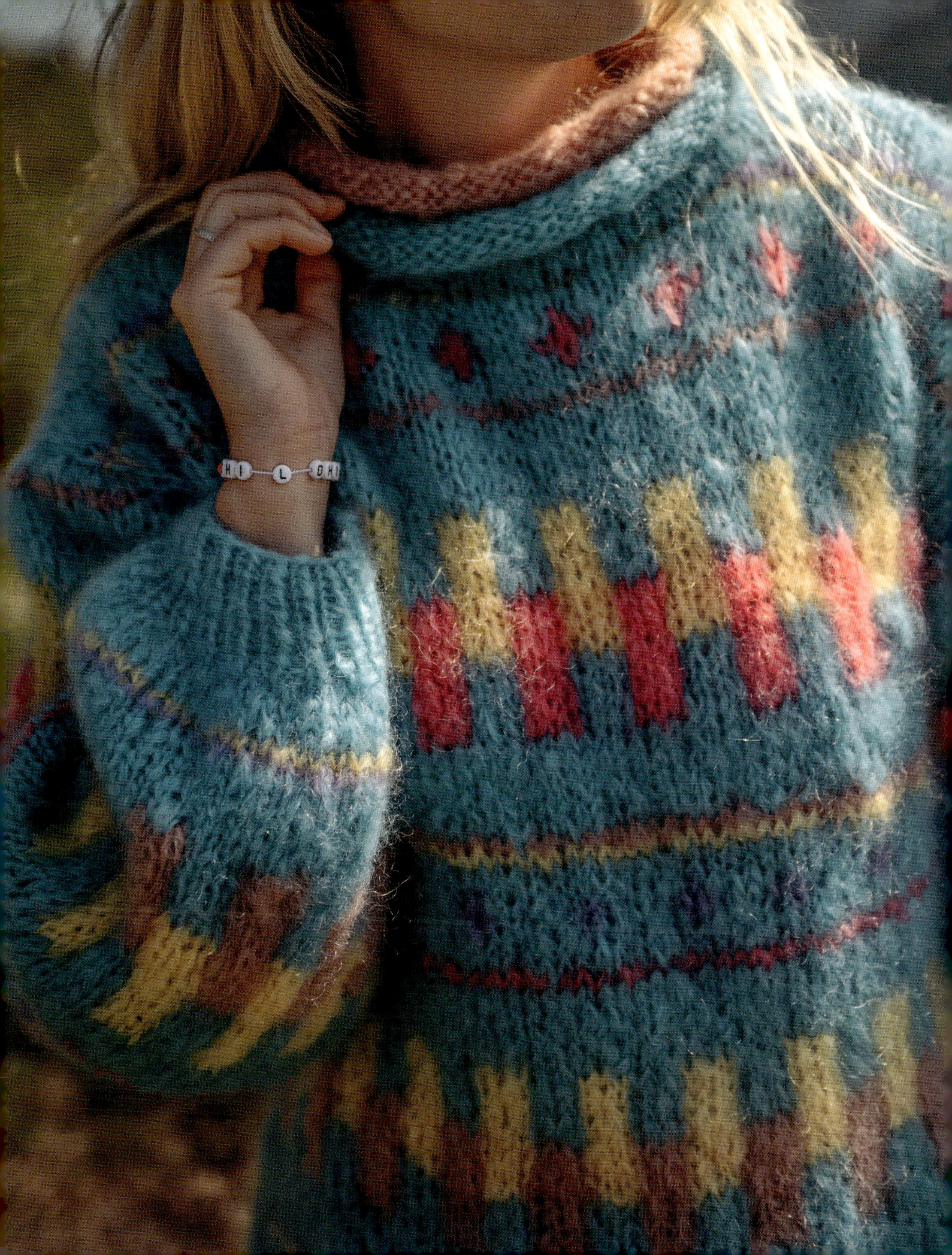

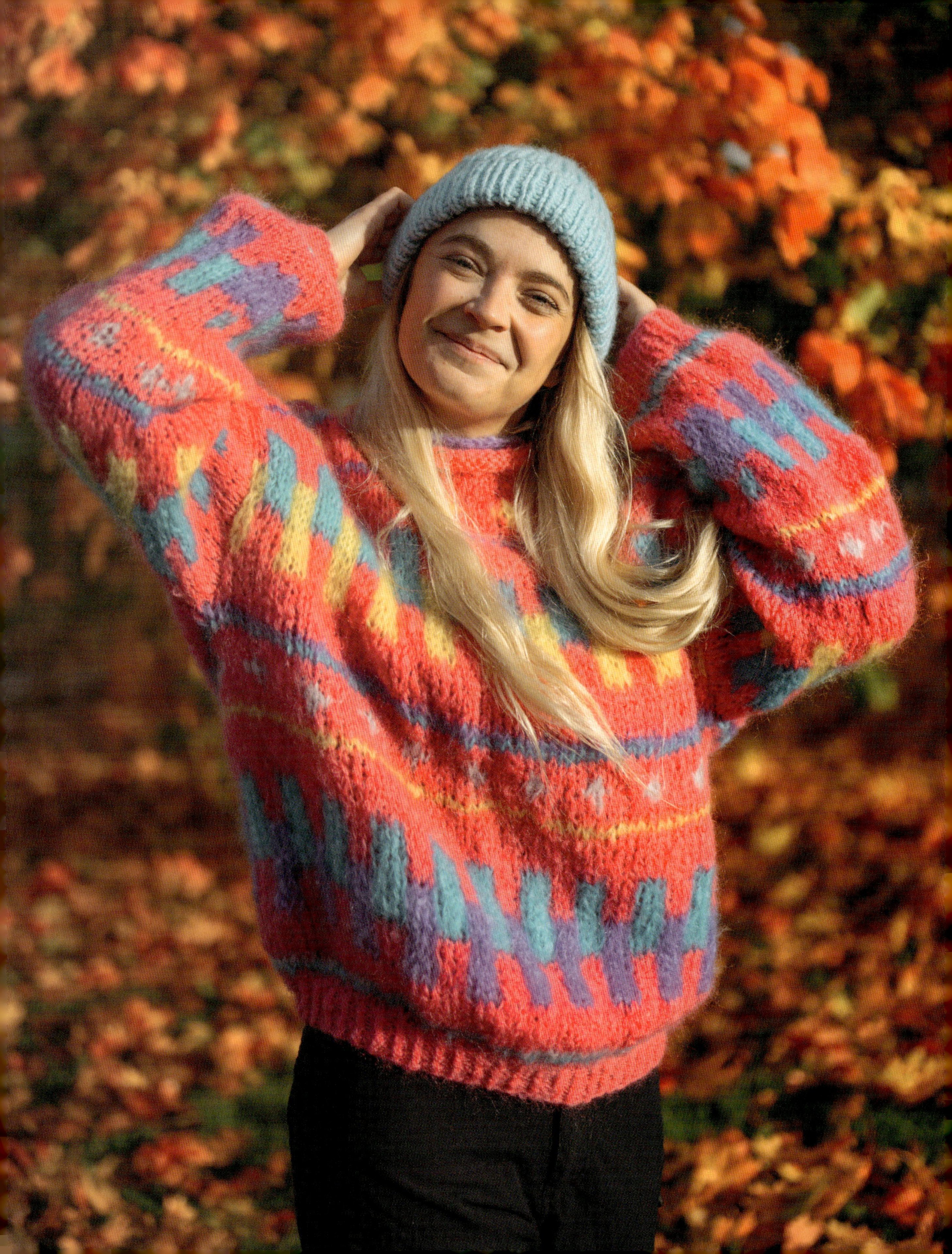

Color 1: Tjukk Mohair, bright rose 106

Color 2: Tjukk Mohair, teal 077

Color 3: Tjukk Mohair, purple 110

Color 4: Tjukk Mohair, lemon yellow 022

Color 5: Tjukk Mohair, rose breeze 184

Left Front

Put all the stitches for the left front back onto the needle. Starting at the neck edge, work 1 wrong-side row and 1 right-side row. Turn and bind off the first 2 stitches on the wrong-side row, then purl to the end of the row. Turn and knit back.

Bind off the first stitch at the beginning of the next 2 wrong-side rows. You have now bound off a total of 4 stitches at the neckline and have 20, 21 (22, 24, 24, 26) (28, 30, 33, 35) stitches remaining. Bind off all stitches on a knit row.

Sleeves

Cast on 32, 34 (36, 38, 40, 42) (42, 44, 44, 46) stitches with color 1 using needle US size 6 double-pointed needles. Place a marker for the beginning of the round. Work knit 1, purl 1 ribbing in the round for 2".

Change to US size 10½ needles. Knit 1 round with color 1, at the same time increasing 13 stitches evenly as follows:

XXS:
Knit 2, increase 1 stitch. *Knit 3, increase 1 stitch, knit 2, increase 1 stitch*. Repeat from * to * 6 times.

XS:
Knit 4, increase 1 stitch. *Knit 3, increase 1 stitch, knit 2, increase 1 stitch*. Repeat from * to * 6 times.

S:
Knit 2, increase 1 stitch. *Knit 3, increase 1 stitch*. Repeat from * to * 5 times.
Knit 2, increase 1 stitch. *Knit 3, increase 1 stitch*. Repeat from * to * 5 times. Knit 2, increase 1 stitch.

M:
Knit 2, increase 1 stitch. *Knit 3, increase 1 stitch*. Repeat from * to * 12 times.

L:
Knit 1. *Knit 3, increase 1 stitch*. Repeat from * to * 13 times.

XL and 2XL:
Knit 4, increase 1 stitch. *Knit 3, increase 1 stitch*. Repeat from * to * 5 times.
Knit 4, increase 1 stitch. *Knit 3, increase 1 stitch*. Repeat from * to * 5 times.
Knit 4, increase 1 stitch.

3XL and 4XL:
Knit 3, increase 1 stitch, knit 3, increase 1 stitch. *Knit 4, increase 1 stitch, knit 3, increase 1 stitch*. Repeat from * to * 5 times. Knit 3, increase 1 stitch.

5XL:
Knit 4, increase 1 stitch. *Knit 3, increase 1 stitch, knit 4, increase 1 stitch*. Repeat from * to * 6 times.

You now have 45, 47 (49, 51, 53, 55) (55, 57, 57, 59) stitches on the needles.

Knit the pattern following the chart as follows: Beginning with stitch 4, 3 (2, 1, 6, 5) (5, 4, 4, 3) of each chart round, knit to stitch 6, then repeat stitches 1–6 to the end of the round. The round will not end with a complete repeat. Start with row 1 of the chart and work as many rows as needed to reach desired length.

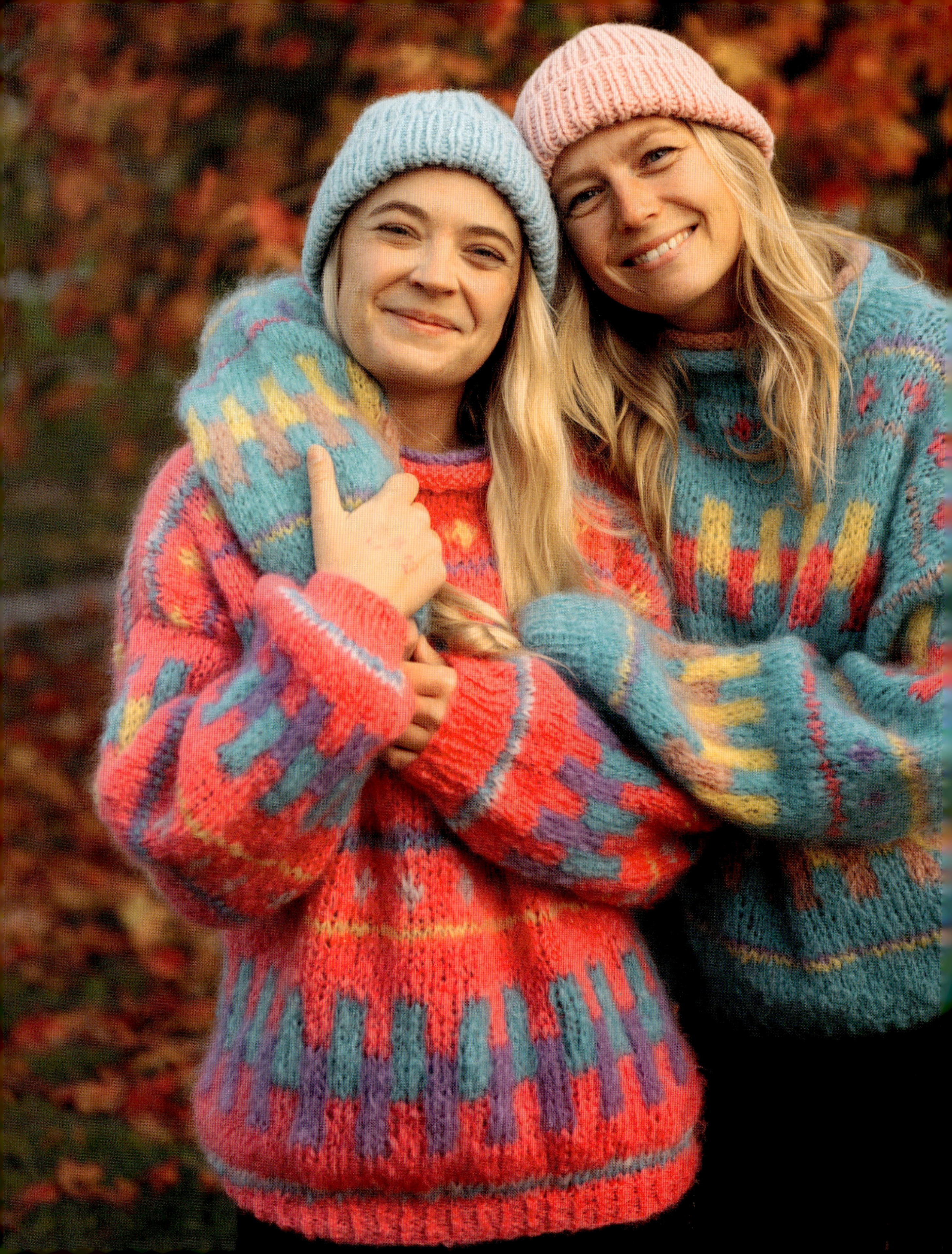

At the same time, when sleeve measures 1½, 1½ (1½, 1½, 1½, 1½) (1¼, 1¼, 1¼, 1¼)" after the ribbing, increase 2 stitches in the next round as follows: Knit the first stitch, pick up the strand between stitches front to back with the left needle, and knit it through the back loop. Knit the pattern until 1 stitch remains, pick up the strand between stitches from back to front with the left needle and knit it. The increased stitches are knitted as an extension of the pattern.

Continue increasing 2 stitches on the sleeve every 1½, 1½ (1½, 1½, 1½, 1½) (1¼, 1¼, 1¼, 1¼)" 17, 17 (17, 17, 17, 17) (19, 21, 23, 23) more times. You now have 63, 65 (67, 69, 71, 73) (75, 79, 81, 83) stitches on the needle. Continue knitting in chart pattern without increasing until the sleeve measures 17, 17 (17¾, 18, 18½, 19¼) (19¾, 19¾, 20, 20)" or to the desired length. Knit 1 round with color 1.

Bind off all stitches. Knit the second sleeve the same way.

Finishing
Use mattress stitch to sew the front shoulders to the corresponding back shoulders (see page 170). Sew in the sleeves (see page 175).

Double Collar
With color 1 and the shorter US size 6 circular needle, pick up and knit 60, 64 (64, 68, 68, 72) (72, 76, 76, 80) stitches evenly around the neckline. Place a marker for the beginning of the round. Knit stockinette in the round for about 2½". Bind off all stitches loosely.

With color 3 and the shorter US size 6 circular needle, pick up and knit 60, 64 (64, 68, 68, 72) (72, 76, 76, 80) stitches evenly around the neckline along the same rows where you picked up for the first part of the collar. Knit stockinette in the round for about 2½". Bind off all stitches loosely.

Weave in all loose ends. Rinse the sweater to get an even finish.

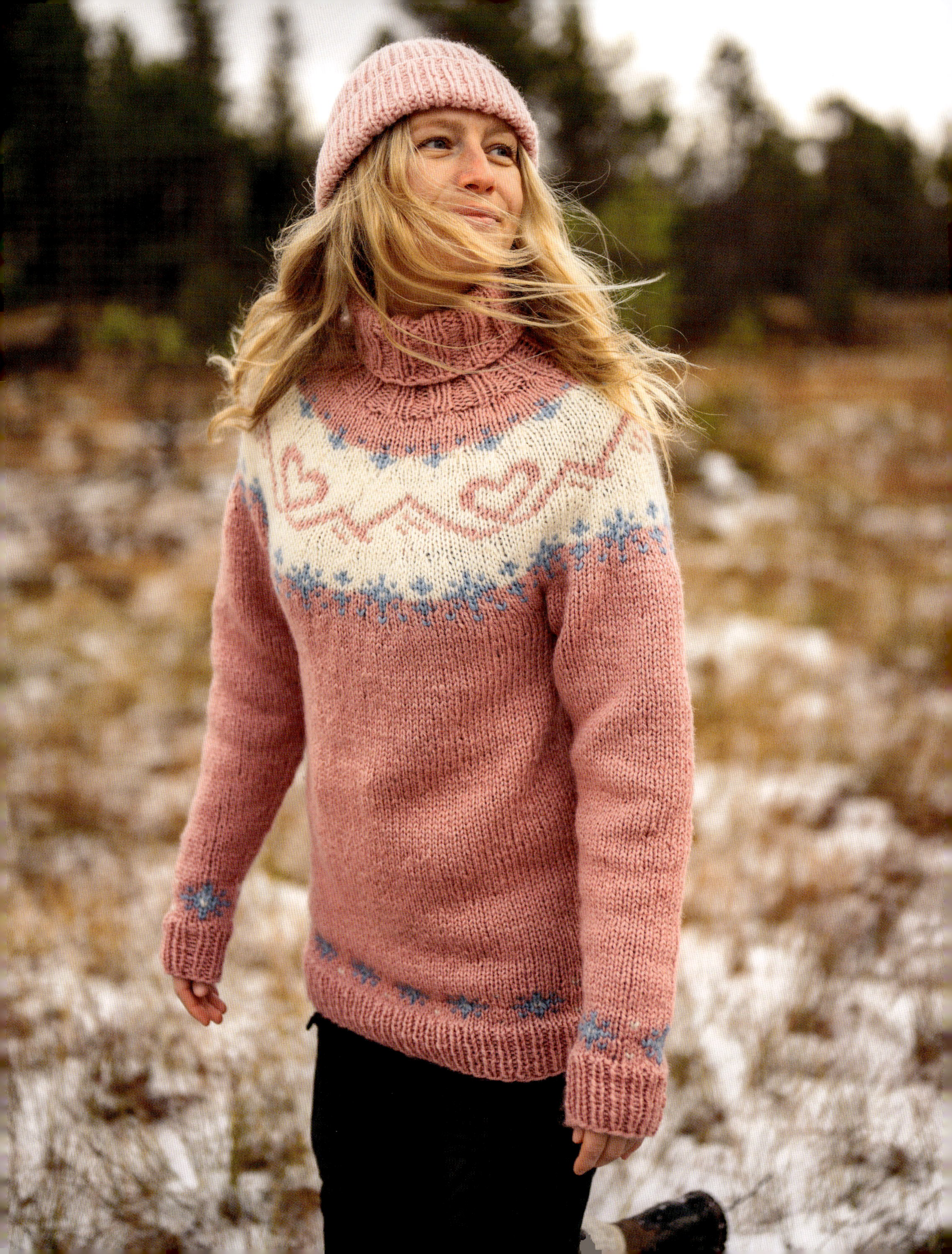

Mountain Sweater

Since we were little girls, my sister Stine and I have worked with yarn and needles making knitted projects. As adults, we've traditionally knit something for each other for Christmas and birthdays. Our favorite activity is to sit down to indulge in a *Harry Potter* marathon with some treats in a bowl, and, of course, our knitting. Knitting takes us right back to our childhood and the sense of security we had together as a family. No one laughs like Stine and I do together, and our sisterly bond has become even stronger through our shared hobbies.

In 2009, we started a small project we called Strikkeriet, where we found a creative outlet making handcrafts that we sold on a small scale at markets. That was the beginning of our first collaboration in the knitting world, and since then, we've achieved a lot together. Nine years later, the idea for the Mountain Sweater came to life. I was looking for a warm hiking sweater that reflected my love of nature, the mountains, and the woods. It had to be warm and durable. I knew the qualities the garment needed and had some ideas about the design, while Stine had the technical skills required to create a good, functional, and beautiful garment. After quite a bit of trial, calculation, ripping, and failure, we finally ended up with a sweater we were both happy with. This is the garment I have used most often on my hikes since then.

Mountain Sweater is the only design in this book that has already been on the market for a long time. It's a very popular design that many have already knitted. It's incredibly thrilling to see our design being knitted by someone else and, not least, to see their versions of the sweater. Mountain Sweater is knitted in thick Norwegian yarn and is made to be worn a lot. It has an incredibly cozy and warm neck, which is especially comforting on cold winter days. The sweater is perfect for hikes, in the sleeping bag, and at the cabin.

Sizes
XXS, XS (S, M, L, XL) (2X, 3X, 4X, 5X)

Garment Measurements
This sweater is designed to have approximately 1½" of positive ease.
Bust: 31, 34 (36½, 39¾, 42, 44½) (47, 50, 53, 56)"
Total length: 22½, 22¾ (23¾, 24¾, 25½, 26) (27, 27½, 28, 28¼)" or desired length
Sleeve length: 19, 19 (19¾, 20, 20½, 21¼) (21¾, 21¾, 22, 22)" or desired length

Yarn
Rauma Vams (100% Norwegian wool: 91 yd [83 m]/50 g)

Actual Yarn Amounts
Color 1: 400, 400 (450, 500, 550, 600) (650, 700, 750, 800) g
Color 2: 100, 100 (100, 100, 150, 150) (200, 200, 200, 200) g
Color 3: 50, 50 (50, 50, 50, 50) (100, 100, 100, 100) g

Needles
US size 10: 16" and 32" circular needles and set of double-pointed needles
Adjust needle size as necessary to obtain gauge.

Gauge
14 stitches × 18 rows in stockinette = 4 × 4"

Tip: In some rows, the yarn not in use must travel a long distance on the wrong side. To avoid overly long floats, twist the yarns together on the wrong side.

How to Knit This Sweater

The sweater is knitted from the bottom up to the armholes in the round. The sleeves are knitted from the cuffs to the armholes. The sleeves and body are then joined together, and the circular yoke is knitted in the round to the neck while decreasing. The neckline is knitted at the end.

Body

Cast on 110, 120 (130, 140, 150, 160) (170, 180, 190, 200) stitches on US size 10 (6 mm) circular needles with color 1. Place a marker to mark the beginning of the round. Work knit 1, purl 1 ribbing in the round for 2½". Knit 1 round.

Knit the pattern following Chart 1. Repeat stitches 1–10 of chart for each round. Work rounds 1–7 of chart one time.

Continue in stockinette stitch with color 1 until the piece measures 14½, 14½ (15, 15½, 16½, 18) (18, 18½, 19, 19¼)" or to the desired length to armholes.

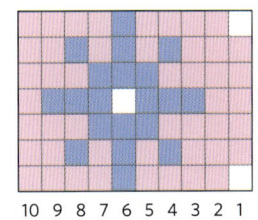

CHART 1

On the next round, bind off 6, 6 (6, 8, 8, 8) (10, 10, 10, 10) stitches on each side for the armholes as follows: Bind off the first 3, 3 (3, 4, 4, 4) (5, 5, 5, 5) stitches of the round. Knit 49, 54 (59, 62, 67, 72) (75, 80, 85, 90) stitches, bind off the next 6, 6 (6, 8, 8, 8) (10, 10, 10, 10) stitches. Knit to the last 3, 3 (3, 4, 4, 4) (5, 5, 5, 5) stitches, bind off these stitches. You now have a total of 98, 108 (118, 124, 134, 144) (150, 160, 170, 180) stitches remaining.

Cut the yarn, set the piece aside, and knit the sleeves.

Sleeves

Cast on 22, 24 (24, 26, 28, 28) (30, 30, 32, 32) stitches on US size 10 double-pointed needles with color 1. Place a marker to mark the beginning of the round. Work knit 1, purl 1 ribbing in the round for 2½".

Knit 1 round while increasing 8, 6 (6, 4, 2, 2) (10, 10, 8, 8) stitches as follows:

Knit 2, 4 (4, 6, 14, 14) (3, 3, 4, 4) stitches, increase 1, knit 3, 4 (4, 7, 14, 14) (3, 3, 4, 4) stitches, increase 1. Repeat from * to * 3, 2 (2, 1, 0, 0) (4, 4, 3, 3) more times, then finish by knitting 2, 0 (0, 0, 0, 0) (0, 0, 0, 0) stitches.

You now have 30, 30 (30, 30, 30, 30) (40, 40, 40, 40) stitches on the needles.

Knit the pattern following Chart 1. Repeat stitches 1–10 of chart for each round. Work rounds 1–7 of chart one time.

Continue in stockinette stitch with color 1. On the next round, increase 2 stitches as follows: Knit the first stitch, pick up the strand between stitches from front to back with the left needle, and knit it through the back loop. Knit the pattern until 1 stitch remains, pick up the strand between stitches from back to front with the left needle and knit it, then knit the last stitch.

Continue to increase in the same way every 1¼, 1¼ (1, 1, 1, 1) (1, 1, 1, ¾)" until you have 50, 52 (58, 60, 64, 68) (72, 74, 80, 82) stitches on the needle. Continue knitting without increasing until the piece measures 19, 19 (19¾, 20, 20½, 21¼) (21¾, 21¾, 22, 22)" or to the desired length to the armhole.

On the next round, bind off 6, 6 (6, 8, 8, 8) (10, 10, 10, 10) stitches for the armhole as follows: Bind off the first 3, 3 (3, 4, 4, 4) (5, 5, 5, 5) stitches of the round. Knit until 3, 3 (3, 4, 4, 4) (5, 5, 5, 5) stitches remain on the needle and bind them

Color 1: Vams, rose 606

Color 2: Vams, white 01

Color 3: Vams, light denim 50

— Knit 2 together

off. You now have 44, 46 (52, 52, 56, 60) (62, 64, 70, 72) stitches remaining on the needles. Knit a second sleeve in the same way.

Yoke

Now, you will knit the stitches from the body and sleeves together on the same needle as follows: Knit the stitches of one sleeve onto the needle. Knit the stitches from the front of the body to the next armhole. Knit the stitches of the second sleeve. Knit the stitches from the back of the body to the end. Place a marker for the beginning of the round. You should now have 186, 200 (222, 228, 246, 264) (274, 288, 310, 324) stitches on the needle.

Knit ½, ½ (½, ½, ½, ¾) (¾, ¾, ¾, 1¼)" with color 1.

On the next round, decrease 4, 4 (12, 4, 8, 12) (8, 8, 2, 2) stitches evenly distributed as follows: *Knit 44, 48, (16, 55, 28, 20) (32, 34, 153, 160) stitches, knit 2 together, knit 45, 48 (17, 55, 29, 20) (32, 34, 153, 160) stitches, knit 2 together*. Repeat from * to * 1, 1 (5, 1, 3, 5) (3, 3, 0, 0) more times. Finish by knitting 0, 0 (0, 0, 2, 0) (2, 0, 0, 0) stitches. You now have 182, 196 (210, 224, 238, 252) (266, 280, 308, 322) stitches remaining.

Knit ½" with color 1.

Knit the pattern following Chart 2 and decreasing as shown in chart. Repeat stitches 1–14 of chart for each round. Work rounds 1–9 of chart one time. You now have 156, 168 (180, 192, 204, 216) (228, 240, 264, 276) stitches remaining.

Knit 2, 3 (3, 4, 4, 4) (4, 5, 5, 5) rounds with color 2.

On the next round, decrease 28, 40 (20, 32, 12, 24) (4, 16, 8, 20) stitches evenly distributed as follows: *Knit 3, 2 (7, 4, 15, 7) (55, 13, 31, 11) stitches, knit 2 together, knit 4, 2 (7, 4, 15, 7) (55, 13, 31, 12) stitches, knit 2 together*. Repeat from * to * 13, 19 (9, 15, 5, 11) (1, 7, 3, 9) more times. Finish by knitting 2, 8 (0, 0, 0, 0) (0, 0, 0, 6) stitches. You now have 128, 128 (160, 160, 192, 192) (224, 224, 256, 256) stitches remaining.

Knit the pattern following Chart 3. Repeat stitches 1–32 of chart for each round. Work rounds 1–1 of chart one time.

Knit 3, 3 (3, 4, 4, 4) (4, 4, 5, 5) rounds with color 2.

CHART 2

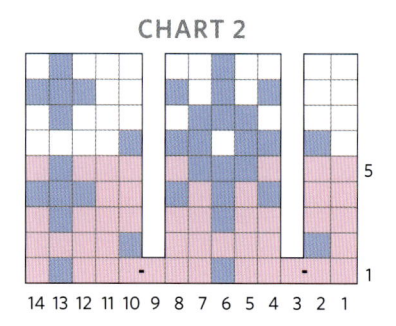

CHART 3

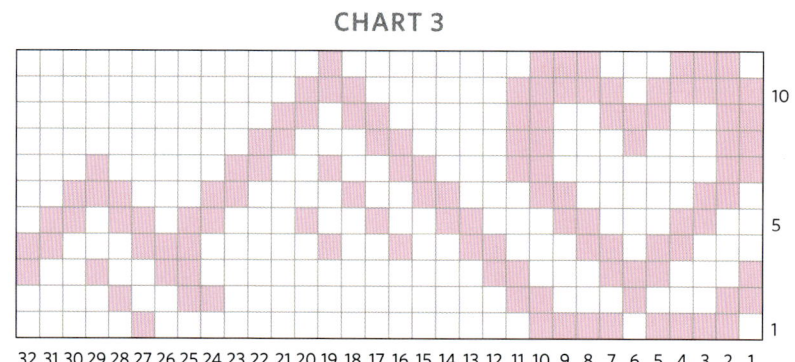

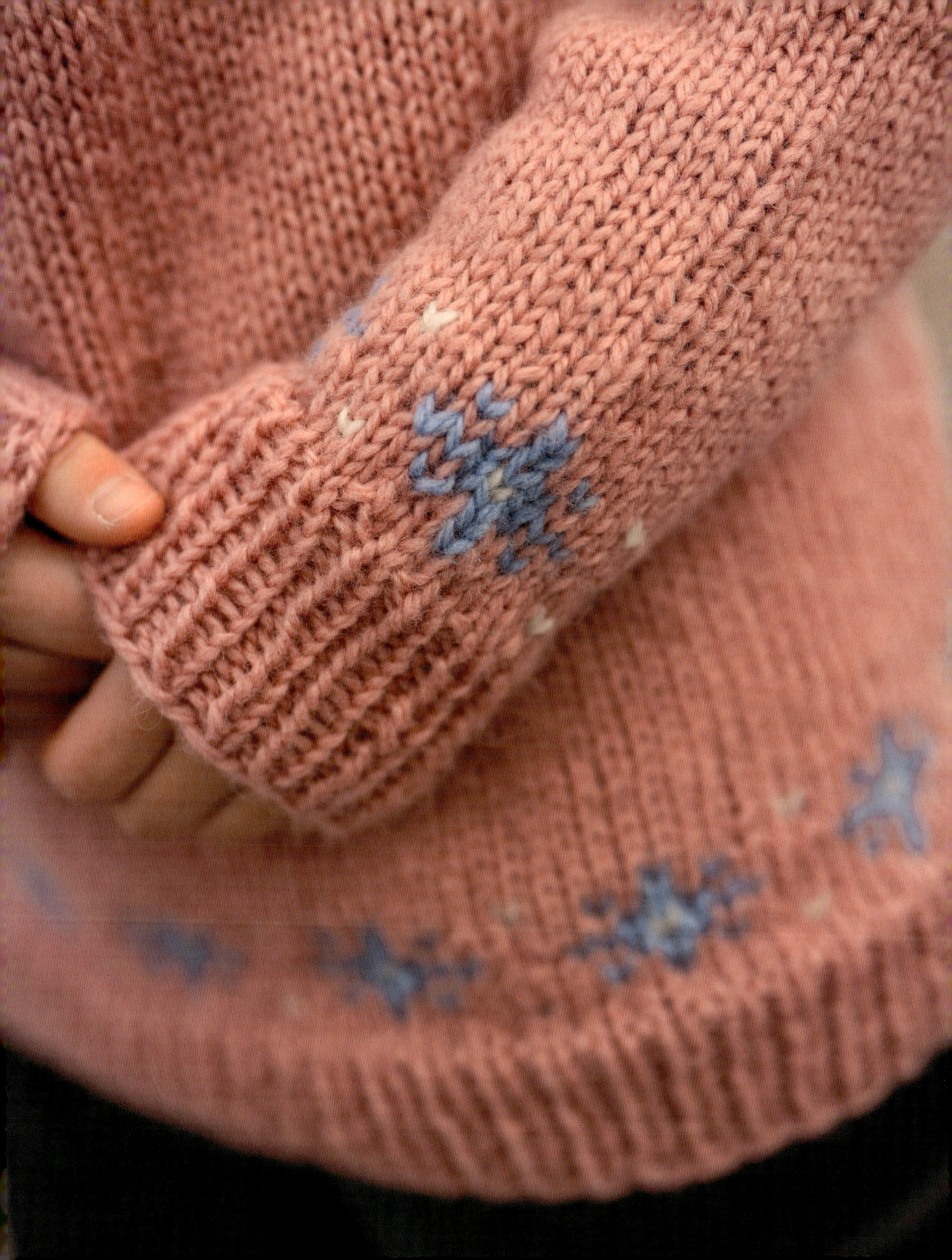

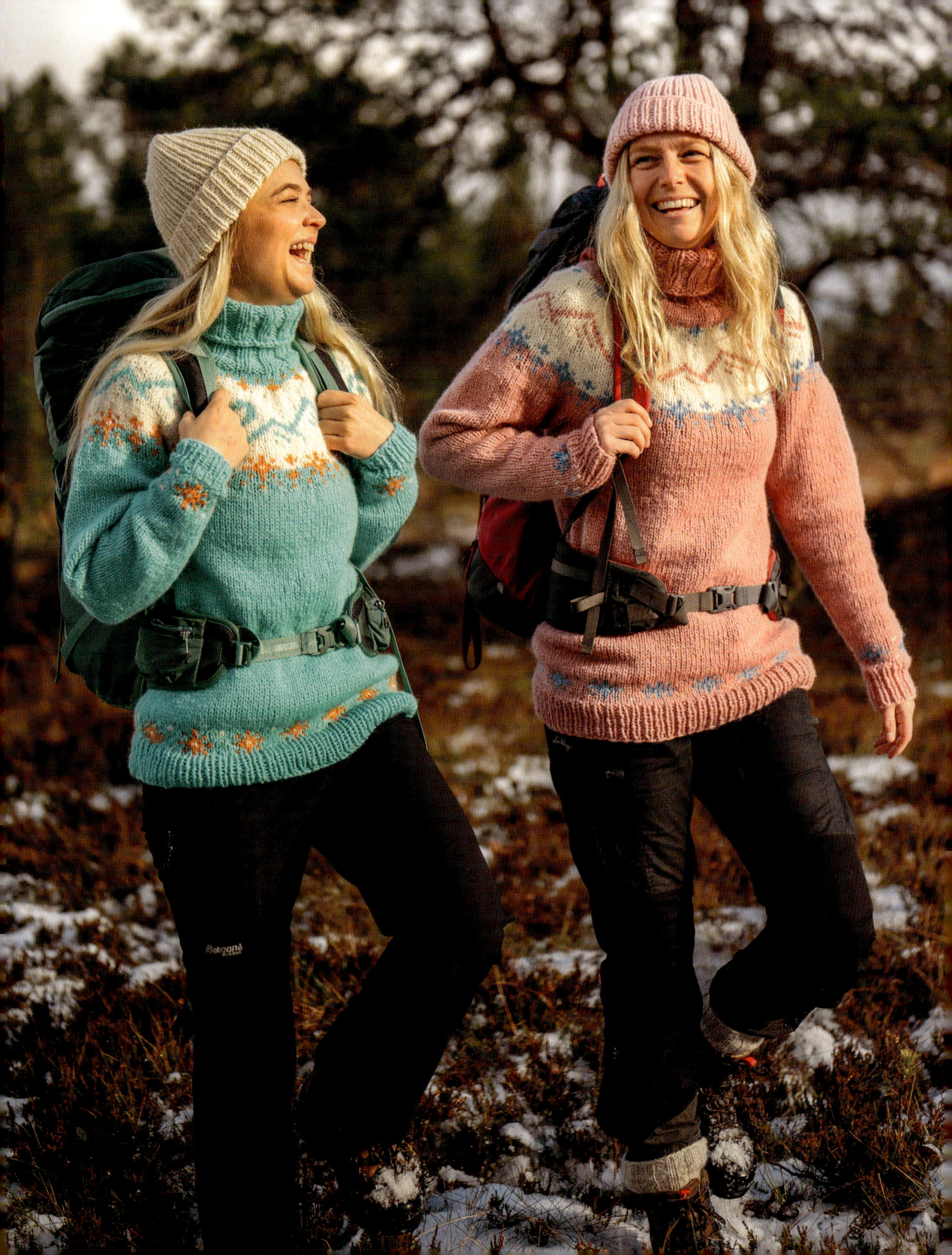

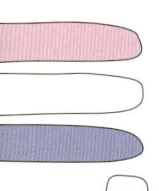

Color 1: Vams, rose 606
Color 2: Vams, white 01
Color 3: Vams, light denim 50
– Knit 2 together

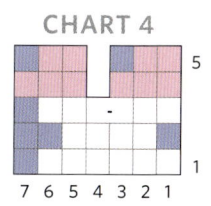

CHART 4

On the next round, decrease 30, 30 (41, 41, 52, 52) (63, 63, 74, 74) stitches evenly distributed as follows:

XXS and XS:
Knit 2, knit 2 together. Repeat from * to * 15 times.
Knit 4 stitches.
Knit 2, knit 2 together. Repeat 15 times.
Knit 4.

S and M:
Knit 2, knit 2 together. Repeat from * to * 18 times.
Knit 1, knit 2 together. Repeat from * to * 2 times.
Knit 2, knit 2 together. Repeat from * to * 19 times. *Knit 1, knit 2 together*. Repeat from * to * 2 times.

L and XL:
Knit 2, knit 2 together, knit 2, knit 2 together. *Knit 2, knit 2 together, knit 2, knit 2 together, knit 1, knit 2 together*. Repeat from * to * 16 times. Knit 2, knit 2 together, knit 2, knit 2 together.

2XL and 3XL:
*Knit 2, knit 2 together. Repeat from * to * 3 times.
Knit 2, knit 2 together, 1 knit, knit 2 together. Repeat from * to * 28 times.
Knit 2, knit 2 together. Repeat from * to * 4 times.

4XL and 5XL:
Knit 1, knit 2 together. Repeat from * to * 3 times.
Knit 2, knit 2 together, 1 knit, knit 2 together. Repeat from * to * 34 times.
Knit 1, knit 2 together. Repeat from * to * 3 times.

You now have 98, 98 (119, 119, 140, 140) (161, 161, 182, 182) stitches remaining on the needles.

Knit the pattern following Chart 4 and decreasing as shown in chart. Repeat stitches 1-7 of chart for each round. Work rounds 1-5 of chart one time. You now have 84, 84 (102, 102, 120, 120) (138, 138, 156, 156) stitches left.

Knit 1, 2 (2, 2, 5, 5) (5, 5, 5, 5) rounds with color 1.

Knit 1, 2 (2, 2, 5, 5) (5, 5, 5, 5) rounds with color 1.

On the next round, decrease 24, 24 (38, 38, 52, 52) (66, 62, 76, 76) stitches evenly distributed as follows:

XXS and XS:
Knit 2, knit 2 together, knit 1, knit 2 together. Repeat from * to * 12 times.

S and M:
Knit 1, knit 2 together. Repeat from * to * 7 times.
Knit 1, knit 2 together, knit 2 together. Repeat from * to * 6 times.
Knit 1, knit 2 together. Repeat from * to * 7 times.
Knit 1, knit 2 together, knit 2 together. Repeat from * to * 6 times.

L and XL:
Knit 2 together. Repeat from * to * 10 times.

Knit 1, knit 2 together, knit 2 together. Repeat from * to *
8 times.
Knit 2 together. Repeat from * to * 10 times.
Knit 1, knit 2 together, knit 2 together. Repeat from * to *
8 times.

2XL:
Knit 2 together. Repeat from * to * 30 times.
Knit 1, knit 2 together. Repeat from * to * 3 times.
Knit 2 together. Repeat from * to * 30 times.
Knit 1, knit 2 together. Repeat from * to * 3 times.

3XL:
Knit 2 together. Repeat from * to * 17 times.
Knit 1, knit 2 together, knit 2 together. Repeat from * to *
7 times.
Knit 2 together. Repeat from * to * 17 times.
Knit 1, knit 2 together, knit 2 together. Repeat from * to *
7 times.

4XL and 5XL:
Knit 2 together. Repeat from * to * 36 times.
Knit 1, knit 2 together. Repeat from * to * 2 times.
Knit 2 together. Repeat from * to * 36 times.
Knit 1, knit 2 together. Repeat from * to * 2 times.

You now have 60, 60 (64, 64, 68, 68) (72, 76, 80, 80) stitches.

On the next round, bind off the 16, 16 (16, 16, 18, 18) (18, 18, 20, 20) stitches at center front for the neckline as follows: Knit the first 13, 13 (15, 15, 15, 15) (17, 19, 20, 20) stitches of the round. Bind off the next 16, 16 (16, 16, 18, 18) (18, 18, 20, 20) stitches. Knit to the end of the round. Cut the yarn.

You now have 44, 44 (48, 48, 50, 50) (54, 58, 60, 60) stitches on the needles.

Knit back and forth in stockinette stitch while decreasing stitches on each side of the front neck as follows:

Start the next row at the right neck edge with a right-side row. Bind off the first 2 stitches of the row. Knit to the end of the row. Turn. Bind off the first 2 stitches of the row. Purl back. Turn. Repeat these 2 rows 2, 2 (2, 2, 3, 3) (3, 3, 3, 3) more times. You have now decreased a total of 6, 6 (6, 6, 8, 8) (8, 8, 8, 8) stitches on each side and have 32, 32 (36, 36, 34, 34) (38, 42, 44, 44) stitches on the needle.

Collar

You will now pick up stitches over the bound-off stitches as follows: Using the shorter circular needle, knit across the row to the left front neck edge. Pick up and knit 28, 28 (28, 28, 34, 34) (34, 34, 36, 36) stitches evenly over the bound-off front neck stitches. You now have a total of 60, 60 (64, 64, 68, 68) (72, 76, 80, 80) stitches on the needle. Place a marker for the beginning of the round. Work knit 2, purl 2 ribbing in the round for 10", or to the desired length.

Bind off loosely, knitting the knit stitches and purling the purl stitches. Fold the neckline outwards. Sew underarm seams and weave in all ends. Steam or wet block the sweater for an even finish.

Color 1: Vams, light teal 69
Color 2: Vams, white 01
Color 3: Vams, melon 113

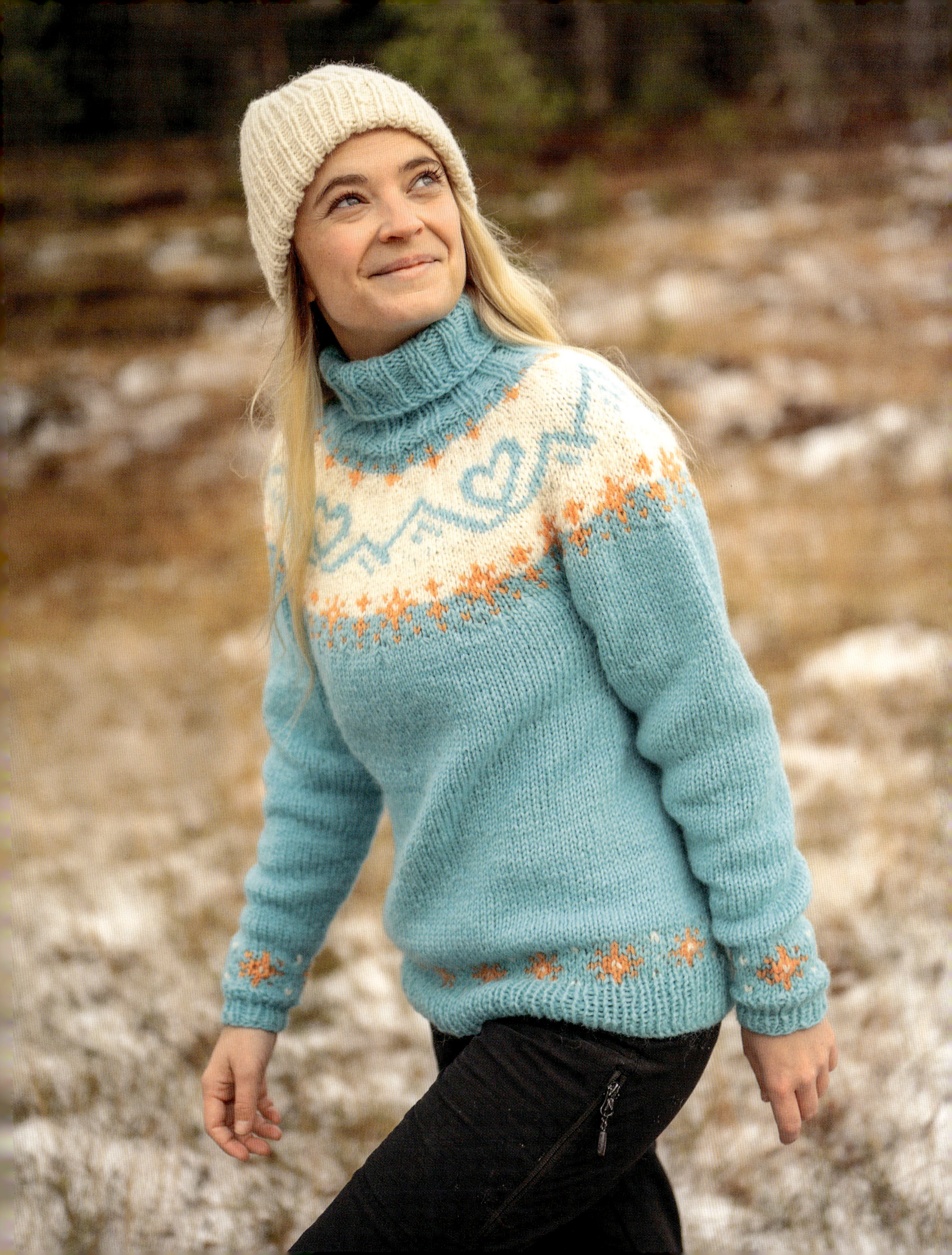

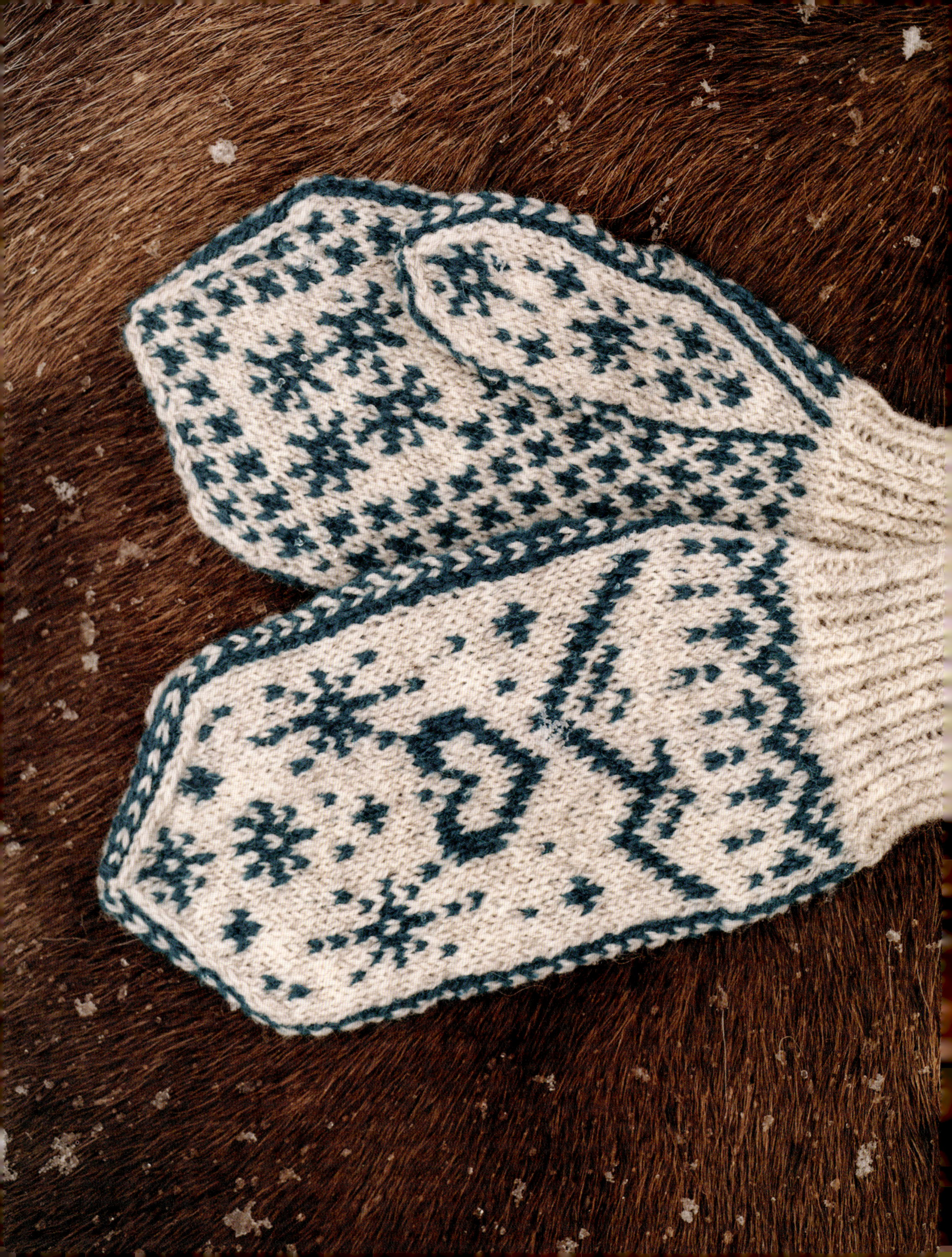

Mountain Mittens

As a continuation of the Mountain Sweater, the Mountain Mittens came along. They are lighter-weight mittens, perfect for walking the dog or for cross-country skiing.

Sizes
S/M (L/XL)

Measurements
Length from top of ribbing to tip: about 7½ (8¼)"
Width (after the thumb): about 4 (4⅜)"

Yarn
Rauma Finull (100% Norwegian wool: 110 yd [100 m]/50 g)

Actual Yarn Amounts
Color 1: 50 g all sizes
Color 2: 50 g all sizes

Needles
US size 1: set of 5 double-pointed needles
US size 3: set of double-pointed needles
Adjust needle size as necessary to obtain gauge.

Gauge
30 stitches × 32 rows in pattern = 4 × 4"

How to Knit These Mittens

Left Mitten

Cast on 50 (56) stitches on US size 1 double-pointed needles with color 1. Place marker for the beginning of the round. Work knit 1 through the back loop, purl 1 ribbing in the round for 3½ (4)".

Switch to US size 3 double-pointed needles and knit 1 round increasing 5 (5) stitches evenly distributed as follows: Knit 10 (11) stitches, increase 1 stitch. Repeat from * to * 4 more times. Finish by knitting 0 (1) stitch. You now have 55 (61) stitches on the needles.

Distribute the stitches so that the stitches on needles 1 and 2 become the top of the mitten, and needles 3 and 4 become the underside of the mitten like so:

Needle 1: 15 (17) stitches.
Needle 2: 15 (17) stitches.
Needle 3: 16 (17) stitches.
Needle 4: 9 (10) stitches.

Knit the pattern following the chart for your size, reading each round of the chart from right to left increasing as shown in the chart. At the orange line in the chart, mark the position of the thumb: Knit the 13 stitches with a strand of contrasting color scrap yarn. Slide the scrap yarn stitches back onto the left needle and knit them with color 1, then continue to the end of the round.

Decrease for tip of mitten as shown in the chart. When the last round of the chart is complete, 10 stitches will remain. Cut the yarn and pull it through the remaining stitches.

Thumb

Remove the scrap yarn and place the 13 stitches above and below the opening on US size 3 double-pointed needles. Pick up 1 extra stitch on each side of the thumb opening. You now have 28 stitches on the needle. Distribute the stitches onto 2 needles, with 14 stitches on each needle.

Knit the pattern following the thumb chart for your size, reading each round of the chart from right to left and decreasing as shown in the chart. Center the pattern on the thumb to align with the gusset pattern. When the last round of the chart is complete, 8 stitches will remain. Cut the yarn and pull it through the remaining stitches.

Right Mitten

Knit the ribbing in the same way as for the left mitten. Knit 1 round of stockinette, increasing as on the left mitten.

Distribute the stitches so that the stitches on needles 1 and 2 become the underside of the mitten, and needles 3 and 4 become the top of the mitten like so:

Needle 1: 9 (10) stitches.
Needle 2: 16 (17) stitches.
Needle 3: 15 (17) stitches.
Needle 4: 15 (17) stitches.

Knit the right mitten the same as the left, but mirrored, so that the pattern is mirrored and the thumb is on the correct side as follows: Knit the pattern following the chart for your size, reading each round of the chart from left to right and increasing as shown in the chart and knit the thumb the same as for the left mitten.

Weave in all loose ends. Steam or wash the mittens for an even finish.

Color 1: Finull, light gray mélange 403

Color 2: Finull, petrol 484

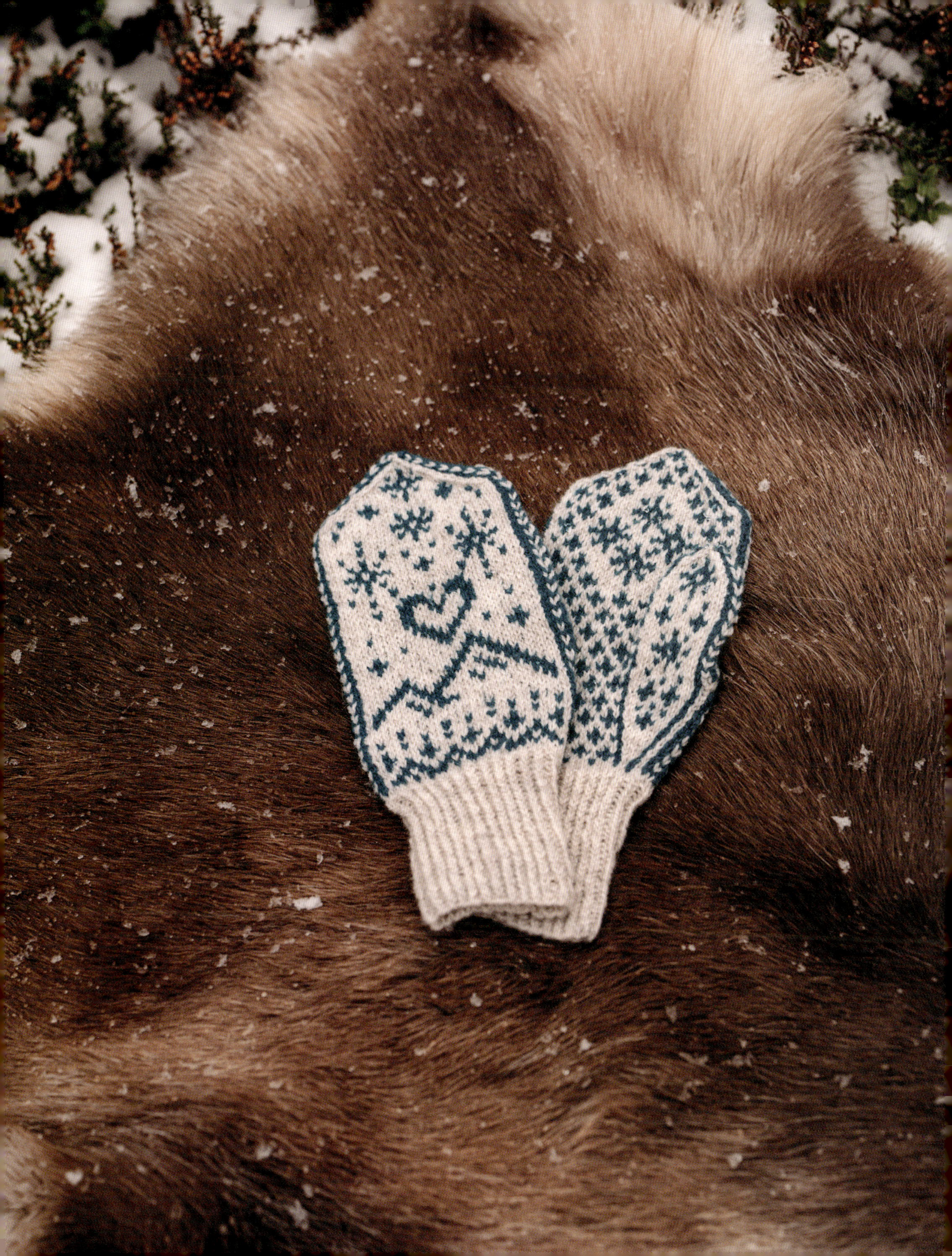

CHART S/M THUMB

Y	Pick up the strand between stitches and knit it through the back loop.
X	At the beginning of needles 1 and 3: Knit 2 together through the back loop. At the end of needles 2 and 4: Knit 2 together.
∧	Slip the first stitch without knitting it, knit 2 together, and lift the slipped stitch over the knit stitch.

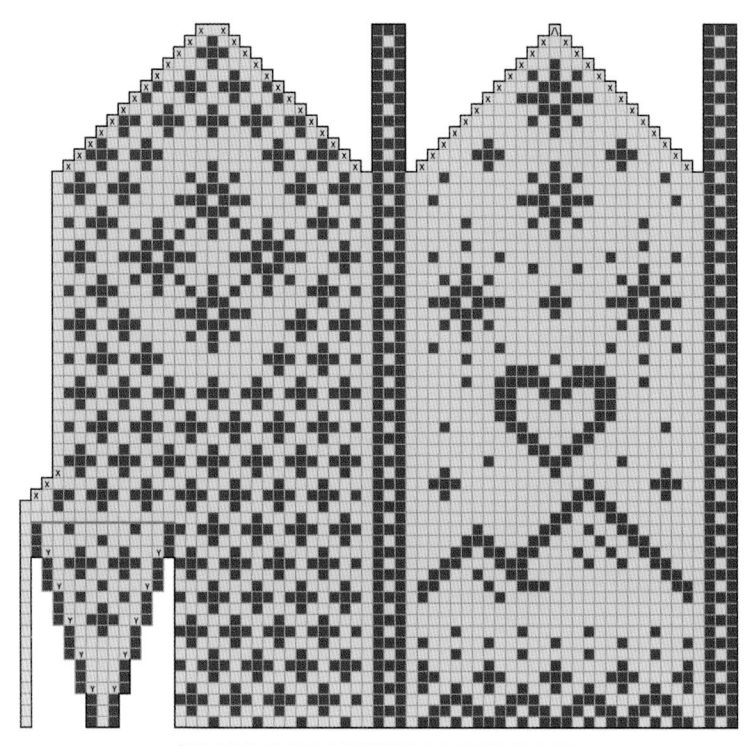

CHART S/M MITTEN, LEFT HAND

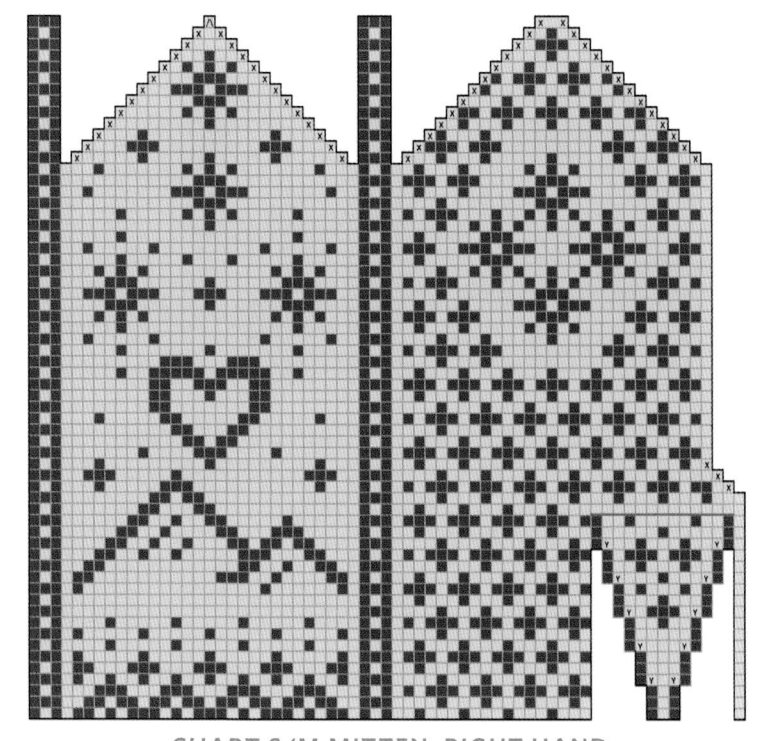

CHART S/M MITTEN, RIGHT HAND

Scan the QR code with your smartphone or visit www.quarto.com/files/HappyNordicKnits.com to download enlarged, printable charts for this project.

CHART, M/L THUMB

CHART M/L MITTEN, LEFT HAND

CHART M/L MITTEN, RIGHT HAND

73

Maddis Sweater

I have always looked up to my older sister, Stine. She was good at so many things and was allowed to do everything I wasn't. She was my role model when I was little. For her, I was probably the annoying little sister who didn't understand or want to accept that I was five years younger. Our age difference led to an imbalance during childhood. But at the same time, we had moments when we were on the same wavelength, and the common meeting point was usually knitting and cozy times together in the living room at home.

When Stine moved out, and I finally became a teenager, we found more balance and harmony in our relationship. Suddenly, we could talk about everything, and the older we got, the closer we grew. That's when the strong sibling relationship came into its own, a solid bond, and the truth that we are one was strengthened. We belong together on another level, not just physically and mentally, but spiritually. Stine and I understand each other without words and finish each other's sentences. Cliché, I know, but that's how it is with us. We understand things about each other that no one else can, and it feels like we are one.

In 2017, Stine became a mother for the first time, and the symbiosis between us changed. Suddenly, there was a new person who needed to find their place in our pack. That little person was Madelen, my beautiful niece. As Madelen has grown up, I see more and more of both Stine and myself in her. Yet, she is completely her own person: creative, warm-hearted, kind, funny, independent, tough, and colorful.

When I designed this sweater, I used the colors of the rainbow, or as Madelen would say: unicorn colors—her favorites. So, I couldn't help giving this design her nickname—Maddis. Now, Madelen has started school and has her own annoying little sister, the tough, fantastic, and independent Andrea. It's like seeing Stine and me thirty years ago. I have no words for how much these girls mean to me, and I am forever a proud aunt.

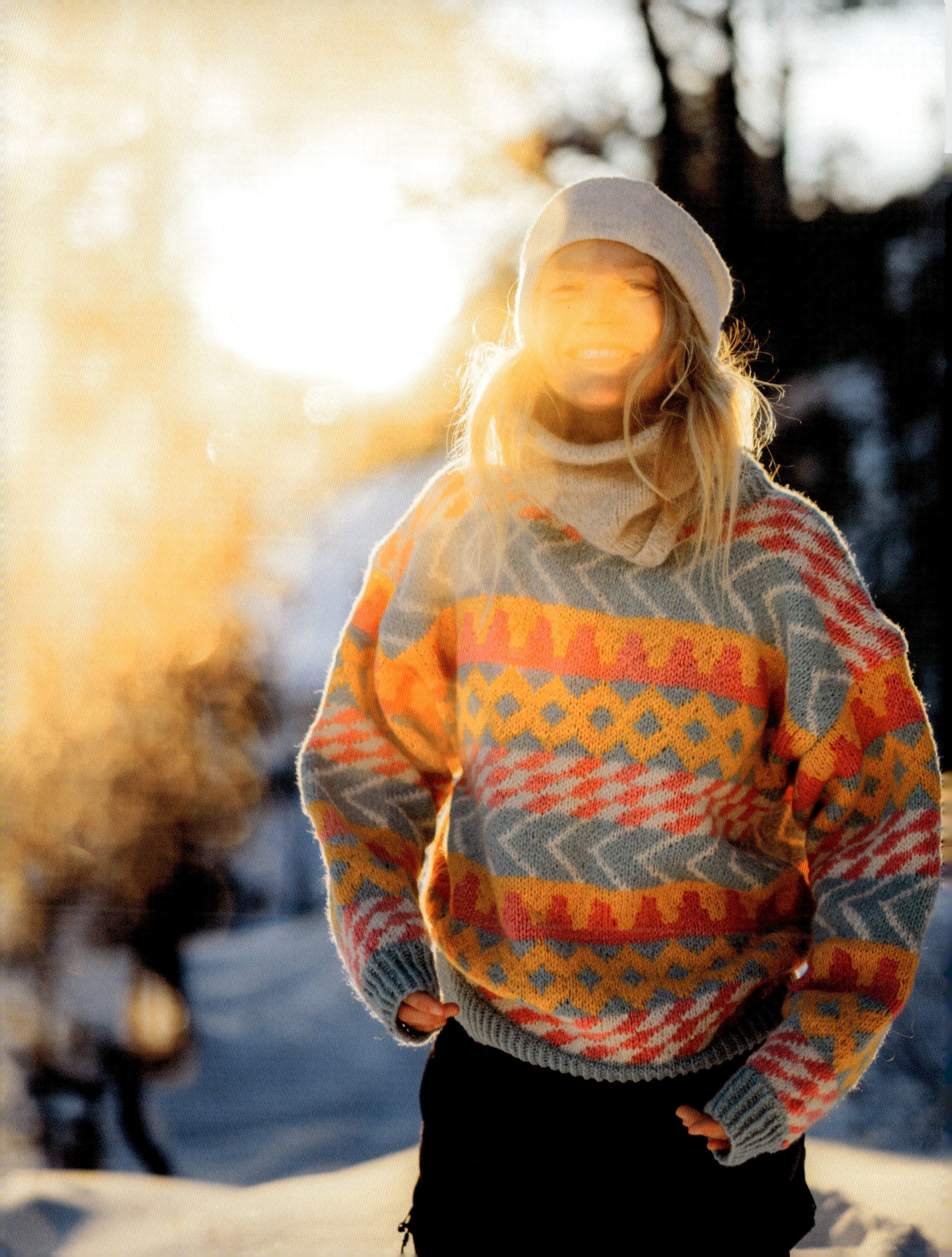

Color 1: Luna, minty green 4444
Color 2: Luna, rose 447
Color 3: Luna, unbleached white 400
Color 4: Luna, warm yellow 421

Size
XXS, XS (S, M, L, XL) (2X, 3X, 4X, 5X)

Garment Measurements
This sweater is designed to have approximately 8" of positive ease.
Bust: 38½, 42 (43¾, 47¼, 48¾, 52¼) (55¾, 57¾, 61½, 63)"
Total length: 22½, 22¾ (24, 24¾, 25½, 26½) (27¼, 27½, 28, 28¼)" or desired length
Sleeve length: 17, 17 (17¾, 18, 18½, 19¼) (19¾, 19¾, 20, 20)" or desired length
Notice that the shoulder sits a bit down on the arm and is part of the sleeve length.

Yarn
Hillesvåg Luna (100% Norwegian wool: 220 yd [200 m]/100 g) or
Hillesvåg Vidde (100 %% Norwegian wool: 220 yd [200 m]/100 g) or
Hillesvåg Varde (100% Norwegian wool: 220 yd [200 m]/100 g)

Actual Yarn Amounts
Color 1: 300, 300 (300, 300, 300, 300) (400, 400, 400, 400) g
Color 2: 200, 200 (200, 200, 200, 200) (200, 200, 300, 300) g
Color 3: 200 g all sizes
Color 4: 200 g all sizes

Needles
US size 2: 16" and 32" circular needles and set of double-pointed needles
US size 7: 16" and 32" circular needles and set of double-pointed needles
Adjust needle size as necessary to obtain gauge.

Gauge
18 stitches × 24 rows in stockinette = 4 × 4"

How to Knit This Sweater

You will knit the body, yoke, and sleeves from the bottom up to the total length. You will cut steeks for the armholes and sew in the sleeves. You'll knit the collar last.

Body

Cast on 176, 192 (200, 216, 224, 240) (256, 264, 280, 288) stitches on US size 2 circular needles with color 1. Place a marker to mark the beginning of the round. Work knit 1 through the back loop, purl 1 ribbing in the round for 2½".

Switch to US size 7 circular needles and knit 1 round with color 1.

Knit the pattern following the chart. Repeat stitches 1–8 of chart for each round. Repeat rounds 1–52 of chart until the piece measures 11¾, 11¾ (13, 13½, 13¾, 14½) (14½, 14½, 14½, 14½)" or to desired length to the armholes.

You will now cast on 5 new stitches on each side for the steeks. These are the stitches that will be cut for armholes later, and they are not included in the total stitch count. You will not knit the pattern over these stitches. Place a marker on each side of the steek stitches as follows:

Knitting the chart pattern over the first 88, 96 (100, 108, 112, 120) (128, 132, 140, 144) stitches. Place 1 marker. Cast on 5 new stitches with the main color for the pattern repeat you are knitting. Place 1 marker. Finish knitting the round in the chart pattern. Place 1 marker and then cast on 5 new stitches at the end of the needle. The steek stitches are now marked on each side.

Continue knitting in pattern as before but knit the steek stitches either in a solid color or by alternating the colors used for that round for each stitch. Continue working in the established pattern until the piece measures 9½, 9¾ (9¾, 10¼, 10½, 11) (11⅜, 11¾, 12¼, 12¾)" from the beginning of the steek stitches.

In the next round, bind off the center 34, 34 (36, 36, 38, 38) (40, 40, 42, 42) stitches for the neckline as follows: Knit the first 27, 31 (32, 36, 37, 41) (44, 46, 49, 51) stitches of the round. Bind off the next 34, 34 (36, 36, 38, 38) (40, 40, 42, 42) stitches. Continue knitting in pattern to the end of the round. You now have 142, 158 (164, 180, 186, 202) (216, 224, 238, 246) stitches left on the needle. Cut the yarn.

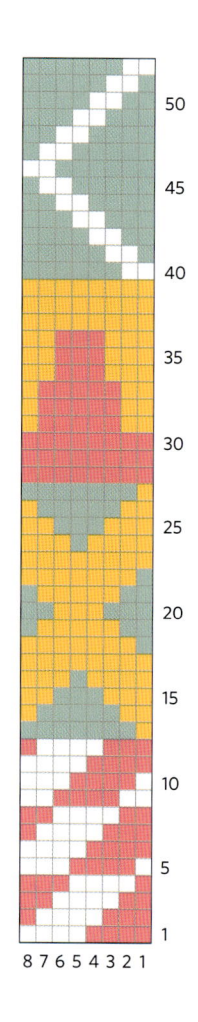

Knit back and forth in stockinette, continuing the chart pattern, while shaping the neckline as follows: Start the next row at the right neck edge with a right-side row. Bind off 1 stitch by slipping 1 stitch onto the right needle without knitting it. Knit the next stitch and pass the first stitch over the second stitch and off the needle. Continue knitting the pattern for the rest of the row. Turn and bind off 1 stitch by slipping 1 stitch onto the right needle without

78

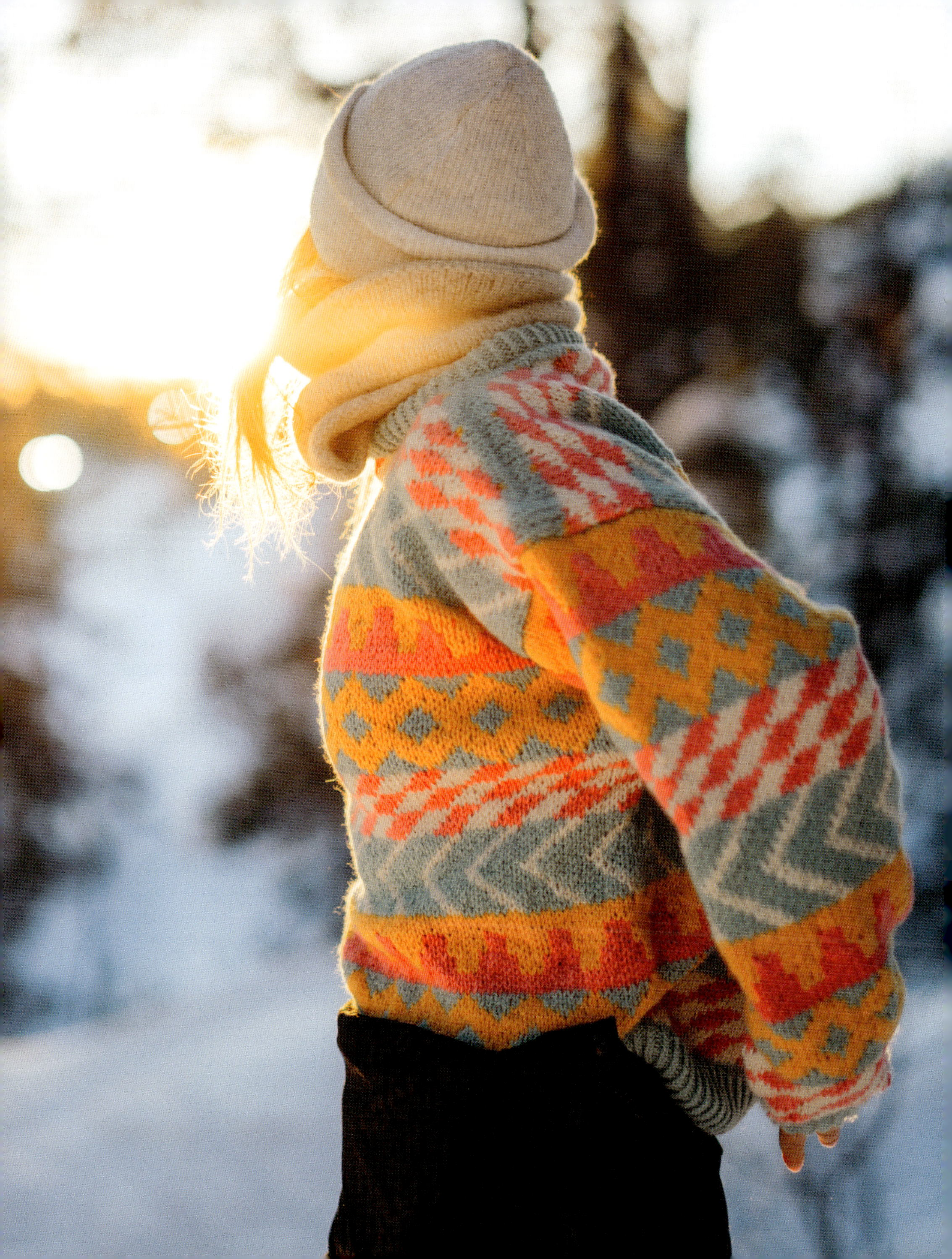

Color 1: Luna, dark burgundy 426
Color 2: Luna, warm yellow 421
Color 3: Vidde, nature gray 321
Color 4: Varde, gray violet 2111

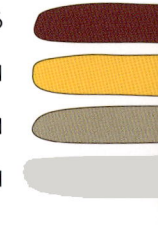

knitting it. Purl the next stitch and pass the first stitch over the second stitch and off the needle. Continue purling the pattern for the rest of the row. Repeat these 2 rows once more. You have now bound off a total of 4 stitches (2 on each side), and you have 138, 154 (160, 176, 182, 198) (212, 220, 234, 242) stitches remaining on the needle.

Knit 2 rows in color 1. Bind off all stitches.

Sleeves
Cast on 36, 36 (40, 40, 44, 44) (46, 46, 48, 50) stitches on US size 2 double-pointed needles with color 1. Place a marker to mark the beginning of the round. Work knit 1 through the back loop, purl 1 ribbing in the round for 2".

In the next round, switch to US size 7 needles and knit 1 round with color 1, while increasing 10 stitches evenly as follows: *Knit 3, 3 (4, 4, 4, 4) (4, 4, 4, 5) stitches, increase 1 stitch, knit 4, 4 (4, 4, 4, 4) (5, 5, 5, 5) stitches, increase 1 stitch*. Repeat from * to * 5 times. Finish the round by knitting 1, 1 (0, 0, 4, 4) (1, 1, 3, 0) stitch(es). You now have 46, 46 (50, 50, 54, 54) (56, 56, 58, 60) stitches on the needles.

Knit the pattern following the chart. Repeat stitches 1–8 of chart for each round. The rounds may not end with a complete pattern repeat. Repeat rounds 1–52 of the chart.

At the same time, when the piece measures 2½", increase 2 stitches as follows: Knit the first stitch, pick up the strand between stitches from front to back with the left needle, and knit it through the back loop. Knit the pattern until 1 stitch remains, pick up the strand between stitches from back to front with the left needle and knit it, then knit the last stitch.

Continue knitting the pattern and increasing in the same way every ½" until you have 98, 100 (100, 104, 108, 112) (116, 118, 122, 126) stitches on the needle. The increased stitches are worked as an extension of the pattern repeat on each side.

Continue knitting the chart pattern without further increases until the sleeve measures 17, 17 (17¾, 18, 18½, 19¼) (19¾, 19¾, 20, 20)" or to the desired length.

Knit 1 round with color 1. Bind off all stitches. Knit another sleeve in the same way.

Finishing
Sew 2 seams on your sewing machine on each side of the steek stitches and steek the armholes (see page 174). Sew the front shoulder stitches to the back shoulder stitches (see page 169). Sew in the sleeves (see page 175).

Collar
Pick up and knit 80, 80 (84, 84, 88, 88) (92, 92, 96, 96) stitches evenly around the neckline using the shorter US size 2 circular needle and color 1. Place a marker to mark the beginning of the round. Work knit 1 through the back loop, purl 1 ribbing in the round for 1½". Bind off loosely, knitting twisted knit over twisted knit and purl over purl. Fold the neckline inward and loosely sew the bound-off edge to the first round of the collar.

Weave in all loose ends.

Steam or wet block the sweater for an even finish.

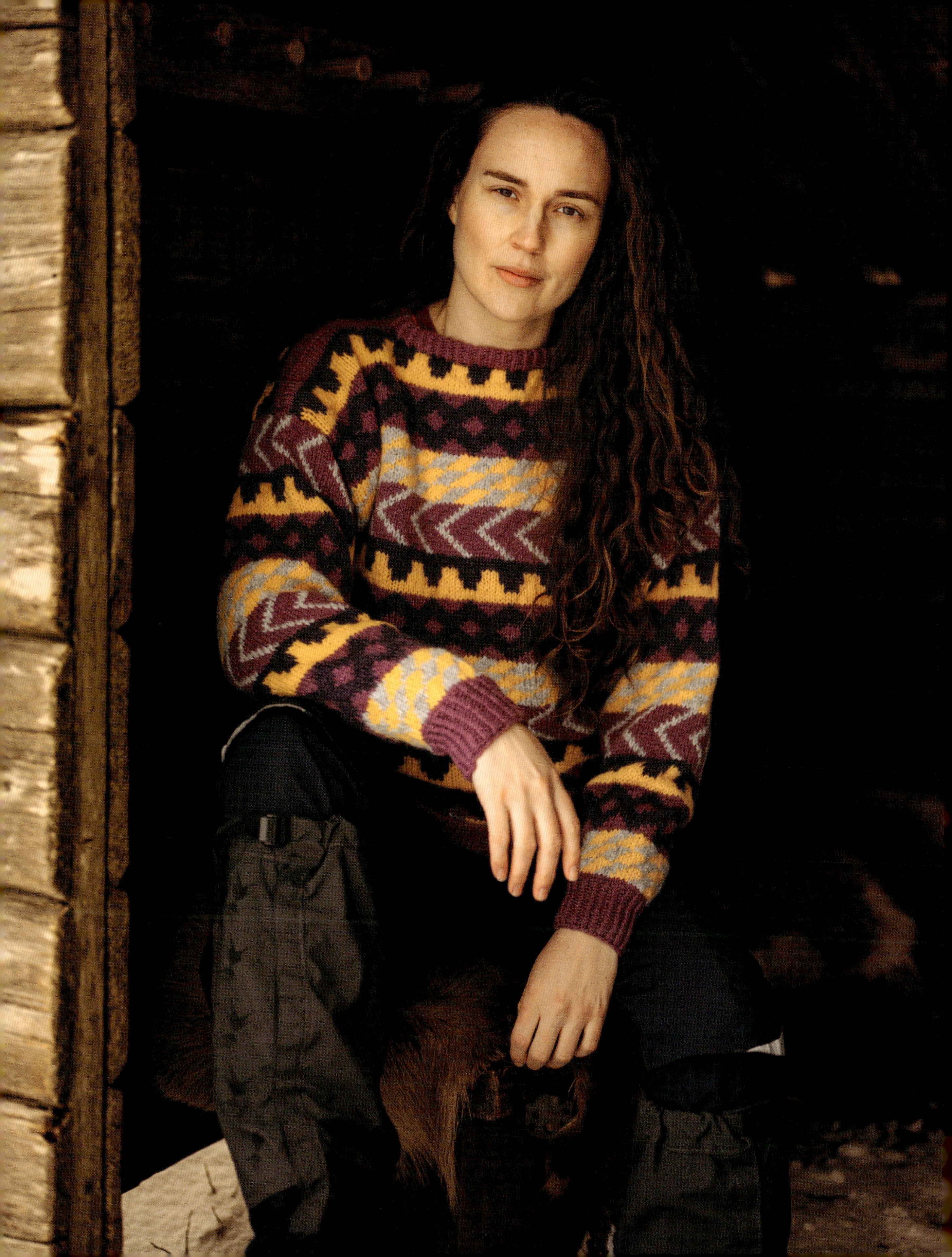

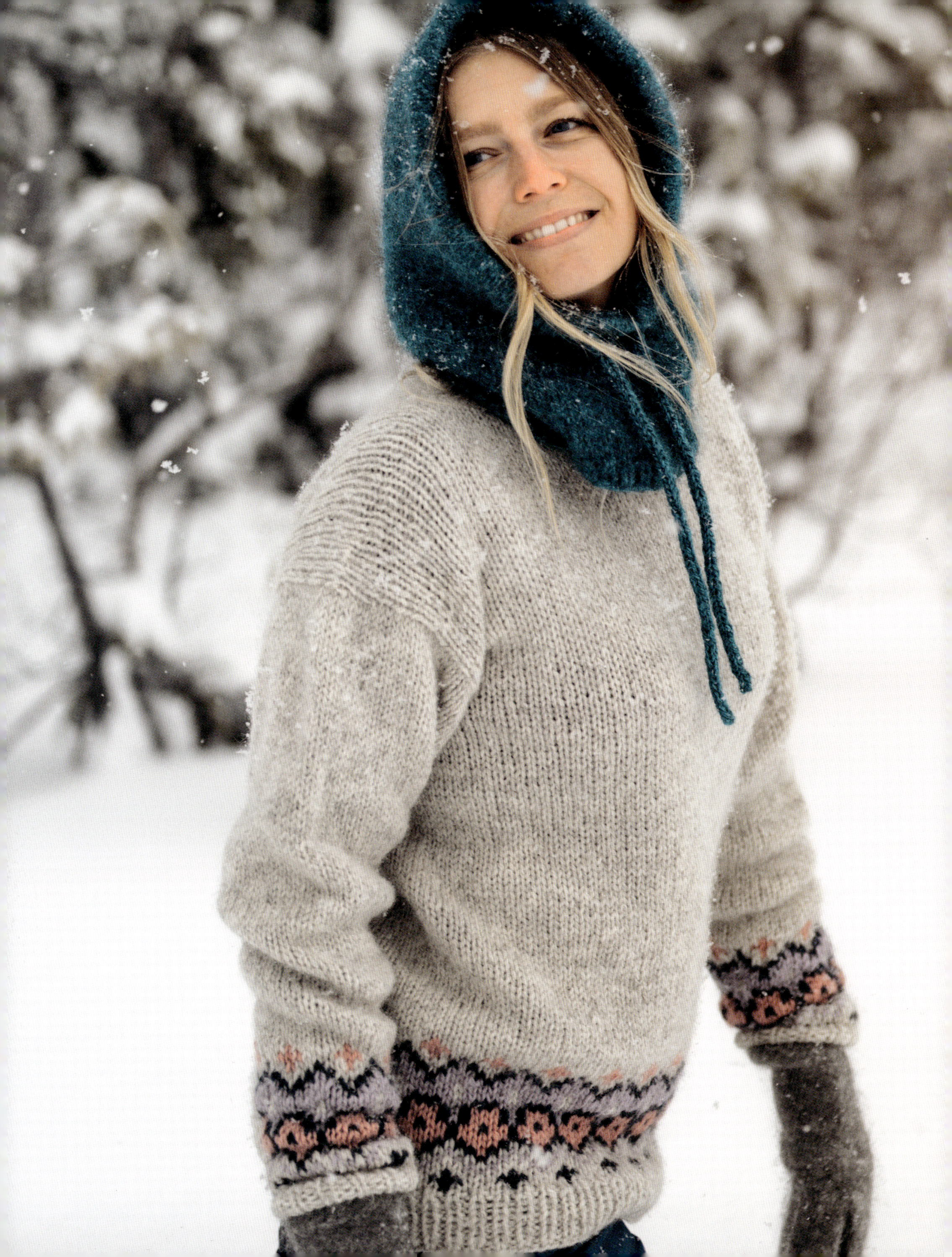

Bitter Cold Collection

A few winters ago, it was unusually cold here in Trondheim. The cold came over us like a frozen blanket, casting a kind of calm over the city. Everything moved in second gear, the countryside turned into a winter wonderland, and we had no choice but to go out on hikes every day to enjoy the cold and gather the few rays of sunshine we could before darkness took over again. There was little snow, making the terrain perfect for getting lost in the woods with Juster. The thermometer dipped below −4°F, and it was so cold that it took much more than just a simple hat and high-necked wool sweater to keep warm, even while active. That winter, I longed for a good neck warmer, something to keep my face and neck warm when my nose froze and my eyelashes turned white with frost.

As usual when I needed new woolen gear for hiking, I called Stine and shared my idea of a felted neck warmer. She didn't think the neck warmer idea was too far-fetched. Just a few days later, I was happily wandering through the winter wonderland, warm and content with a cozy, felted neck warmer. This is where the adventure of the Bitter Cold Collection began. These are durable, felted accessories: balaclava, neck warmer, headband, and mittens. Completely indispensable on the coldest days, but also great to wear in milder weather.

Bitter Cold Balaclava

I wanted to develop an even warmer and more specialized accessory to keep me warm on the coldest and harshest days. I wanted the ultimate hiking garment for cold and windy trips. The result was the Bitter Cold Balaclava. It's a fantastic piece of clothing that I use throughout the winter. It can be cinched shut, left open, worn with or without a hat or headband. On the warmer spring days, it's perfect to wear as a neck warmer with the hood pushed down.

Size
S/M (M/L)
Fits head circumference of 21–22¾ (22¾– 4½)"

Measurements Before Felting
Circumference top of neckline: 23½ (25½)"
Circumference hood (excluding edging): 23¼ (24½)"
Total length: 20½ (22½)"

Measurements After Felting
Circumference top of neckline: 19¾ (20½)"
Circumference hood (excluding edging): 19¾ (20½)"
Total length: 15 (16½)"

Yarn
Hillesvåg Blåne (100% Norwegian wool: 125 yd [114 m]/100 g) or
Hillesvåg Troll (100% Norwegian wool: 125 yd [114 m]/100 g)

Actual Yarn Amounts
300 g both sizes

Needles
US size 10: 16" circular needles
US size 6: set of double-pointed needles (for drawstring)
Adjust needle size as necessary to obtain gauge.

Gauge
114 stitches × 18 rows = 4 × 4"

Color:
Blåne, teal 2106

Color:
Troll, ochre 713

How to Knit this Balaclava

The balaclava is knit from the bottom up. First, the neck warmer is knit in the round, and then stitches are bound off under the chin. Next, the hood is knit back and forth. The edging around the face is picked up and knit at the end.

Neck Warmer

Cast on 100 (108) stitches on US size 10 circular needles, Place a marker for the beginning of the round. Work knit 1, purl 1 ribbing in the round for 4 rounds.

Continue in the round in stockinette stitch while decreasing as follows: Knit 2 rounds. On the next round, decrease 4 stitches as follows: *Knit 2 together, knit 23 (25) stitches*. Repeat from * to * 3 more times. You now have 96 (104) stitches. Knit 2 rounds. On the next round, decrease 4 stitches as follows: *Knit 2 together, knit 22 (24) stitches*. Repeat from * to * 3 more times. You now have 92 (100) stitches. Repeat the same process with 2 rounds of knitting followed by one decrease round, working 1 stitch fewer between the decreases, 4 more times. You now have 76 (84) stitches on the needle. Continue in stockinette stitch in the round until the piece measures 6 (6¼)".

On the next round, bind off 6 stitches under the chin as follows: Bind off the first 6 stitches on the needle and knit the rest of the round as usual. You now have 70 (78) stitches on the needle.

Hood

Now you will knit the hood back and forth in stockinette stitch, knitting on the right side and purling on the wrong side, beginning with a wrong-side purl row. Each time you start a new row, create 1 edge stitch as follows:

On the right side: Slip the first stitch as if to knit, without knitting it.
On the wrong side: Slip the first stitch as if to purl, without purling it.

On the first right side knit row, increase 16 (14) stitches as directed for your size using the following increase method: Increase 1 stitch by picking up the strand between stitches with the left needle from front to back and knitting this stitch through the back loop.

S/M:
Knit 5, increase 1 stitch. *Knit 4, increase 1*. Repeat from * to * 14 more times. Knit the last 5 stitches of the row.

M/L:
Knit 6, increase 1 stitch. *Knit 5, increase 1 stitch*. Repeat from * to * 12 more times. Knit the last 7 stitches of the row.

You now have 86 (92) stitches on the needle.

Knit stockinette stitch back and forth until the piece measures 13½ (15)" from the bound-off stitches under the chin, ending with a right side knit row.

On the next row, purl 43 (46) stitches, place a marker for center back of hood, then purl to the end of the row.

Decrease stitches at the center back of the hood as follows: Knit until 2 stitches remain before the marker. Knit these 2 stitches together through the back loops, knit the 2 stitches after the marker together. Knit to the end of the row. Turn and purl back. Repeat these two rows 6 more times. You now have 72 (78) stitches on the needle.

You can now either bind off all stitches and sew the top together or graft the stitches together.

Option 1, bind off: Bind off all stitches. Fold the hood in half with the wrong sides and sew the bound off edges together with mattress stitch (see page 169).

Option 2, graft together (see page 170): Grafting forms a new row of stitches, creating a seamless join.

Edging Around the Face

Using US size 10 circular needles, pick up and knit 100 (108) stitches evenly along the side edges of the hood, place a marker, then pick up and knit 1 stitch in each of the 6 bound-off stitches under the chin. Place a marker for the beginning of the round. You have 100 (108) stitches on the needle. Knit 2 rounds in stockinette stitch. On the next round, create holes for the drawstring as follows: Knit to the marker before the stitches under the chin. Knit 2 together, yarn over, knit 2 stitches, yarn over, knit 2 together. Knit 5 more rounds in stockinette stitch. Bind off all stitches.

Finishing

Fold the edging to the wrong side and sew the bound-off edge loosely to the row where you picked up stitches. Weave in all loose ends on the inside/wrong side.

Felt the balaclava. See page 179 for felting instructions. Once the balaclava is felted, shape it and lay it flat to dry.

I-Cord

Cast on 3 stitches on US size 6 needle. Knit all stitches. Slide the stitches to the other end of the needle. Bring the yarn behind the stitches, knit the stitches again. Continue until the cord measures 43" or the desired length. Bind off and weave in the loose ends. Thread the drawstring through the edging around the face.

The balaclava is amazing to wear inside a sleeping bag when you sleep outdoors.

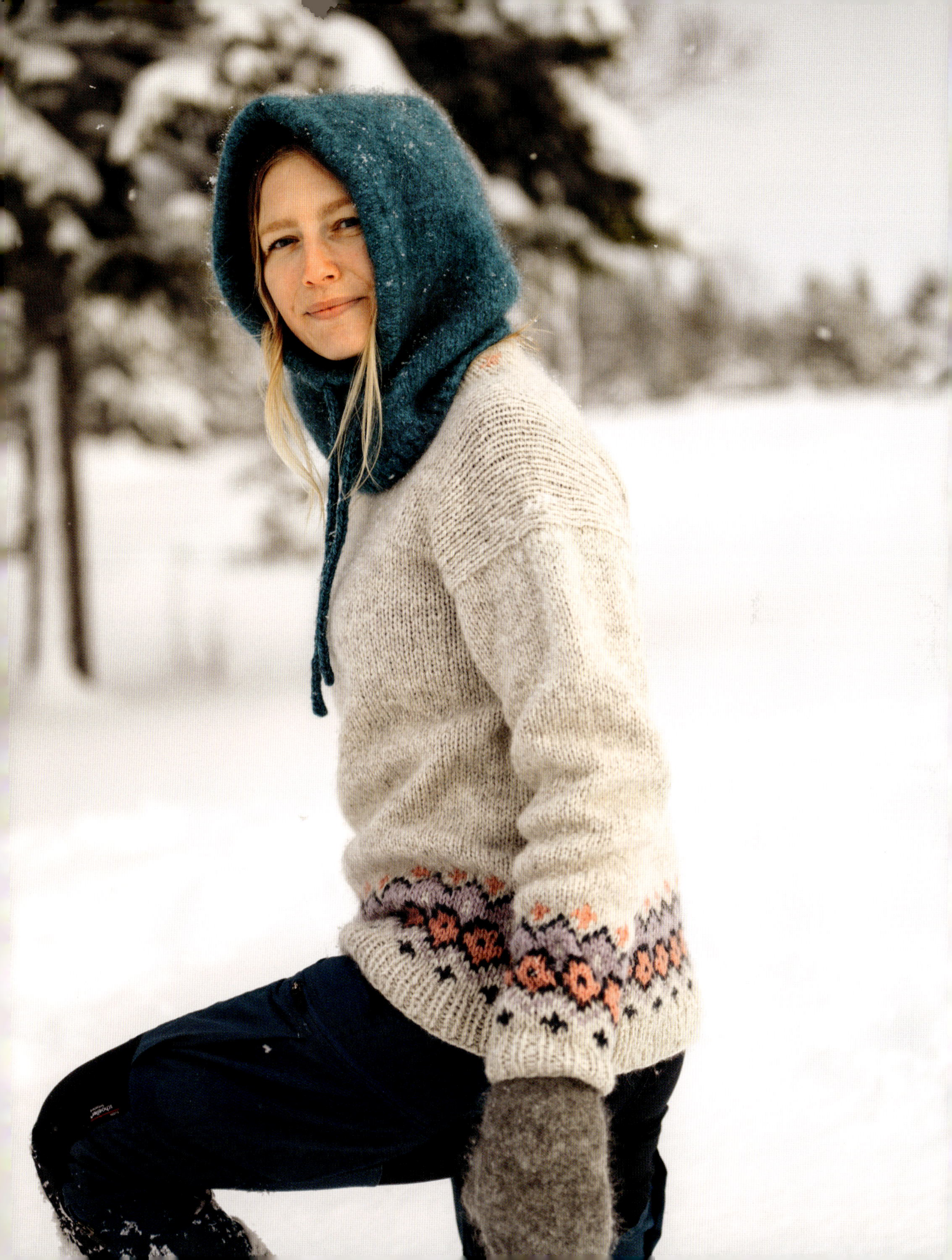

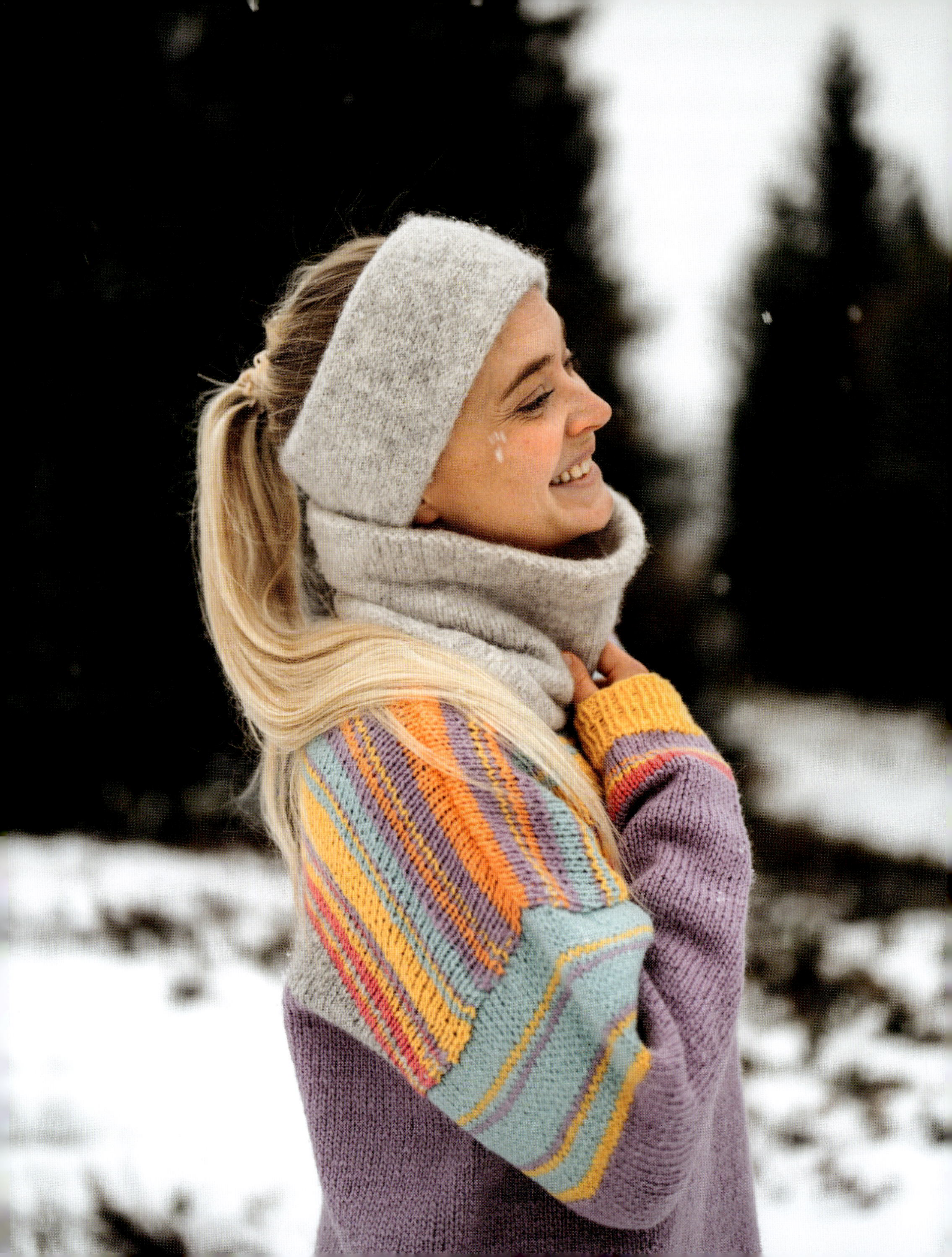

Bitter Cold Neck Warmer and Headband

My Bitter Cold Neck Warmer has accompanied me on countless trips, and I've worn it year-round, whether for camping, skiing, snowboarding, city outings, or walks with Juster. On windy days, the headband has also been my lifesaver. The last thing I want is to wear a headband that lets the wind blow right through. The Bitter Cold Headband is warm and windproof, so you won't have to worry about gusts. It's knit in two layers and felted, so it keeps both your ears and your head well-protected and warm, even on those bone-chilling cold days.

Another great thing about felted projects is that if they stretch over time with use, you can felt them again to tighten them (just be gentle and felt carefully). In other words, these are everlasting garments that keep you warm, are windproof, and are a must for all of us who love outdoor adventures!

BITTER COLD NECK WARMER

Sizes
One size

Measurements Before Felting
Height: 11¾"
Width: 23½"

Measurements After Felting
Height: 10"
Width: 20"

Yarn
Rauma Finull held double (100% Norwegian wool: 191 yd [175 m]/ 50 g) or Rauma Vams single strand (100% Norwegian wool: 91 yd [83 m]/50 g)

Actual Yarn Amount
100 g

Needles
US size 10: 16" circular needles
Adjust needle size as necessary to obtain gauge.

Gauge
14 stitches in stockinette before felting = 4"

How to Knit This Neck Warmer

The neck warmer is knitted from the bottom up. The lower edge has ribbing, while the top edge has a folded hem. The neck warmer is felted at the end.

With yarn held double, cast on 100 stitches with US size 10 needle. Place a marker to mark the beginning of the round. Work knit 1, purl 1, rigging in the round for 4 rounds. Knit 2 rounds.

On the next round, decrease 4 stitches as follows: *Knit 2 together, knit 23 stitches. Repeat from * to * 3 more times. You now have 96 stitches on the needle. Knit 2 rounds. On the next round, decrease 4 stitches as follows: *Knit 2 together, knit 22 stitches*. Repeat from * to * 3 more times. You now have 92 stitches on the needle.

Repeat the decrease round every third round 2 more times, knitting 1 fewer stitch between decreases each time. You now have 84 stitches left on the needle.

Continue in stockinette stitch until the piece measures approximately 11¾" from the cast-on edge.

Purl 1 round to create the turning ridge.

Continue in stockinette stitch until piece measures 2" from the turning ridge. Bind off all stitches.

Finishing
Fold the top edge to the wrong side at the turning ridge and sew down the bound-off edge, stitch by stitch, to the wrong side of the piece.

Weave in all loose ends on the wrong side.

Lightly felt the neck warmer. See page 179 for the felting guide.

Color:
Finull, light gray mélange 403

BITTER COLD HEADBAND

Sizes
XS (S, M, L)
Fits head circumference of 21–22 (22–22¾, 22¾–23½, 23½–24½)"

Measurements Before Felting
Height: 4¾" all sizes
Width: 22½ (23½, 24½, 25½)"

Measurements After Felting
Height: 4" all sizes
Width: 19 (20, 20½, 21¼)"

Yarn
Rauma Finull held double (100% Norwegian wool: 191 yd [175 m]/ 50 g) or
Rauma Vams single strand (100% Norwegian wool: 91 yd [83 m]/50 g)

Actual Yarn Amounts
100 g all sizes

Needles
US size 10: set of double-pointed needles
Adjust needle size as necessary to obtain gauge.

Gauge
14 stitches in stockinette before felting = 4"

How to Knit this Headband

The headband is knitted in the round on double-pointed needles (or your preferred needle style), forming a tube so it becomes double-layered. The cast-on and bound-off edges are sewn together at the end.

Cast on 34 stitches with two strands of Finull held double. Place a marker for the beginning of the round. Knit in stockinette stitch in the round until the work measures 22½ (23½, 24½, 25½)" or the desired pre-felting length. Bind off all stitches. Weave in all loose ends on the wrong side of the headband.

Finishing
Sew the ends of the headband together with the right side facing. Take care to align the beginning of the round at each end and sew each stitch to the corresponding stitch all the way around.

Felt the headband. See page 179 for the felting guide.

Color:
Finull, light gray mélange 403

Bitter Cold Mittens

These mittens are perfect for everyday use, dog walks, or on a trip in the mountains. I've worn mine for many, many years, and I've given them as gifts to friends for Christmas and birthdays. They are relatively quick to knit and can easily be spiced up with bold color choices—it's entirely up to you!

Color: Troll, unbleached white 702

Sizes
XS/S (M/L)

Measurements Before Felting
Length (from the cuff to the top of the mitten): 12½ (13⅓)"
Width (below the thumb): 5 (5½)"

Measurements After Felting
Length (from the cuff to the top of the mitten): 8⅔ (9½)"
Width (below the thumb): 4 (4⅓)"

Yarn
Rauma Vams (100% Norwegian wool: 91 yd [83 m]/50 g)

Actual Yarn Amounts
150 (150) g

Needles
US size 10: set of double-pointed needles
Adjust needle size as necessary to obtain gauge.

Gauge
14 stitches in stockinette before felting = 4"

How to Knit these Mittens

Right Mitten

Cast on 30 (32) stitches on double-pointed needles as follows: Cast on 7 (8) stitches on the first needle, cast on 8 (8) stitches on the next needle. Repeat on the remaining two needles. You now have 15 (16) stitches on for each side of the mitten. Knit in seed stitch for 6 rounds as follows:

Round 1: * Knit 1, purl 1*. Repeat from * to * to the end of the round.
Round 2: * Purl 1, knit 1*. Repeat from * to * to the end of the round
Repeat Rounds 1 and 2 two more times.

Knit 22 (22) rounds in stockinette stitch.

On the next round, increase 6 stitches evenly as follows: *Knit 5 (5) stitches, increase 1 stitch*. Repeat from * to * 5 more times. End by knitting 0 (2) stitches. You now have 36 (38) stitches on the needles. Knit 6 (6) rounds.

On the next round, mark the position of the thumb with scrap yarn as follows: Knit the first 6 (7) stitches on needle 1 with a piece of scrap yarn (preferably in a different color). Slide the scrap yarn stitches back onto the left needle and knit them with the main yarn, then continue to the end of the round.

Knit in stockinette stitch until mitten measures 4¾ (5½)" past the thumb or to your desired length.

On the next round, decrease 8 stitches evenly as follows: *Knit 2, knit 2 together, knit 3, knit 2 together*. Repeat from * to * 3 more times. End by knitting 0 (2) stitches. You now have 28 (30) stitches. Knit 3 rounds without decreasing.

On the next round, decrease 8 stitches evenly as follows: *Knit 1, knit 2 together, knit 2, knit 2 together*. Repeat from * to * 3 more times. End by knitting 0 (2) stitches. You now have 20 (22) stitches. Knit 3 rounds without decreasing.

On the next round, decrease 8 stitches evenly as follows: *Knit 1, knit 2 together, knit 2 together*. Repeat from * to * 3 more times. End by knitting 0 (2) stitches. You now have 12 (14) stitches. Knit 1 round without decreasing.

Decrease 4 (6) stitches evenly as follows:

XS/S:
Knit 1, knit 2 together. Repeat from * to * 3 more times.

M/L:
Knit 1, knit 2 together, knit 2 together, knit 2 together. Repeat from * to * one more time.

Cut the yarn and thread it through the remaining 8 stitches.

Thumb

Remove the scrap yarn and place the 6 (7) stitches above and below the opening on two needles, then pick up 1 more stitch on each side of the thumb opening, giving you a total of 14 (16) stitches. Knit in stockinette stitch in the round for 3 (3½)".

Knit 2 together 7 (8) times. You now have 7 (8) stitches left. Cut the yarn and pull it through the remaining stitches.

Left Mitten

Knit the left mitten in the same way as the right mitten except mark the position of the thumb as follows: Knit until there are 6 (7) stitches left on needle 2. Knit the next 6 (7) stitches with a piece of scrap yarn (preferably in a different color). Slide the scrap yarn stitches back onto the left needle and knit them with the main yarn, then continue to the end of the round.

Felt the mittens. See the felting guide on page 179.

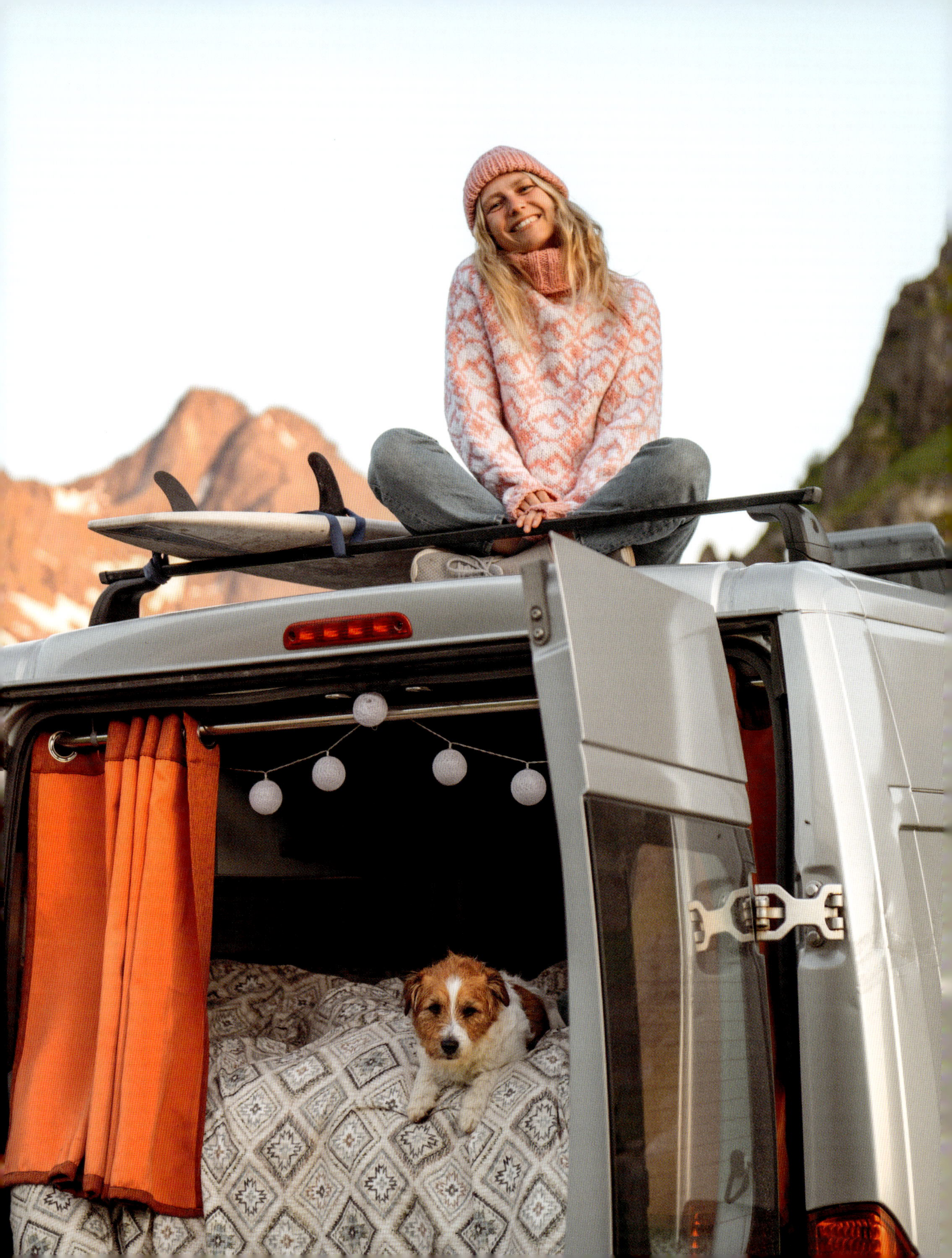

Lofoten Folk Sweater

After much trial and error, I've come to understand that life is not a straight line constantly going upward. Life happens, both to us and around us. We're always in motion and, for better and worse, life brings new insights, experiences, bumps in the road, and mountains to climb.

The same year I fell in love with nature, Stine became pregnant, and we started playing around with hiking knits, I also began a new study program to become a kindergarten teacher with a specialization in outdoor education. I loved that the outdoors was a natural classroom. I learned so much, about both outdoor life and myself, during the training to become a teacher. I was on top of the world, thinking I could do everything at once. That meant being an A student, overachieving, actively participating in classes, maintaining an Instagram account that was growing larger and larger, blogging for companies, having hobbies, being a good dog mom, a great partner, an attentive aunt, and on top of it all, holding down a part-time job. Not to mention maintaining my outdoor refuge, something I had less and less time for.

It may not come as a surprise that it eventually became too much for me. Life consisted of too many "musts," and I completely forgot to replenish myself with what I needed to stay afloat. My body was drained, my mind darkened, and I recognized that darkness too well to ignore it. I quickly realized that enough was enough. In the spring of my second year, I threw in the towel right in the middle of my internship. I quit halfway through, fully aware that it meant I wouldn't be able to start my third and final year the following fall. It felt like a failure, but at the same time, I was proud of listening to my body and taking care of myself.

Suddenly, the possibilities for that fall were wide open. I had time before retaking my internship the following spring. So, I decided to follow my dream of being close to nature, experiencing new adventures, and doing something completely uncharacteristic. My whole life, I had been someone who sought security, afraid to do things without my parents nearby. I had lived in Trøndelag all my life and had barely been north of Steinkjer. But Lofoten was a dream I had carried since I fell in love with nature, and now I had an opportunity that might not come again. I traveled north. Perhaps I was also fleeing from everything I felt I hadn't mastered. Even though I was proud of having made a good decision for my body, I also felt the disappointment and shame of having failed. I longed for time and a new environment to get back on my feet, so I went to a tiny house with Juster, far up north in Lofoten.

Reine, Lofoten

For six months, I lived in that little house in the big mountains. The days were beautiful but tough, because it wasn't just my hiking gear that came with me. Anxiety was also packed in my backpack. Being completely alone, so far from my family and partner, was brutal, even though I was lucky to have them visit me several times. They supported my decision to go and cheered me on as I pursued my dream. Still, I realized that running away from my problems wasn't the best way to handle them. It just felt too scary to face them head-on, and in many ways, it was easier to move a thousand kilometers north for new experiences than to stand in all the painful feelings back home in Trondheim.

Despite that, I made new friends and gained new experiences in the north that I would never trade for anything. I got to live closer to the incredible nature we have in Norway, and not least, I got to experience Lofoten without the tourists, with local residents who are more generous and warmer than you can imagine. Their kindness and willingness to help was truly inspiring!

Lofoten Folk is in honor of the people of Lofoten and the majestic nature of the north. Made with thick Norwegian wool, it's perfect for the northern Norwegian climate and as robust as the people of the north.

Lofoten Folk brings me so much joy and reminds me of the time when I was far, far from home. I learned so much about myself, and looking back, I can hardly believe I dared to make that decision. It will always be an adventure I remember with pride because even though it was scary, I did it.

Color 1: Troll, cotton candy 753

Color 2: Troll, white 701

Tip: In some rows, the yarn not in use must travel a long distance on the wrong side. To avoid overly long floats, twist the yarns together on the wrong side.

Sizes
S (M, L, XL, 2X)

Garment Measurements
This sweater is designed to have 2–4" of positive ease.
Bust: 35½ (39¼, 43¼, 51¼, 55)"
Total length: 22¾ (24¾, 26¾, 28¼, 29¼)" or desired length
Sleeve length: 19, (19¾–20, 20½–21¼, 21¾, 22)" or desired length

Yarn
Hillesvåg Blåne (100% Norwegian wool: 125 y [114 m] /100 g) or Hillesvåg Troll (100% Norwegian wool: 125 y [114 m]/100 g)

Actual Yarn Amounts
Color 1: 400 (400, 500, 600, 600) g
Color 2: 400 (500, 500, 600, 600) g

Needles
US size 9: 16" and 32" circular needles and set of double-pointed needles
US size 10: 16" and 32" circular needles and set of double-pointed needles
Adjust needle size as necessary to obtain gauge.

Gauge
14 stitches × 18 rows in stockinette = 4 × 4"

Color 1: Blåne, burgundy 2104

Color 2: Troll, unbleached white 702

How to Knit this Sweater

You will knit the body in the round from the bottom up to the armholes. The sleeves are knitted from the bottom up to the armholes. From there, the pieces are joined and you'll decrease for the raglan up to the collar, which is knitted last.

Body

Cast on 126 (140, 154, 182, 196) stitches on US size 9 needles with color 1. Place a marker for the beginning of the round. Work knit 1, purl 1 ribbing in the round for 2½".

Switch to US size 10 needles. Knit the pattern following the chart as follows: Beginning with stitch 9 (6, 2, 9, 6) of each chart round, knit to stitch 14, then repeat stitches 1-14 to last 8 (5, 1, 8, 5) stitches, then work stitches 1-8 (1-5, 1, 1-8, 1-5).

Repeat rounds 1-14 of chart until the body measures 15 (16¼, 17, 17¾, 17¼)" or to desired length to armholes. Note which round of chart was worked last.

You will now bind off 6 (8, 10, 10, 12) stitches for the armholes on each side as follows: Bind off the first 3 (4, 5, 5, 6) stitches on the needle. Continuing in chart pattern, knit 57 (61, 67, 81, 85) stitches for front. Bind off the next 6 (8, 10, 10, 12) stitches. Continue in pattern until 3 (4, 5, 5, 6) stitches remain on the needle and bind off these stitches. You now have 114 (124, 134, 162, 172) stitches on the needle: 57 (61, 67, 81, 85) stitches for the front and 57 (63, 67, 81, 87) stitches for the back. Cut yarn and set the piece aside.

Sleeves

Cast on 24 (26, 28, 30, 32) stitches on US size 9 double-pointed needles with color 1. Place a marker for the beginning of the round. Work knit 1, purl 1 ribbing in the round for 2".

Switch to US size 10 needles and knit 1 round while increasing 7 stitches evenly distributed as follows:

S:
Knit 3 stitches, increase 1 stitch. *Knit 4 stitches, increase 1 stitch, knit 3 stitches, increase 1 stitch*. Repeat from * to * 2 more times.

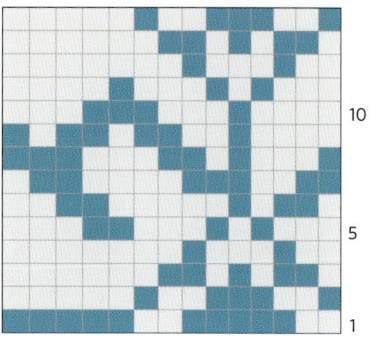

M:
Knit 3 stitches, increase 1 stitch. *Knit 4 stitches, increase 1 stitch*. Repeat from * to * 4 more times. Knit 3 stitches, increase 1 stitch.

L:
Knit 4 stitches, increase 1 stitch. Repeat from * to * 6 more times.

XL:
Knit 5 stitches, increase 1 stitch. *Knit 4 stitches, increase 1 stitch*. Repeat from * to * 4 more times. Knit 5 stitches, increase 1 stitch.

2XL:
Knit 5 stitches, increase 1 stitch. *Knit 4 stitches, increase 1 stitch, knit 5 stitches, increase 1 stitch*. Repeat from * to * 2 more times.

You now have 31 (33, 35) (37, 39) stitches on the needle.

When the sleeve measures ¾" beyond the ribbing, increase 2 stitches in the round as follows: Knit the first stitch, pick up the strand between stitches from front to back with the left needle, and knit it through the back loop. Knit the pattern until 1 stitch remains, pick up the strand between stitches from back to front with the left needle and knit it, then knit the last stitch. The increased stitches should be worked as an expansion of the chart pattern on each side.

Color 1: Blåne, teal 2106

Color 2: Troll, gray mélange 703

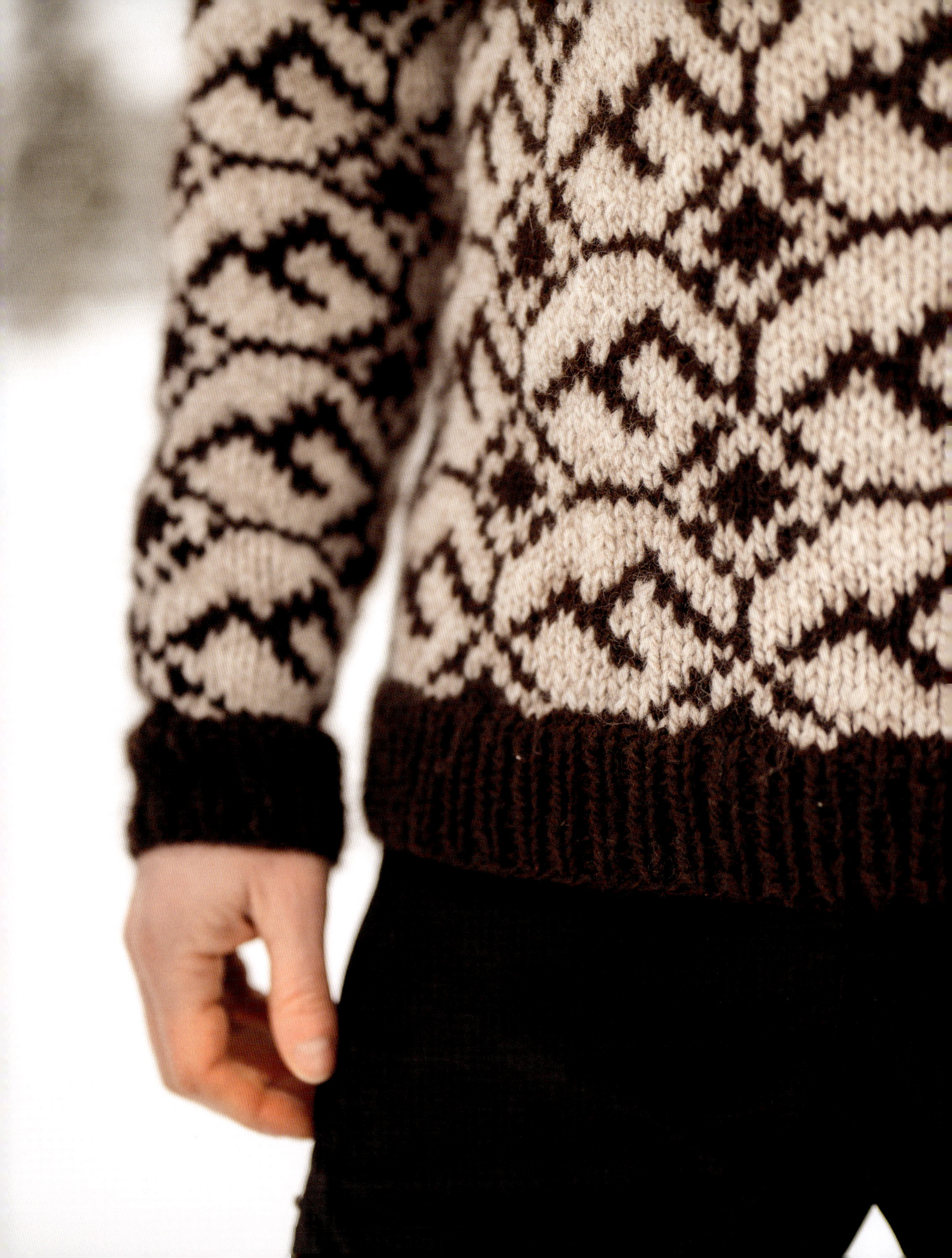

Color 1: Blåne, dark brown 2116

Color 2: Troll, light brown mélange 705

Continue knitting the pattern and increasing in the same way every ¾" until you have 67 (69, 71, 75, 81) stitches on the needle.

Continue knitting in pattern without further increases until the sleeve measures 19 (20, 21¼, 21½, 22)" or the desired length to armholes, ending with same round of chart as for body.

You will now bind off stitches for the armhole on the same round of the chart as for the body. Bind off the first 3 (4, 5, 5, 6) stitches on the needle. Knit until 3 (4, 5, 5, 6) stitches remain, and bind off those. You now have 61 (61, 61, 65, 69) stitches remaining on the needle. Set the work aside and knit the second sleeve in the same way.

Raglan

You will now knit the stitches from the body and sleeves onto the same needle, continuing the chart pattern on the body and sleeves, while placing 4 markers as follows: Knit all the stitches from one sleeve onto the needle. Place a marker. Knit all the stitches from the front section of the body. Place a marker. Knit all the stitches from the second sleeve onto the needle. Place a marker. Knit all the stitches from the back section of the body. Place a marker for the beginning of the round, between the back and the left sleeve. You now have 236 (246, 256, 292, 310) stitches on the needle.

Mark the raglan stitches as follows:
On the next round, knit the 3 stitches before and after each marker as follows: * Knit the first 2 stitches on the needle with color 1. Knit the next stitch with color 2. Knit in pattern until 3 stitches before the next marker. Knit the first stitch with color 2, knit the next 2 stitches with color 1, and slip the marker*. Repeat from * to * 3 more times.

On the next round, decrease for the raglan as follows:
Knit the first 2 stitches on the round together with color 1. Knit the next stitch with color 2. Knit in pattern to 3 stitches before the next marker. Knit the next stitch with color 2. Then, SSK (slip, slip, knit, see page 173) with color 1. Slip the marker. Repeat from * to * 3 more times. You have now decreased 8 stitches, leaving you with 228 (238, 248, 284, 302) stitches on the needle.

Repeat the last 2 rounds 12 (14, 16, 18, 21) more times, ending with a decrease round. You now have 132 (126, 120, 140, 134) stitches on the needle.

On the next round, bind off stitches at center front for the neckline as follows:
Knit the first 44 (40, 36, 40, 37) stitches of the round as usual. Bind off the next 13 (13, 15, 17, 17) stitches. Continue knitting as usual to the end of the round. Cut the yarn.

You now have 119 (113, 105, 123, 117) stitches left on the needle. Slip 44 (40, 36, 40, 37) left sleeve and left front stitches to right needle.

Next, you will knit back and forth in stockinette stitch, continuing the chart pattern, knitting on the right side and purling on the wrong side, and continuing the raglan decreases every other row. At the same time, shape the neckline as follows: Start at the right neck edge with a right-side row. Bind off the first 2 stitches.

Continue knitting the pattern and raglan decreases. Turn and bind off the first 2 stitches on the needle. Purl back, continuing the pattern.

Repeat these 2 rows once more. You have now bound off 4 stitches on each side for the neckline.

Continue in stockinette stitch in pattern for 6 more rows, binding off 1 stitch at the start of each row and continuing the raglan decreases on each right-side row. You now have 71 (65, 55, 69, 63) stitches left on the needle. Cut color 2.

Collar

Continuing with color 1, knit all stitches, then pick up and knit 1 stitch in each of the 27 (27, 29, 31, 31) bound-off stitches at front neck. Place a marker for the beginning of the round. You now have 98 (92, 84, 100, 94) stitches on the needle.

On the next round, decrease 38 (32, 22, 32, 22) stitches evenly distributed as follows:

S:
Knit 1, knit 2 together. Repeat from * to * 2 more times.
Knit 1, knit 2 together, knit 2 together. Repeat from * to * 7 more times.
Knit 1, knit 2 together. Repeat from * to * 2 more times.
Knit 1, knit 2 together, knit 2 together. Repeat from * to * 7 more times.

M:
Knit 2 together, knit 2 together. *Knit 1, knit 2 together*. Repeat from * to * 13 more times.
Knit 2 together, knit 2 together. *Knit 1, knit 2 together*. Repeat from * to * 13 more times.

L:
Knit 1, knit 2 together. *Knit 2, knit 2 together*. Repeat from * to * 9 more times.
Knit 1, knit 2 together. *Knit 2, knit 2 together*. Repeat from * to * 9 more times.

XL:
Knit 1, knit 2 together. Repeat from * to * 13 more times.
Knit 2, knit 2 together. Repeat from * to * 1 more time.
Knit 1, knit 2 together. Repeat from * to * 13 more times.
Knit 2, knit 2 together. Repeat from * to * 1 more time.

2XL:
Knit 2, knit 2 together. Repeat from * to * 7 more times.
Knit 3, knit 2 together. Repeat from * to * 2 more times.
Knit 2, knit 2 together. Repeat from * to * 7 more times.
Knit 3, knit 2 together. Repeat from * to * 2 more times.

You now have 60 (60, 62, 68, 72) stitches on the needle.

Switch to the 16" US size 9 circular needle and work in knit 2, purl 2 ribbing for 10" or to your desired length. Bind off all stitches by knitting knit stitches and purling purl stitches. Sew the underarm seams and weave in all ends.

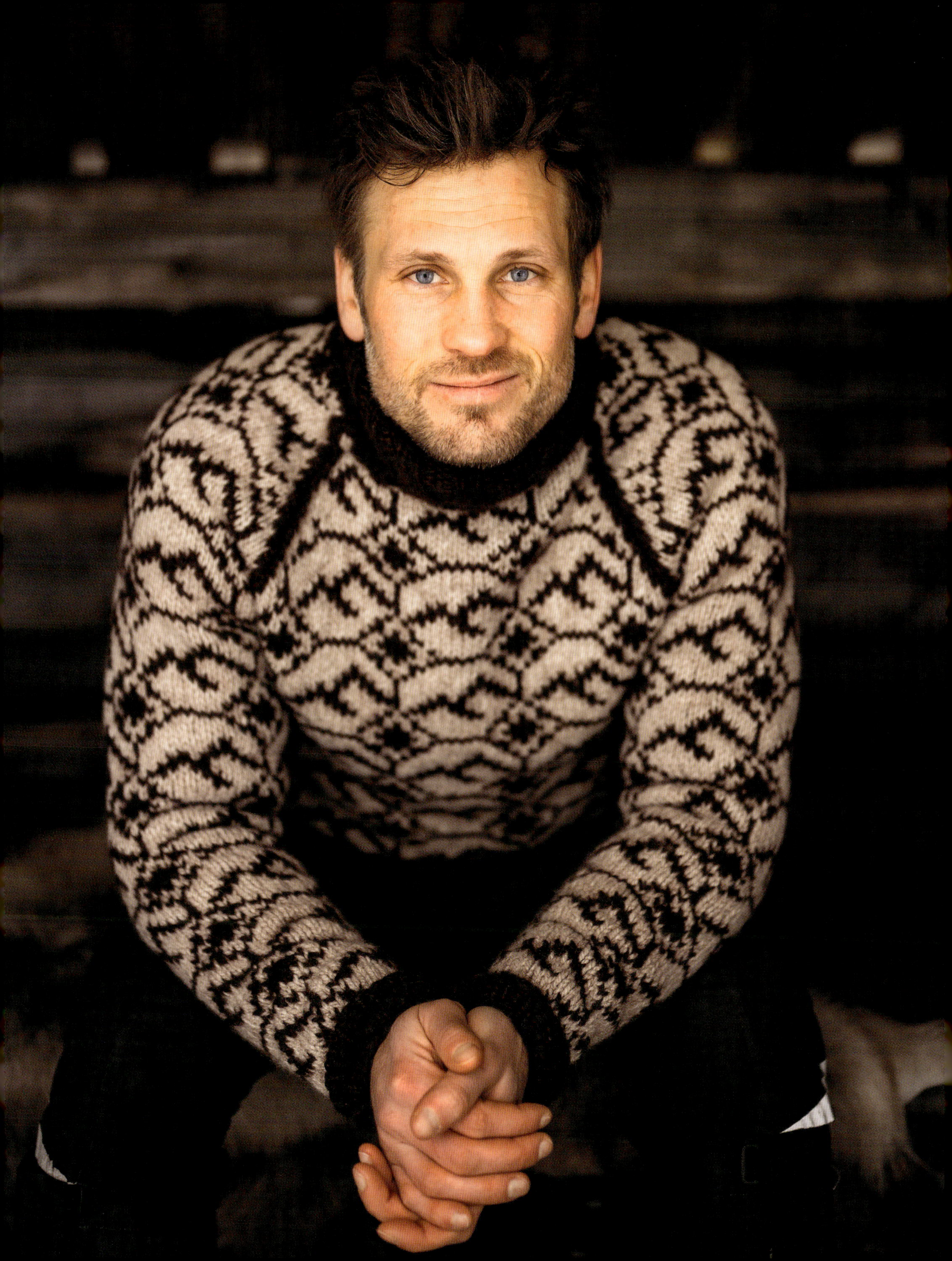

Lofoten Folk Sitting Pad

This sitting pad is perfect to bring along in your backpack. It takes up very little space but provides incredible warmth under your seat. The combination of colorwork knitting and two sides felted together makes this pad thick and cozy. Felted wool is water-resistant, making it suitable for use on damp surfaces like rocks or heather.

Measurements Before Felting
Width: 23"
Height: 16½"

Measurements After Felting
Width: 17¾"
Height: 11¾"

Yarn
Rauma Vams (100% Norwegian wool: 91 yd [83 m]/50 g)

Actual Yarn Amounts
Color 1: 200 g
Color 2: 150 g

Needles
US size 10: 32" circular needles

Gauge
14 stitches × 18 rows in stockinette = 4 × 4"

How to Knit this Sitting Pad

The sitting pad is knitted in the round, similar to the body of a sweater. The pad will be double layered, and the openings at the top and bottom will be sewn together at the end.

Cast on 168 stitches with color 1 on US size 10 circular needles. Place a marker at the beginning of the round. Knit 2 rounds in stockinette stitch.

Knit the pattern following the chart. Repeat stitches 1–14 of chart for each round. Work rounds 1–14 of chart 5 times, then work round 1 one more time.

Knit 2 rounds with color 1. Bind off all stitches. Weave in all loose ends on the inside of the sitting pad.

Flatten the tube of knitting, with the beginning of round along one folded edge. Use whipstitch and color 1 to sew the openings closed, starting at the beginning of round and sewing stitch by stitch to the other fold. See page 169 for more detailed instructions.

Felt the sitting pad either in the washing machine, or by hand. See page 179 for the felting guide.

While the sitting pad is still wet from felting, shape it to the desired length and width and lay it flat to dry.

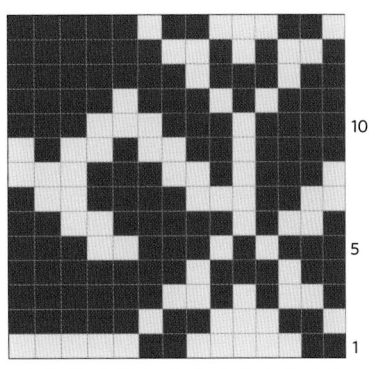

110

Color 1: Vams, dark petrol 53

Color 2: Vams, light gray mélange 03

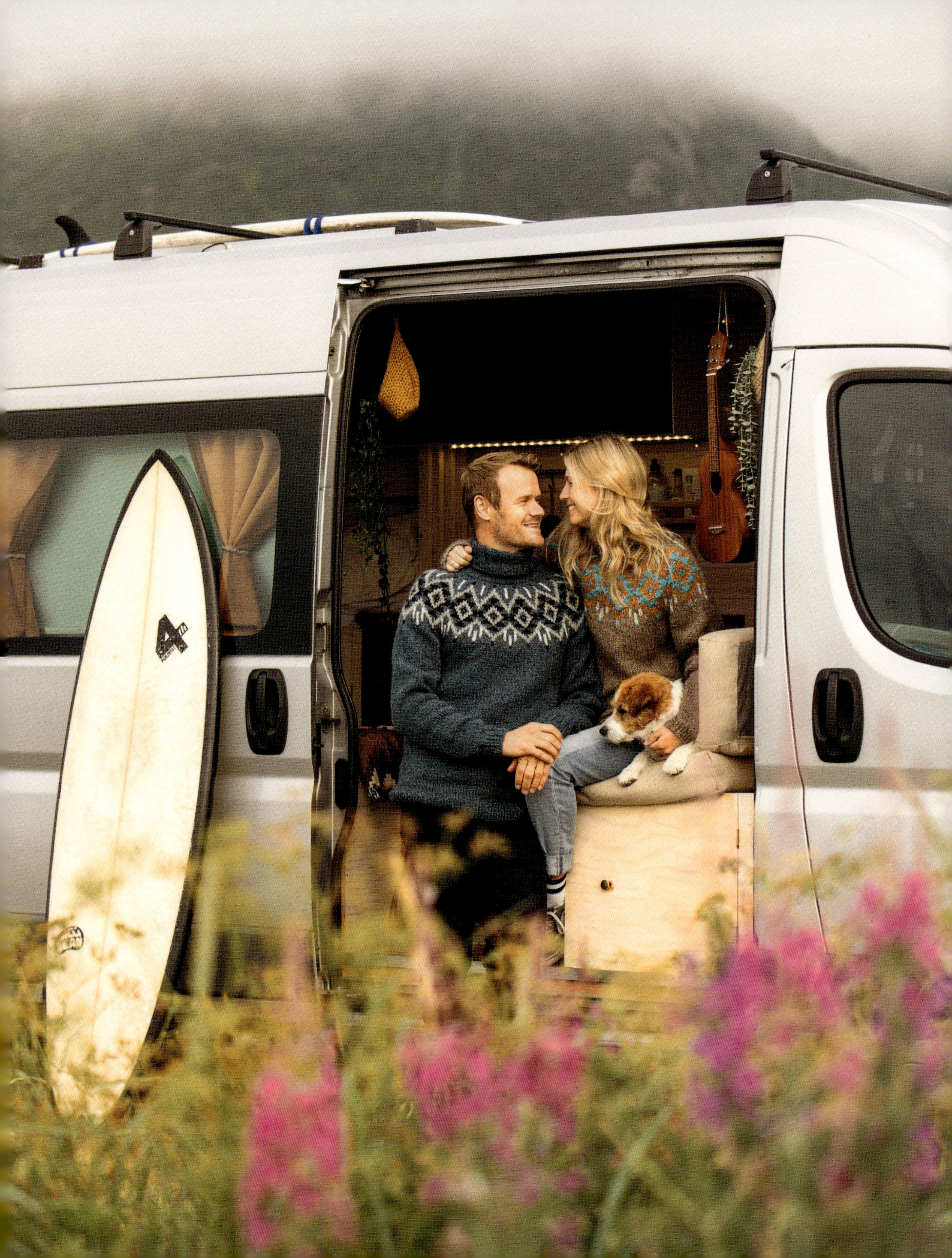

Leif Sweater

After my adventure in Lofoten, I returned to Trondheim and began work on finishing my early childhood education degree. Even though I truly believed that escaping my problems would solve everything, I quickly realized that was a poor strategy. I came back with many accomplishments and experiences, but also with a fragile mental state and an exhausted body after pushing myself too hard for too long.

I did my best to accommodate my limited capacity, and the three-year degree ended up taking me four and a half years. I took two years to complete the final year of education, allowing my body and mind to keep up. In December 2020, I finally received my certification, though it had come at a high cost.

In those months, I felt like I was running on empty. It felt as if my head was filled with cotton, my body ached as if I had a constant fever, and I could barely do anything other than lie in bed, waiting for the pain to ease. But it didn't ease. In fact, the pain hadn't let up once since I returned from the north.

My poor condition had consequences, and I struggled to get outside. It was too demanding, too exhausting, and too painful. In a vicious cycle, things only got worse when I couldn't go on outdoor trips to the places that usually gave me energy and joy. Everyday life felt meaningless. After giving up hope that the pain and fatigue would go away on their own, I went to the doctor and was referred for further tests. That's when I got the diagnosis I didn't want. The pain wasn't from catching the flu every other week or from a vitamin deficiency. The hard truth was that I had pushed myself for too long. Life had become too much for me. I strived to excel, to be the best, and to handle everything, but the opposite happened. My body completely collapsed, and in the winter of 2021, I was diagnosed with Chronic Fatigue Syndrome (CFS).

It felt like my life was over.

I could only manage twenty percent of what I could do in a day when I was healthy a few years earlier. I was a shadow of myself. For a long time, I struggled with my body telling me enough was enough, long before my mind was ready to rest. But now I realized it was serious. Even making dinner was a chore, and some days, that was too much. I felt nauseous, utterly exhausted, and completely drained of energy. Suddenly, my entire life was turned upside down. I was told to rest often, not to overuse my body, walk slowly, and give up the mountain trips that I loved so much.

The outdoors had once been my sanctuary. Now the couch became my own personal hell. I lay there every day, monitoring my energy levels, rationing it for short walks with Juster, perhaps taking a shower or doing a load of laundry between naps and rest. There were few trips into the woods; the pain tore through my body, and my thoughts were darker than ever. If I couldn't do what gave me energy, accomplishment, and joy, what was the point of my life?

Summer came, and normally, Harald, Juster, and I would have gone on a vacation with the car, tent, and hiking boots. But I wasn't in shape for that. I was tired, in pain, and pessimistic about being able to handle an outdoor vacation the way we used to. In the hours I spent on the couch, I scrolled through ad after ad, searching for a camper van that could make travel easier. One day, there it was: a Citroën Jumper, converted into a fantastic little cabin on wheels. We bought it and named it Van Leif.

I felt butterflies in my stomach. I barely dared to hope that Van Leif would give me what I longed for. But I didn't need much, just a taste of the outdoor life we had enjoyed in previous years, with Norwegian nature, drizzle on my face, the sun warming the heather on the mountain, and the majestic waterfalls in grand mountain valleys. If I could just get a taste of it, I'd be happy. For the first time in many months, I felt joy, excitement, and hope.

And what a turning point it was! Van Leif became my salvation, my chance to get back into nature despite the pain and fatigue. Since then, we have traveled around large parts of the country in our little cabin on wheels, and we love every single second.

The Leif Sweater is a tribute to Van Leif, with thanks for the freedom it gives me and the joy I feel every time I sit behind the wheel, ready for new adventures.

The pattern is inspired by the interior of the van, and I absolutely love this sweater. It's warm, cozy, and perfect for camping trips.

Sizes
XXS, XS (S, M, L, XL) (2X, 3X, 4X, 5X)

Garment Measurements
This sweater is designed to have 4" of positive ease.
Bust: 34¼, 37 (39½, 41, 43¼, 45) (47¼, 51¼ 55, 59)"
Total length: 21¾, 22¾ (23½, 24½, 25½, 26½) (27½, 27¾, 28, 28¼)" or desired length
Sleeve length: 19, 19 (19¾, 20, 20½, 21¼) (21¾, 21¾, 22, 22)" or desired length

Yarn
Hillesvåg Troll (100% Norwegian wool: 125 y [114 m]/100 g)
Hillesvåg Blåne (100% Norwegian wool: 125 y [114 m]/100 g)

Actual Yarn Amounts
Color 1: 600, 600 (600, 700, 700, 700) (800, 800, 900, 1000) g
Color 2: 100 g all sizes
Color 3: 100 g all sizes
Color 4: 100 g all sizes

Needles
US size 9: 16" and 32" circular needles and set of double-pointed needles
US size 10: 16" and 32" circular needles and set of double-pointed needles
Adjust needle size as necessary to obtain gauge.

Gauge
14 stitches × 18 rows = 4 × 4"

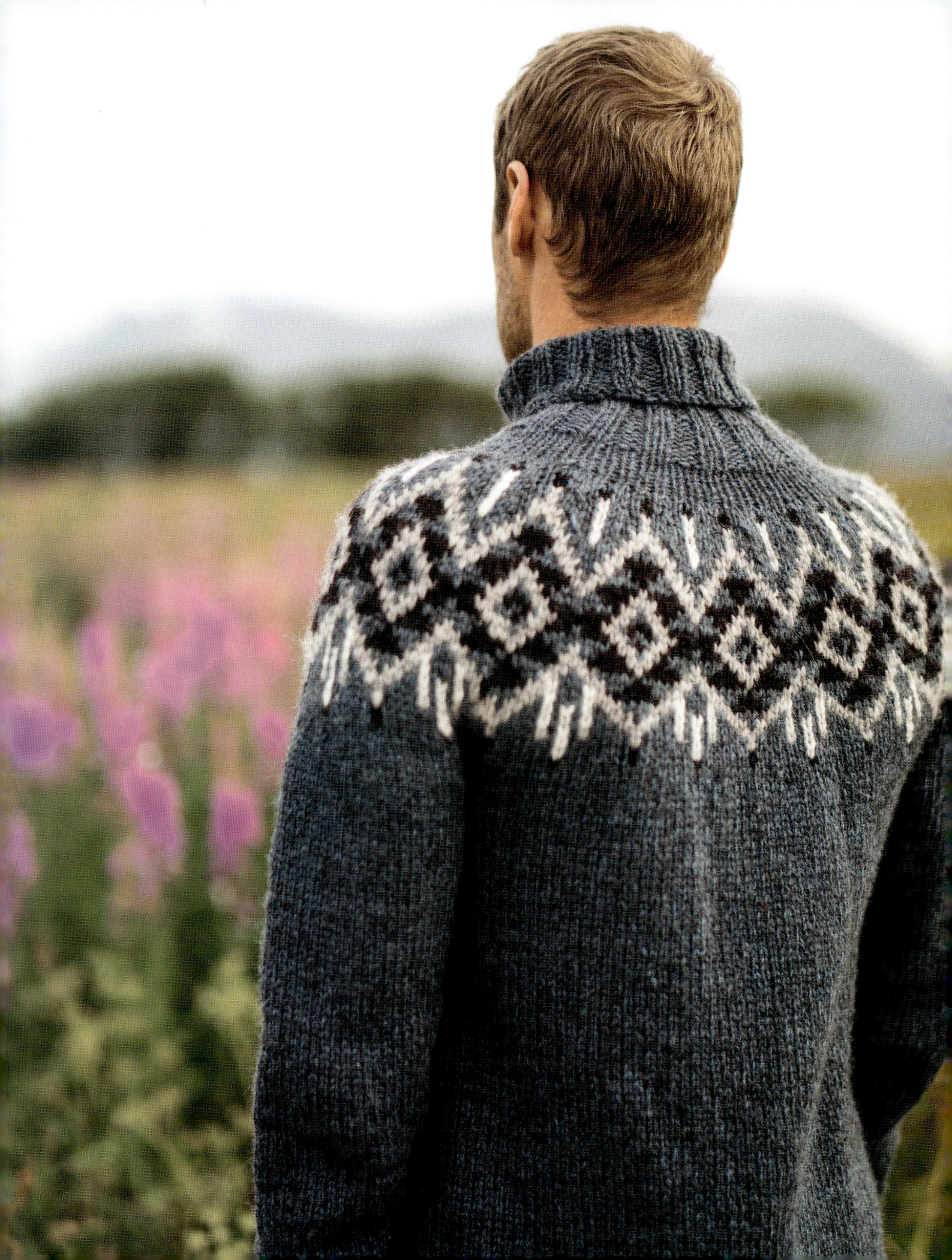

How to Knit this Sweater

The sweater is knitted in the round from the bottom up to the armholes. The sleeves are knitted from the bottom up to the armholes. The sleeves and body are then joined together, and the yoke is knitted in the round towards the neck while decreasing. The collar is knitted at the end.

Body

Cast on 122, 132 (140, 146, 154, 160) (168, 182, 196, 210) stitches on US size 9 circular needles with color 1. Place a marker to mark the beginning of the round. Work in knit 1, purl 1 ribbing for 2½".

Switch to US size 10 (6 mm) circular needles and knit in stockinette stitch in the round until the piece measures 13¾, 15 (15¾, 16½, 17¼, 17¼) (17¾, 17¾, 17¾, 18)" or to desired length to the armholes.

On the next round, bind off 8, 10 (10, 10, 10, 10) (12, 12, 12, 12) stitches for armholes on each side as follows: Bind off the first 4, 5 (5, 5, 5, 5) (6, 6, 6, 6) stitches. Knit 53, 56 (60, 63, 67, 70) (72, 79, 86, 93) stitches for the front and bind off the next 8, 10 (10, 10, 10, 10) (12, 12, 12, 12) stitches. Knit until there are 4, 5 (5, 5, 5, 5) (6, 6, 6, 6) stitches left, and bind off these stitches. You now have 106, 112 (120, 126, 134, 140) (144, 158, 172, 186) stitches left on the needles. Cut yarn and set aside.

Sleeves

Cast on 22, 24 (24, 24, 26, 28) (28, 30, 30, 30) stitches on US size 9 double-pointed needles with color 1. Place a marker to mark the beginning of the round. Work in knit 1, purl 1 ribbing for 2½".

On the next round, switch to needles US size 10 and knit 1 round with color 1, while at the same time increasing 6 stitches evenly as follows:

Knit 3, 4 (4, 4, 4, 4) (4, 5, 5, 5) stitches, increase 1 stitch, knit 4, 4 (4, 4, 4, 5) (5, 5, 5, 5) stitches, increase 1 stitch. Repeat from * to * 2 more times. Finish by knitting 1, 0 (0, 0, 2, 1) (1, 0, 0, 0) stitch(es). You now have 28, 30 (30, 30, 32, 34) (34, 36, 36, 36) stitches on the needles.

Continue knitting stockinette stitch in the round until the sleeve measures 1¼, 1¼ (1, 1, 1, 1) (¾, ¾, ¾, ¾)" past the ribbing. Now, you will increase 2 stitches as follows: Knit the first stitch, pick up the strand between stitches from front to back with the left needle, and knit it through the back loop. Knit the pattern until 1 stitch remains, pick up the strand between stitches from back to front with the left needle and knit it, then knit the last stitch.

Continue increasing in this way every 1¼, 1¼ (1, 1, 1, 1) (¾, ¾, ¾, ¾)" until you have 52, 56 (58, 60, 64, 66) (74, 78, 80, 82) stitches. Continue knitting without increasing until the sleeve measures 19, 19 (19¾, 20, 20½, 21¼) (21¾, 21¾, 22, 22)" or desired length to armhole.

On the next round, bind off 8, 10 (10, 10, 10, 10) (12, 12, 12, 12) stitches for the armholes as follows:

Bind off the first 4, 5 (5, 5, 5, 5) (6, 6, 6, 6) stitches, knit until 4, 5 (5, 5, 5, 5) (6, 6, 6, 6) stitches remain, and bind off these stitches. You now have 44, 46 (48, 50, 54, 56) (62, 66, 68, 70) stitches left on the needles. Set this sleeve aside and knit the second sleeve in the same way.

Yoke

Now you will knit the stitches from the body and sleeves onto the same needle as follows:

Knit the stitches of one sleeve onto the needle. Knit the stitches from the front of the body to the next armhole. Knit the stitches of the second sleeve. Knit the stitches from the back of the body to the end. Place a marker for the beginning of the round. You now have 194, 204 (216, 226, 242, 252) (268, 290, 308, 326) stitches on the needle.

Knit 1, 1 (1, 2, 4, 5) (6, 7, 9, 9) round(s). On the next round, decrease 40, 36 (34, 30, 32, 28) (30, 38, 42, 46) stitches evenly as follows:

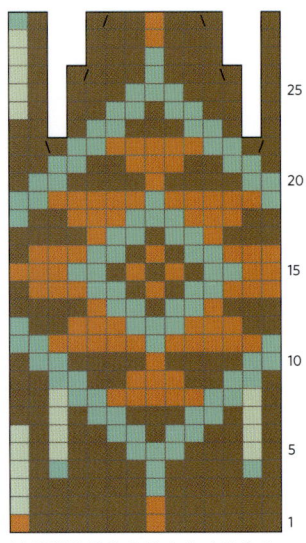

/ Knit 2 together

\ Knit 2 together through the back loop

XXS:

Knit 2, knit 2 together. Repeat from * to * 2 more times.
Knit 3, knit 2 together. Repeat from * to * 16 more times.
Knit 2, knit 2 together. Repeat from * to * 2 more times.
Knit 3, knit 2 together. Repeat from * to * 16 more times.

XS:

Knit 5, knit 2 together, knit 5, knit 2 together.
Knit 3, knit 2 together, knit 4, knit 2 together. Repeat from * to * 15 more times.
Knit 5, knit 2 together, knit 5, knit 2 together.

S:

Knit 5, knit 2 together. Repeat from * to * 5 more times.

Knit 4, knit 2 together. Repeat from * to * 10 more times.
Knit 5, knit 2 together. Repeat from * to * 5 more times.
Knit 4, knit 2 together. Repeat from * to * 10 more times.

M:

Knit 6, knit 2 together, knit 6, knit 2 together.
*Knit 5, knit 2 together, knit 6, knit 2 together *. Repeat from * to * 13 more times.

L:

Knit 6, knit 2 together, knit 6, knit 2 together.
Knit 5, knit 2 together, knit 6, knit 2 together. Repeat from * to * 13 more times.
Knit 6, knit 2 together, knit 6, knit 2 together.

XL:

Knit 7, knit 2 together. Repeat from * to * 27 more times.

2XL:

Knit 6, knit 2 together, knit 6, knit 2 together.
Knit 7, knit 2 together. Repeat from * to * 27 more times.

3XL:

Knit 6, knit 2 together. Repeat from * to * 4 more times.
Knit 5, knit 2 together, knit 6, knit 2 together. Repeat from * to * 13 more times.
Knit 6, knit 2 together. Repeat from * to * 4 more times.

4XL:

Knit 5, knit 2 together. Repeat from * to * 13 more times.
Knit 6, knit 2 together. Repeat from * to * 6 more times.
Knit 5, knit 2 together. Repeat from * to * 13 more times.
Knit 6, knit 2 together. Repeat from * to * 6 more times.

5XL:

Knit 6, knit 2 together. Repeat from * to * 3 more times.
Knit 5, knit 2 together. Repeat from * to * 41 more times.

You now have 154, 168 (182, 196, 210, 224) (238, 252, 266, 280) stitches on the needle.

Knit the pattern following the chart as follows: Beginning with stitch 11, 7 (4, 14, 11, 7) (4, 13, 12, 7) of each chart round, knit to stitch 14, then repeat stitches 1–14 to last 10, 6 (3, 13, 10, 6) (3, 12, 11, 6) stitches, then work stitches 1–10, 1–6 (1–3, 1–13, 1–10, 1–6) (1–3, 1–12, 1–11, 1–6). Work rounds 1–29 of chart, decreasing as shown in rounds 22, 26, and 29.

Work the pattern and decreases as shown in the chart. To center the pattern, start each round on square 11, 7 (4, 14, 11, 7) (4, 13, 12, 7) of the chart. Knit through the chart and repeat from stitch 1 to 14 for the entire round.

Note: For some sizes, the starting stitch will disappear with decreases

118

Color 1: Blåne, beige 2101
Color 2: Troll, light teal mélange 7303
Color 3: Troll, ocher 713
Color 4: Troll, minty green 748

Color 1: Vams, petrol mélange 405
Color 2: Vams, black sheep 10
Color 3: Vams, light grey mélange 03
Color 4: Vams, natural 01

in the pattern. In this case, adjust as needed to ensure the pattern remains aligned as you knit. If the starting stitch must be decreased with the last stitch on the needle, slip the starting stitch without knitting it at the beginning of the round, and knit it together with the last stitch at the end of the round.

You now have 88, 96 (104, 112, 120, 128) (136, 144, 152, 160) stitches left on your needle. Knit 1, 1 (2, 3, 5, 6) (8, 9, 10, 12) rounds in color 1. On the next round, decrease 28, 36 (44, 48, 56, 60) (68, 72, 76, 80) stitches evenly as follows:

XXS:
Knit 2, knit 2 together, knit 2, knit 2 together.
Knit 1, knit 2 together. Repeat from * to * 11 more times.
Knit 2, knit 2 together, knit 2, knit 2 together.
Knit 1, knit 2 together. Repeat from * to * 11 more times.

XS:
Knit 1, knit 2 together, knit 1, knit 2 together, knit 2 together. Repeat from * to * 11 more times.

S:
Knit 2 together. Repeat from * to * 5 more times.
Knit 1, knit 2 together, knit 2 together. Repeat from * to * 15 more times.
Knit 2 together. Repeat from * to * 5 more times.

M:
Knit 1, knit 2 together, knit 2 together, knit 2 together. Repeat from * to * 15 more times.

L:
Knit 1, knit 2 together. Repeat from * to * 3 more times.
Knit 2 together. Repeat from * to * 23 more times.
Knit 1, knit 2 together. Repeat from * to * 3 more times.
Knit 2 together. Repeat from * to * 23 more times.

XL:
Knit 1, knit 2 together. Repeat from * to * 3 more times.
Knit 2 together. Repeat from * to * 25 more times.
Knit 1, knit 2 together. Repeat from * to * 3 more times.
Knit 2 together. Repeat from * to * 25 more times.

2XL, 3XL, 4XL and 5XL:
Knit 2 together for the entire round.

You now have 60, 60 (60, 64, 64, 68) (68, 72, 76, 80) stitches remaining on the round.

On the next round you bind off the 16, 16 (16, 16, 16, 18) (18, 18, 18, 20) center front stitches for the neckline as follows: Knit the first 13, 13 (13, 15, 15, 15) (15, 17, 19, 20) stitches. Bind off the next 16, 16 (16, 16, 16, 18) (18, 18, 18, 20) stitches. Knit to the end of the round. Cut the yarn. Slip the 13, 13 (13, 15, 15, 15) (15, 17, 19, 20) left front stitches to the right needle.

You now have 44, 44 (44, 48, 48, 50) (50, 54, 58, 60) stitches remaining on your needle. Knit back and forth in stockinette, while binding off stitches for the neckline as follows: Start at the right neck edge with a right-side row. Bind off the first 2 stitches of the row. Knit to the end of the row. Turn. Bind off the first 2 stitches of the row. Purl back. Turn. Repeat these two rows 2, 2 (2, 3, 3, 3) (3, 3, 3, 3) more times. You have now bound off a total of 6, 6 (6, 8, 8, 8) (8, 8, 8, 8) stitches on each side and have 32, 32 (32, 32, 32, 34) (34, 38, 42, 44) stitches remaining on the needle.

Collar
Knit to the end of the row, then pick up and knit a total of 28, 28 (28, 32, 32, 34) (34, 34, 34, 36) stitches over the bound-off front neck stitches. Place marker for new beginning of round. You now have a total of 60, 60 (60, 64, 64, 68) (68, 72, 76, 80) stitches on your needle.

Switch to 16" US size 9 needles and work in knit 2, purl 2 ribbing for 8" or to desired length. Bind off loosely working knit over knit and purl over purl.

Finishing
Weave in all loose ends. Sew the underarm seams. Steam or wet block the sweater for an even finish.

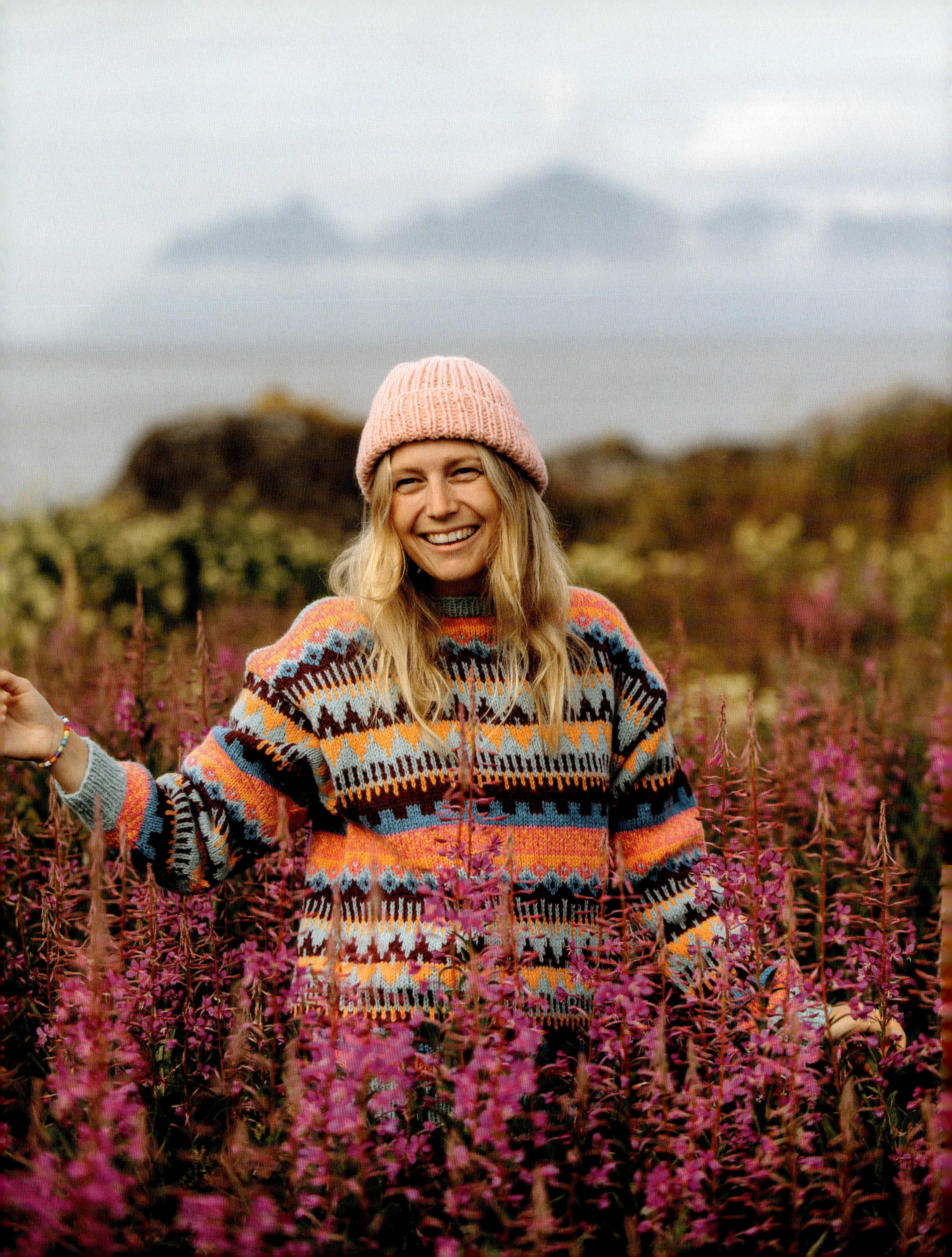

Une Sweater

Finding Van Leif in the summer of 2021 became a crucial bright spot in my otherwise dark existence with a fresh CFS diagnosis. For four months, I had barely left the couch, and I felt sicker than ever. I thought I would never again be able to go on a trip like I used to, but with Van Leif, the world opened up for me. The bed in the living area of the van became my salvation, allowing me to rest whenever I needed to.

On our first trip, we headed south toward Hardanger. I was anxious about whether I could even get out of the vehicle, and the idea of a hike seemed completely unattainable. To my great surprise, it was as if the illness had stayed behind on the couch at home. During the trip, we camped at stunning spots high up in the mountains by blue waters. We took the time to be outside, slow down, and fully immerse ourselves in nature and in the moment. With new landscapes, amazing nature, fresh air, and a new environment, my body felt healthier than it had in a long time. The brain fog was gone, the pain had almost disappeared, and the constant feverish feeling subsided. I felt so well that when we finally arrived in Kinsarvik, I dared to attempt a hike up to a viewpoint along Dronningstien.

It was a gravel road, and I walked with light steps the whole way. Harald reminded me to take it easy and to listen to my body. But for the first time in years, I felt full of energy! I reached the top after a few hours of walking and was incredibly happy. My whole body was filled with a bubbling sense of euphoria, and I smiled from ear to ear. Never had I imagined I would experience this again, but there I stood, sweaty, face flushed, and with tears of joy rolling down my cheek.

I had forgotten that I was sick. I had left the focus on my illness behind. Standing there with rosy cheeks and a pounding heart, I realized that much of the reason I had been getting worse was that everything in my life had revolved around my illness.

It was in that moment that I understood that if I wanted to get better, I needed to focus less on being sick. It would be better to slowly, but surely, continue doing the things I loved. I had to fill my soul to heal my body.

It was one of the most powerful experiences of my life. That's why I wanted to immortalize it in the Une sweater. It is full of energy, joy, and colors that reflect this life-changing experience. I wanted to change my life and how I lived with my illness, one step at a time, in the right direction. My direction.

Sizes
XXS, XS (S, M, L, XL) (2XL, 3XL, 4XL, 5XL)

Garment Measurements
This sweater is designed to be oversized with 6–8" of positive ease.
Bust: 38¼, 40½ (43¼, 46, 48½, 52¼) (55, 57¾, 60¼, 63)"
Total length: 22½, 22¾ (24, 24¾, 25½, 26½) (27, 27½, 28, 28¼)" or desired length
Sleeve length: 17, 17 (17¾, 18, 18½, 19¼) (19¾, 19¾, 20, 20)" or desired length
Notice that the shoulder sits down on the arm and adds to the sleeve length.

Yarn
Hillesvåg Luna (100% Norwegian wool: 220 yd [200 m]/100 g) or Hillesvåg Vidde (100% Norwegian wool: 220 yd [200 m]/100 g) or Hillesvåg Varde (100% Norwegian wool: 220 yd [200 m]/100 g)

Actual Yarn Amounts
Color 1: 200, 300 (300, 300, 300, 300) (400, 400, 400, 400) g
Color 2: 200, 200 (200, 200, 200, 200) (300, 300, 300, 300) g
Color 3: 100, 200 (200, 200, 200, 200) (200, 200, 200, 200) g
Color 4: 100 g all sizes
Color 5: 100 g all sizes

Needles
US size 2: 16" and 32" circular needles and set of double-pointed needles
US size 7: 16" and 32" circular needles and set of double-pointed needles
Adjust needle size as necessary to obtain gauge.

Gauge
18 stitches × 24 rows in stockinette = 4 × 4"

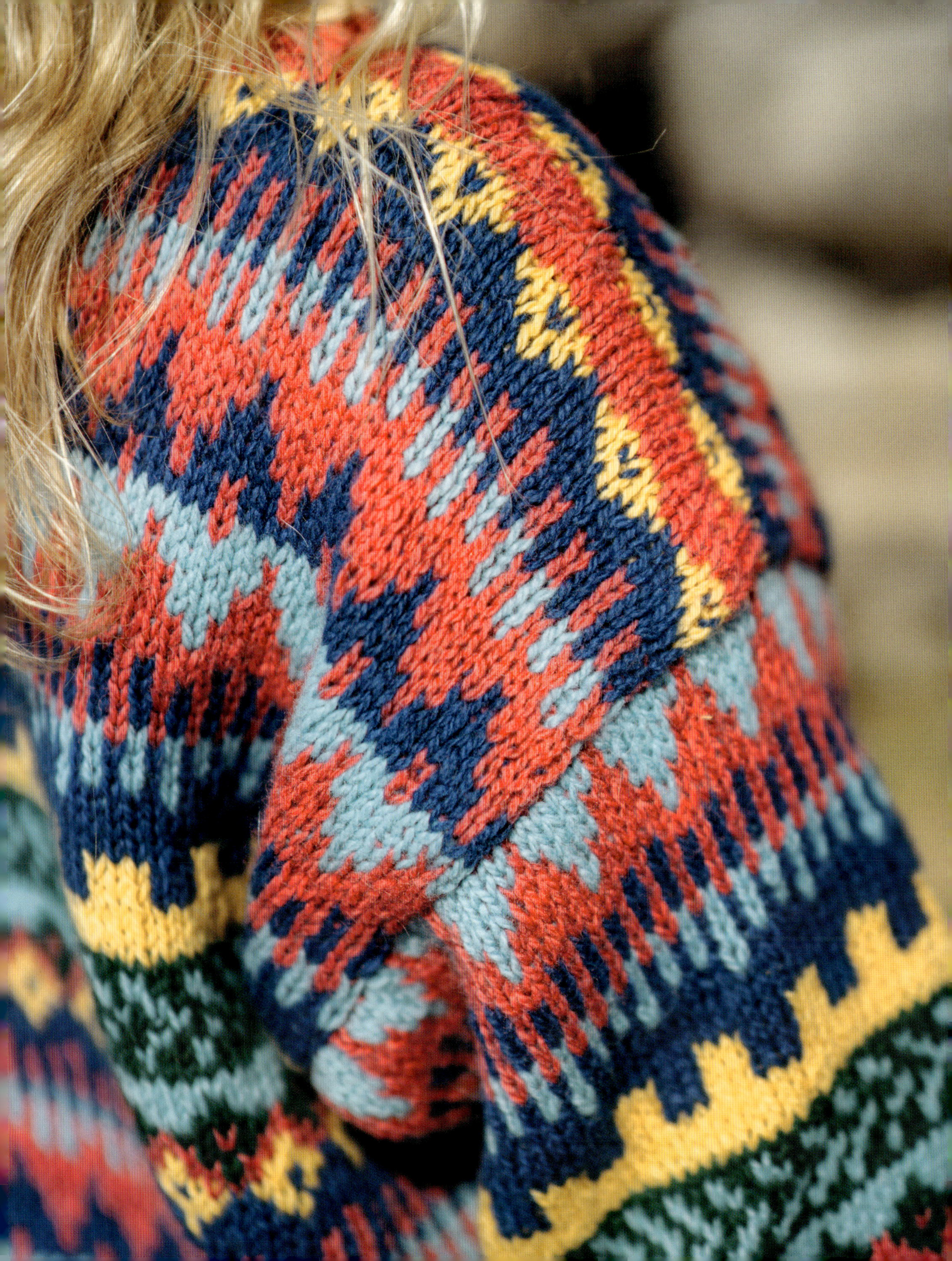

Color 1: Luna, minty green 444
Color 2: Vidde, dark plum red 327
Color 3: Luna, light orange 428
Color 4: Luna, light blue 411
Color 5: Luna, rose 447

How to Knit this Sweater

You will knit the body in the round to the shoulders. You will knit the sleeves in the round from the cuff to the armholes. You will cut steeks for the armholes and sew in the sleeves. You'll knit the neckline last.

Body

Cast on 174, 186 (198, 210, 222, 240) (252, 264, 276, 288) stitches on US size 2 circular needles with color 1. Place a marker to indicate the beginning of the round. Work in knit 1, purl 1 ribbing for 2½". Change to US size 7 circular needles and knit 1 round with color 1.

Knit the pattern following the chart as follows: Beginning with stitch 1, 4 (1, 4, 1, 3) (6, 3, 6, 3) of each chart round, knit to stitch 6, then repeat stitches 1-6 to last 6, 3 (6, 3, 6, 2) (5, 2, 5, 2) stitches, then work stitches 1-6, 1-3 (1-6, 1-3, 1-6, 1-2) (1-5, 1-2, 1-5, 1-2).

Repeat rounds 1-59 of chart until the piece measures 11¾, 11¾ (13, 13½, 14, 14½) (14½, 14½, 14½, 14½)" or desired length to the armholes.

You will now cast on 5 new stitches on each side for the steeks. These are the stitches that will be cut for armholes later, and they are not included in the total stitch count. You will not knit the pattern over these stitches. Place a marker on each side of the steek stitches as follows:

Knit the first 87, 93 (99, 105, 111, 119) (125, 131, 137, 143) stitches in the established pattern. Place a marker. Cast on 5 new stitches using the main color for the pattern row you are knitting. Place a marker. Continue knitting to the end of the round. Place a marker and cast on 5 new stitches at the end of the round. The steek stitches are now marked on each side.

Continue knitting in pattern as before, but knit the steek stitches either in a solid color or by alternating the colors used for that round for each stitch. Continue working in the established pattern until the piece measures 9½, 9¾ (9¾, 10¼, 10½, 11) (11¾, 12, 12¼, 12½)" from the beginning of the steek stitches.

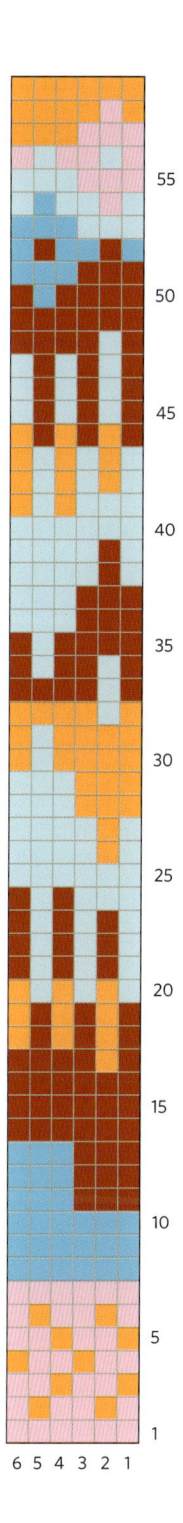

In the next round, bind off the 33, 33 (35, 35, 37, 37) (39, 39, 41, 41) stitches at center front for the neckline as follows: Knit the first 27, 30 (32, 35, 37, 41) (43, 46, 48, 51) stitches of the round. Bind off the next 33, 33 (35, 35, 37, 37) (39, 39, 41, 41) stitches. Continue knitting in pattern to the end of the round. You now have 141, 153 (163, 175, 185, 203) (213, 225, 235, 247) stitches left on the needle. Cut the yarn. Slip the 27, 30 (32, 35, 37, 41) (43, 46, 48, 51) left front stitches to the right needle.

You will knit the rest of the sweater back and forth in stockinette stitch, while shaping the neckline as follows: Start at the right front neck edge with a right-side row. Continuing in pattern, bind off 1 stitch by slipping the first stitch onto the right needle without knitting it. Knit the next stitch and lift the slipped stitch over the second stitch and off the needle. Continue knitting the pattern to the end of the row.

Turn, and bind off 1 stitch on the wrong-side row by slipping the first stitch onto the right needle without knitting it. Purl the next stitch, then lift the slipped stitch over the second stitch and off the needle. Continue purling the pattern to the end of the row.

Repeat these 2 rows one more time. You have now bound off a total of 4 stitches (2 on each side) and have 137, 149 (159, 171, 181, 199) (209, 221, 231, 243) stitches remaining on the needle. Finish by knitting 2 rows with color 1. Bind off all stitches.

Sleeves

Cast on 36, 36 (40, 40, 44, 44) (46, 46, 48, 50) stitches on US size 2 double-pointed needles with color 1. Place a marker to indicate the beginning of the round. Work in knit 1, purl 1 ribbing for 2".

Change to US size 7 circular needles and knit 1 round with color 1, while increasing 9 stitches evenly distributed as follows: *Knit 4, 4 (4, 4, 5, 5) (5, 5, 6, 6) stitches, increase 1 stitch, knit 4, 4 (5, 5, 5, 5) (5, 5, 5, 5) stitches, increase 1 stitch*. Repeat from * to * 3 more times. End the round by knitting 4, 4 (4, 4, 4, 4) (6, 6, 4, 6) stitches, increase 1 stitch. You now have 45, 45 (49, 49, 53, 53) (55, 55, 57, 59) stitches on the needles.

Knit the pattern following the chart as follows: Beginning with stitch 4, 4 (2, 2, 6, 6) (5, 5, 4, 3) of each chart round, knit to stitch 6, then repeat stitches 1–6 to last 0, 0 (2, 2, 4, 4) (5, 2, 0, 1) stitch(es), then work stitches 0, 0 (1-2, 1-2, 1-4, 1-4) (1-5, 1-2, 0, 1). Repeat rounds 1–59 of chart.

When piece measures ½" after the ribbing, you will increase 2 stitches as follows: Knit the first stitch, pick up the strand between stitches from front to back with the left needle, and knit it through the back loop. Knit the pattern until 1 stitch remains, pick up the strand between stitches from back to front with the left needle and knit it, then knit the last stitch. The increased stitches should be worked as an extension of the chart pattern on each side.

Continuing in pattern, increase in the same way every ½" until you have a total of 97, 99 (99, 103, 107, 111) (115, 117, 121, 125) stitches on the needles.

Continue in pattern without further increasing until the sleeve measures 17, 17 (17¾, 18, 18½, 19¼) (19¾, 19¾, 20, 20)" or the desired length to the armholes. Knit 1 round with color 1. Bind off all stitches. Knit the second sleeve in the same way.

Finishing

Sew 2 seams on your sewing machine on each side of the steek stitches and steek the armholes (see page 174). Sew the front shoulder stitches to the back shoulder stitches (see page 169). Sew in the sleeves (see page 175).

Neckline

Using a 16" US size 2 circular needle and color 1, pick up and knit 80, 80 (84, 84, 88, 88) (92, 92, 96, 96) stitches evenly around the neck opening. Place a marker to indicate the beginning of the round. Work in knit 1, purl 1 ribbing for 1¼". Bind off all stitches loosely, knitting knit stitches and purling purl stitches.

Weave in all loose ends. Steam or wet block the sweater for an even finish.

Color 1: Vidde, cerise 315

Color 2: Vidde, navy blue 301

Color 3: Luna, light teal 435

Color 4: Luna, warm yellow 421

Color 5: Varde, green 2126

Color:
Fjell, unbleached white 100

Reading Socks

I often talk about taking things one step at a time, whether it comes to facing challenges in life or practicing something you don't know or of which you are afraid. It can mean learning step by step to achieve as much mastery as possible. That's why it felt natural for me to include the pattern for a good, warm pair of socks, or "læsta" as we say in Trøndelag. The Reading Socks can be your companion for all the steps you take on your journey. They are perfect in hiking boots when the weather gets colder, or as an extra layer inside your sleeping bag slippers. I also use mine indoors during winter and at the cabin where the floors are cold.

Sizes
S (M, L)
The sizes correspond to women's shoe sizes 6-7½ (8½-9½, 10-12).

Finished Size
Foot length: Approx. 8½-9½ (10-10½, 11-11½)"

Yarn
Hillesvåg Fjell (80% wool, 20% nylon: 183 yd [167 m]/100 g)

Actual Yarn Amounts
200 g all sizes

Needles
US size 4: set of double-pointed needles.

Gauge
22 stitches × 29 rows in stockinette = 4 × 4"

How to Knit these Socks

The socks are knitted in the round. The leg is worked in ribbing to the top of the heel. The heel is worked back and forth over half the stitches. You then pick up stitches around the heel to knit the foot in stockinette stitch.

Leg

Cast on 44 (48, 52) stitches on US size 4 double-pointed needles. Distribute the stitches with 11 (12, 13) stitches on each of 4 needles. Place a marker for the beginning of the round. Work in knit 1, purl 1 ribbing in the round for 5½ (6, 6¼)".

Heel Flap

Now, knit the heel over the first 22 (24, 26) stitches (needles 1 and 2). Let the remaining stitches, which will form the front of the sock, rest on needles 3 and 4. The heel is knitted back and forth in stockinette (knit on the right side, purl on the wrong side) with edge stitches on each side, as follows:

Start by knitting the 22 (24, 26) stitches on needles 1 and 2 onto a single needle. Turn, make an edge stitch by slipping the first stitch as if to purl without knitting it, and then purl to the end of the row. Turn and make an edge stitch by slipping the first stitch as if to knit without knitting it, then knit to the end of the row. Repeat these two rows, working back and forth with edge stitches, until the heel measures 2 (2½, 2½)", finishing with a purl row.

Heel Turn

On the next right-side row, knit until there are 8 (8, 9) stitches left on the needle. Knit the next two stitches together through the back loops. Turn, and slip the first stitch as if to purl, purl until 8 (8, 9) stitches remain on the needle, and purl the next two stitches together.

Turn, and slip the first stitch as if to knit, knit until there is one stitch left before the gap from the previous turn, knit the next two stitches together through the back loops to close the gap. Turn, and slip the first stitch as if to purl, purl until there is one stitch left before the gap from the previous turn, purl the next two stitches together to close the gap.

Repeat the last two rows 5 (5, 6) more times. You now have 8 (10, 10) stitches remaining on the heel needle. Cut the yarn.

Gusset

With the right side facing, starting where the heel flap meets the resting instep stitches, use an extra needle to pick up and knit 10 (12, 12) stitches along the edge of the heel flap, then knit 4 (5, 5) stitches from the heel needle. This is now needle 1. Use another needle to knit remaining 4 (5, 5) heel stitches, then pick up and knit 10 (12, 12) stitches along other side edge of heel flap. This is needle 2. Knit the resting instep stitches onto needles 3 and 4. You are now at the beginning of the round. You have 50 (58, 60) stitches in total, with 28 (34, 34) stitches for the heel and gusset on needles 1 and 2, and 22 (24, 26) stitches for the top of the foot on needles 3 and 4.

Work in stockinette stitch in the round while decreasing the gusset as follows: Knit the first 2 stitches of needle 1 together. Knit until there are 2 stitches left on needle 2 and knit these 2 stitches together through the back loop. Knit the rest of the round. You now have 48 (56, 58) stitches remaining. Knit 1 round.

Decrease 2 stitches in this manner every other round 4 (6, 5) more times. You now have 40 (44, 48) stitches in total. Redistribute the stitches so there are 10 (11, 12) stitches on each needle, with the beginning of the round side of the sock, the sole of the sock on needles 1 and 2, and the top of the foot on needles 3 and 4.

132

Foot

Continue knitting in stockinette stitch until the foot measures 6¾-7½ (7½-8, 8½-9)" from the back of the heel, or 1¾ (1¾, 2)" less than desired finished length.

Toe

Decrease 4 stitches on the next round as follows: Knit the first 2 stitches of needle 1 together, knit to the last 2 stitches on needle 2 and SSK (slip, slip, knit—see page 173). Then knit the first 2 stitches of needle 3 together, knit to the last 2 stitches on needle 4 and SSK. You have now decreased 4 stitches, leaving you with 36 (40, 44) stitches. Knit 1 round without decreasing.

Repeat the last 2 rounds, decreasing 4 stitches every other round, 3 (3, 4) more times. You now have 24 (28, 28) stitches left.

Decrease 4 stitches every round 4 (5, 5) times. You now have 8 stitches remaining. Cut the yarn and pull it through all the remaining stitches.

Knit the second sock in the same way. Weave in all loose ends.

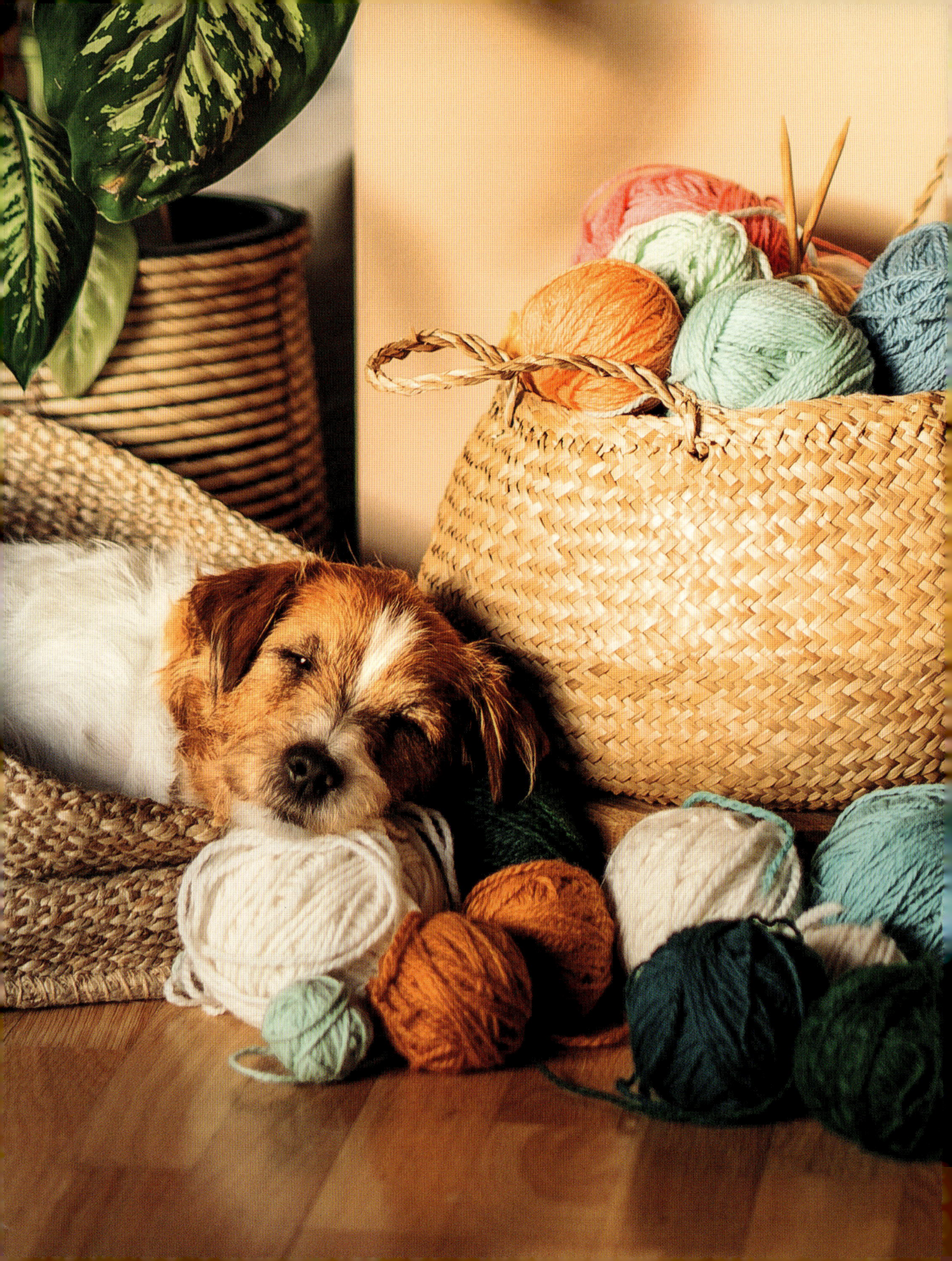

ZERO-WASTE PROJECTS

Like most other knitters, I have a sea of leftover yarn from all the projects, big and small, I've knit over the years. After working on this book, where for the first time I designed and knitted many new garments in a short time, I realized just how much yarn you can have left over. Especially after knitting garments with many different colors.

I've always had the philosophy that reuse is not only important, but it can also be fun and innovative.

That's why it was important for me to create several designs that could utilize most of the yarn leftovers you have after finishing a few projects from this book. Some of them, such as the Frostbite Mittens, are already presented in the previous chapter in connection with similar patterns. The rest, you are getting here.

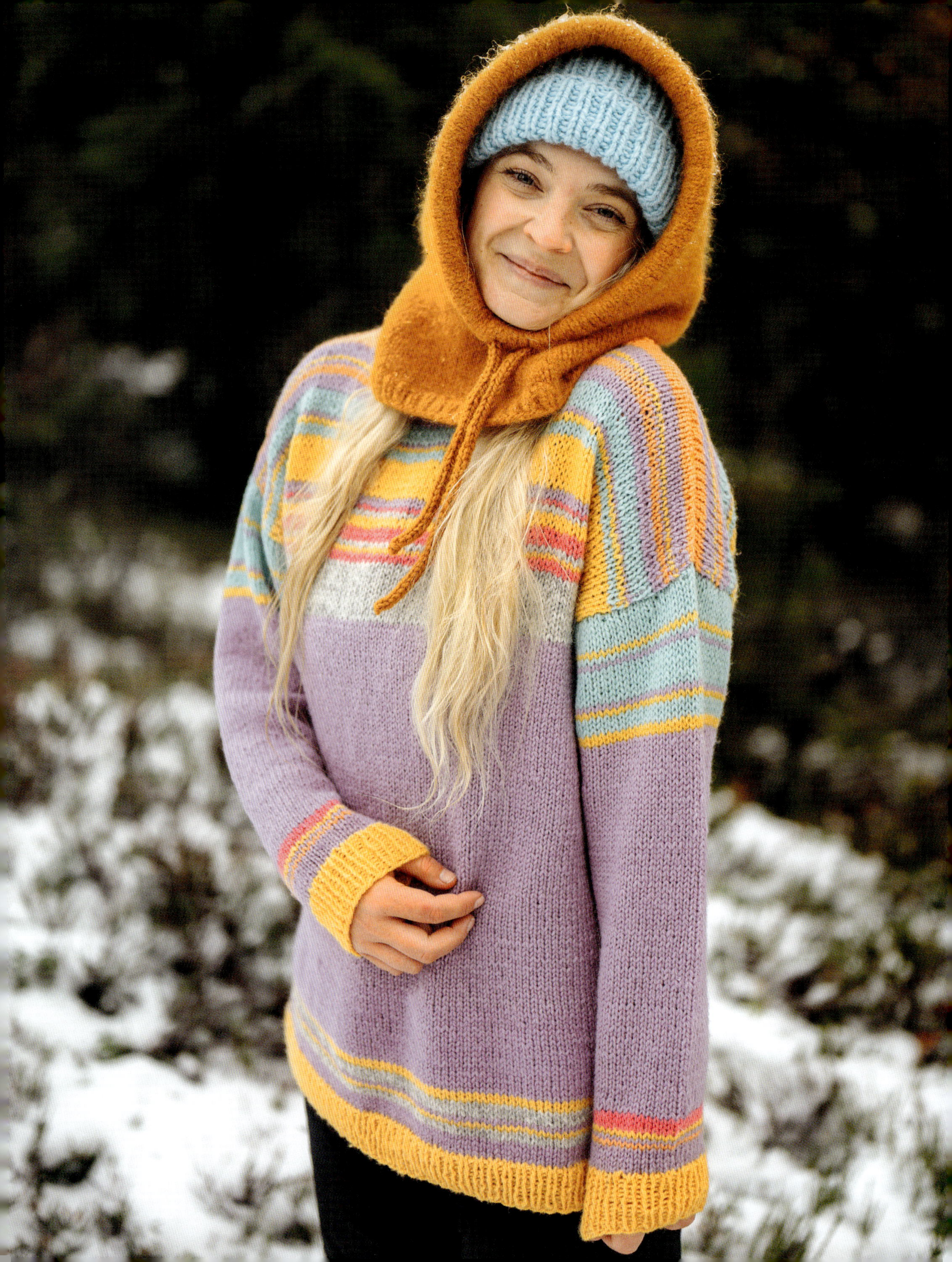

Scrap Sweater

We've created a pattern for both a bulky-weight and a worsted-weight version of a sweater made with leftover yarn. This allows yarn from most of the garments in the book to be used here. These instructions are simply templates for you to use to create your very own version, exactly as you like, with the leftover yarn you have on hand. There are no patterned borders in these sweaters, just the total amount of yarn, stitch counts, and instructions. They're also designed to be as simple as possible, without requiring special skills for assembly or challenging techniques. Even beginners can master this project.

So be creative, be bold, be wild, and enjoy making this leftover sweater. No two sweaters will be alike. You have everything you need to create your own unique design.

You can be creative with this sweater!

Worsted-Weight Scrap Sweater

Sizes
XXS, XS (S, M, L, XL) (2XL, 3XL, 4XL, 5XL)

Garment Measurements
This sweater is designed to be worn with 6" of positive ease.
Bust: 37, 39¼ (41, 43¼, 45¾, 47¼) (48¾, 52¾, 56¾, 60¾)"
Total length: 22½, 22¾ (24, 24¾, 25½, 26½) (27, 27½, 28, 28¼)" or desired length
Sleeve length: 17, 17 (17¾, 18, 18½, 19¼) (19¾, 19¾, 20, 20)" or desired length
Note that the shoulder sits down on the arm and adds to the sleeve length.

Yarn
Use what you have of leftover yarn from Hillesvåg Luna, Vidde, or Varde and Rauma Fivel. These are worsted-weight, or medium-weight, yarns.

Total Yarn Amount
Approx. 420, 445 (465, 490, 515, 535) (555, 600, 645, 690) g

Needles
US size 6: 16" and 32" circular needles and set of double-pointed needles
US size 7: 16" and 32" circular needles and set of double-pointed needles
Adjust needle size as necessary to obtain gauge.

Gauge
18 stitches × 24 rows in stockinette = 4 × 4"

How to Knit this Sweater

You will knit this sweater in the round from the bottom up to the armholes. You will divide the stitches for front and back and finishing each part separately, knitting back and forth. Then, you'll knit the sleeves from the cuffs up to the armholes before you sew in the sleeves. The neckline is finished at the end.

No instructions are given for how to arrange the colors or the stripes. Change colors and knit your stripes in any way you please to make the best use of your collection of yarn leftovers.

Body
Cast on 170, 180 (188, 198, 208, 216) (224, 242, 260, 278) stitches on US size 6 circular needles. Place a marker to mark the beginning of the round. Work in knit 1, purl 1 ribbing in the round for 2½".

Switch to US size 7 needles and knit in stockinette stitch in the round until the piece measures 14¼, 14¼ (14½, 15¼, 15¾, 16) (16½, 16½, 16½, 16½)" or desired length to the armholes.

On the next round, divide the stitches for the front and back as follows: Knit 85, 90 (94, 99,

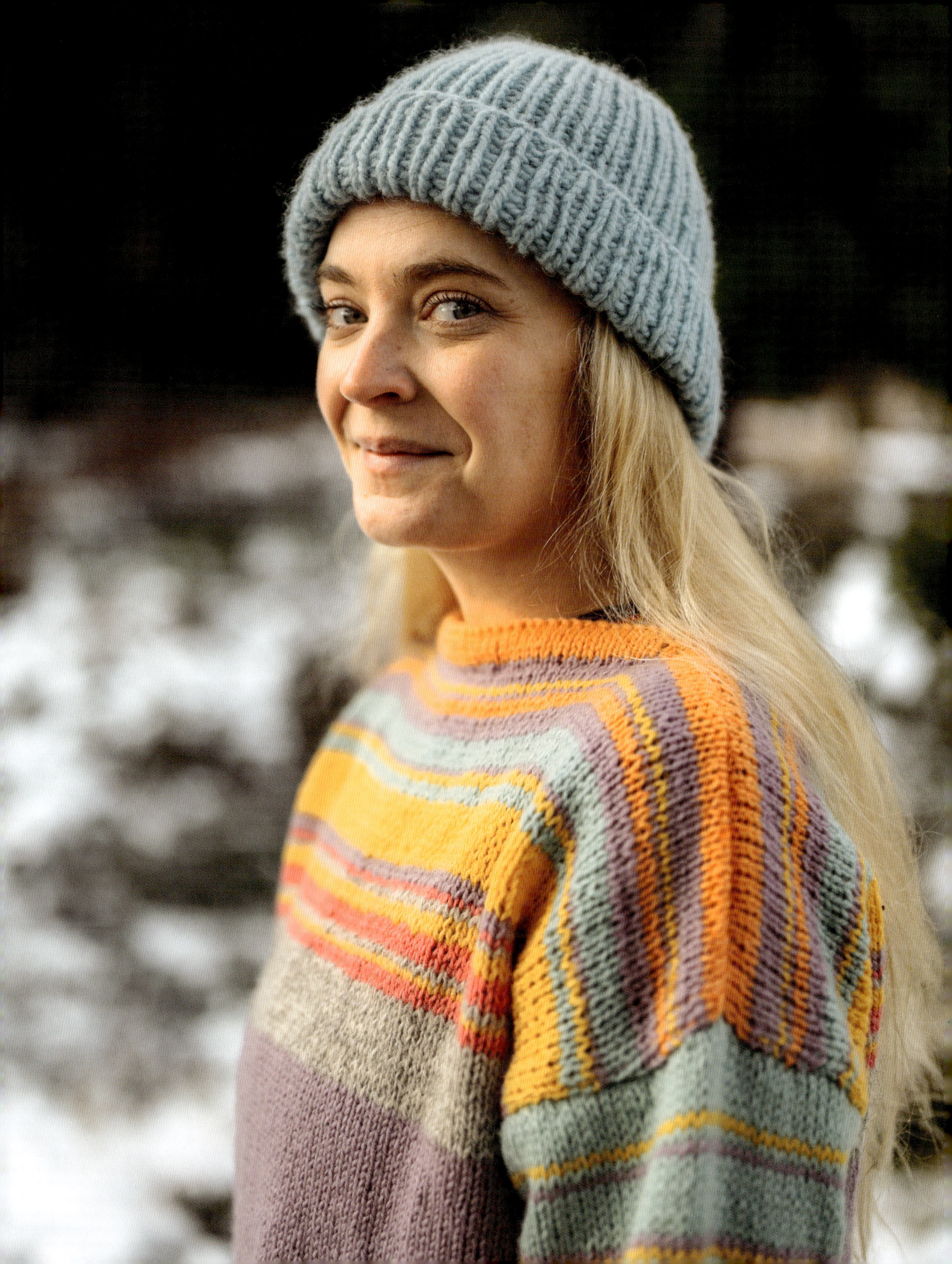

104, 108) (112, 121, 130, 139) stitches for the front and place these stitches on a stitch holder or a piece of scrap yarn. Continue knitting the remaining 85, 90 (94, 99, 104, 108) (112, 121, 130, 139) stitches to the end of the round for the back.

Back

Continue working back and forth in stockinette stitch over the back stitches until the piece measures 8¼, 8¾ (9, 9½, 9¾, 10¼) (10¾, 11, 11½, 11¾)" from the division. Bind off all stitches.

Front

Before knitting the front, you need to decide if you want a boat neck (as shown in the photos), a crew neck, or a turtleneck.

FOR A BOAT NECK:
Knit the front in the same way as the back. Omit the front neck shaping. Bind off all stitches when the front measures the same length as the back.

FOR CREW NECK OR TURTLENECK:
Continue back and forth in stockinette stitch over the front stitches until the piece measures measures 7, 7½ (7¾, 8¼, 8¾, 9) (9½, 10, 10¼, 10¾)" from the division.

On the next right-side row, bind off the center 29, 30 (32, 33, 34, 34) (36, 37, 38, 39) stitches for the neckline as follows: Knit the first 28, 30 (31, 33, 35, 37) (38, 42, 46, 50) stitches on the needle. Bind off the next 29, 30 (32, 33, 34, 34) (36, 37, 38, 39) stitches. Knit to the end of the row. Finish each side of the front separately as follows:

Right Front
Turn and purl the first wrong-side row back to the neckline. Turn and bind off the first 2 stitches on the right-side row, then knit to the end of the row. Repeat these 2 rows 1 more time.

On the next right-side row, bind off 1 stitch at the start of the row, then knit to the end of the row. You have now bound off 5 stitches, and the right front has 23, 25 (26, 28, 30, 32) (33, 37, 41, 45) stitches remaining. Turn and bind off all stitches with purl.

Left Front
Starting at the armhole edge with a right-side row, knit to the end of the row. Turn and bind off the first 2 stitches of the wrong-side row, then purl to the end of the row. Repeat these 2 rows 1 more time.

On the next wrong-side row, bind off 1 stitch at the start of the row, then purl to the end of the row. You have now bound off 5 stitches, and the left side of the front has 23, 25 (26, 28, 30, 32) (33, 37, 41, 45) stitches remaining. Turn and bind off all stitches with knit.

Sleeves
Cast on 32, 32 (36, 40, 42, 44) (44, 46, 46, 48) stitches on US size 6 double-pointed needles. Place a marker to mark the beginning of the round. Work in knit 1, purl 1 ribbing in the round for 2".

On the next round, switch to US size 7 needles. Knit 1 row, while increasing 6 stitches evenly as follows: *Knit 5, 5 (6, 6, 7, 7) (7, 7, 7, 8) stitches, increase 1 stitch*. Repeat from * to * 5 more times. Finish by knitting 2, 2 (0, 4, 0, 2) (2, 4, 4, 0) stitches. You now have 38, 38 (42, 46, 48, 50) (50, 52, 52, 54) stitches.

Continue in stockinette stitch in the round. When you have knitted ½" after the ribbing, increase 2 stitches as follows: Knit the first stitch, pick up the strand between stitches from front to back with the left needle, and knit it through the back loop. Knit the pattern until 1 stitch remains, pick up the strand between stitches from back to front with the left needle and knit it, then knit the last stitch. Increase in the same way every ½" until you have 76, 80 (84, 86, 90, 94) (98, 102, 104, 108) stitches on the needle.

Continue in stockinette stitch without increasing until the sleeve measures 16¼, 16½ (17, 17¼, 17¾, 18¼) (18½, 19, 19¼, 19¾)" or desired length to the armhole. Knit 1 more round and then bind off all stitches. Knit another sleeve in the same way.

Finishing
Each shoulder on the front and back has 23, 25 (26, 28, 30, 32) (33, 37, 41, 45) stitches. Sew the shoulder stitches of the front to the corresponding stitches on the back (see page 169). Sew in the sleeves (see page 175).

Neck Edging or Collar
BOAT NECK:
You have knitted the front piece to the same length as the back piece. Using a 16" US size 7 circular needle, pick up and knit 78, 80 (84, 86, 88, 88) (92, 94, 96, 98) stitches evenly around the neckline. Purl 1 round. This is the turning ridge. Knit 4 rounds, then bind off all stitches. Fold the

neck edging to the wrong side at the turning ridge and sew it down with loose stitches.

CREW NECK:

Using a 16" US size 6 circular needle, pick up and knit 80, 80 (84, 84, 88, 88) (92, 92, 96, 96) stitches evenly around the neckline. Place a marker to mark the beginning of the round. Work in knit 1, purl 1 ribbing in the round for 2½". Bind off all stitches in ribbing. Fold the collar to the wrong side and sew the bound-off edge to the first round of the collar with loose stitches.

TURTLENECK:

Using a 16" US size 6 circular needle, pick up and knit 80, 80 (84, 84, 88, 88) (92, 92, 96, 96) stitches evenly around the neckline. Place a marker to mark the beginning of the round. Work in knit 1, purl 1 ribbing in the round for 8" or to the desired length. Bind off all stitches in ribbing. Fold the collar to the right side.

Weave in all loose ends. Steam or wet block the sweater for a more even result.

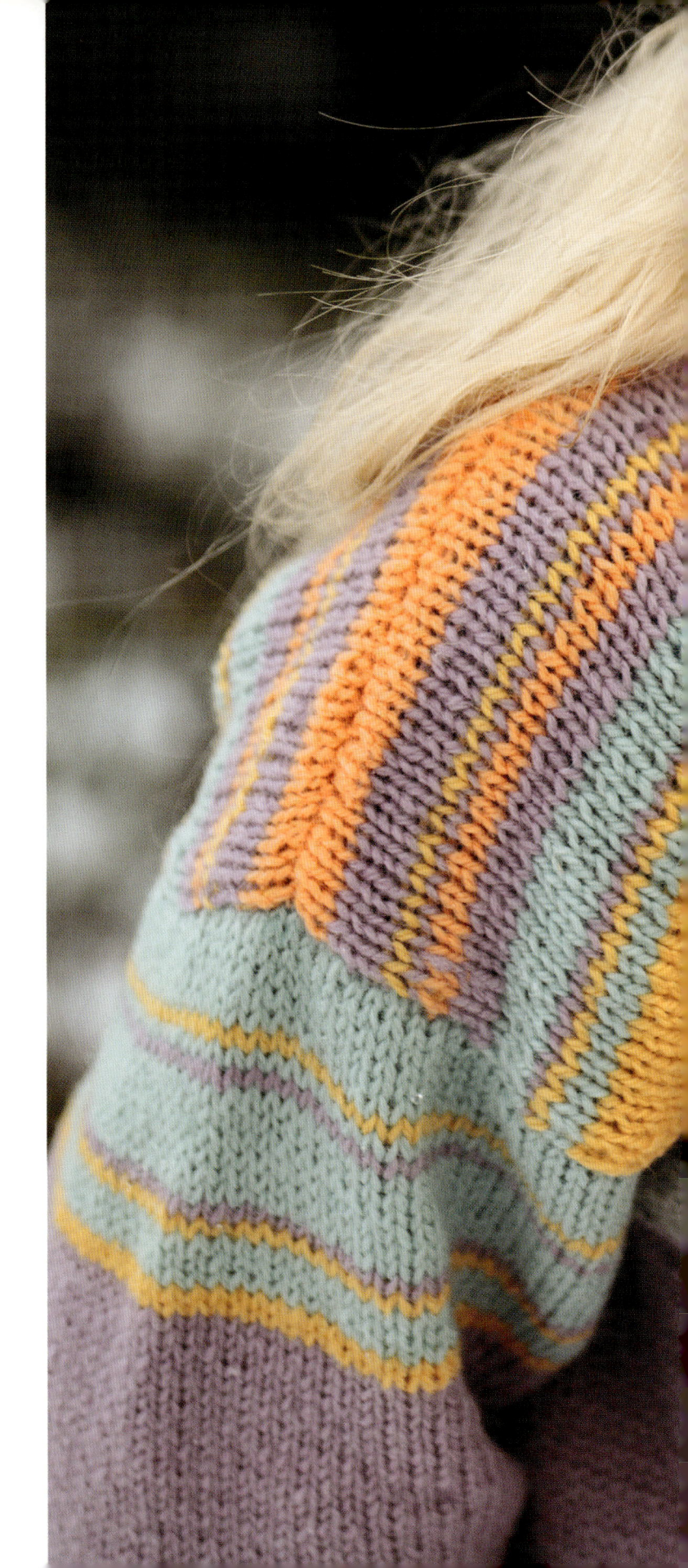

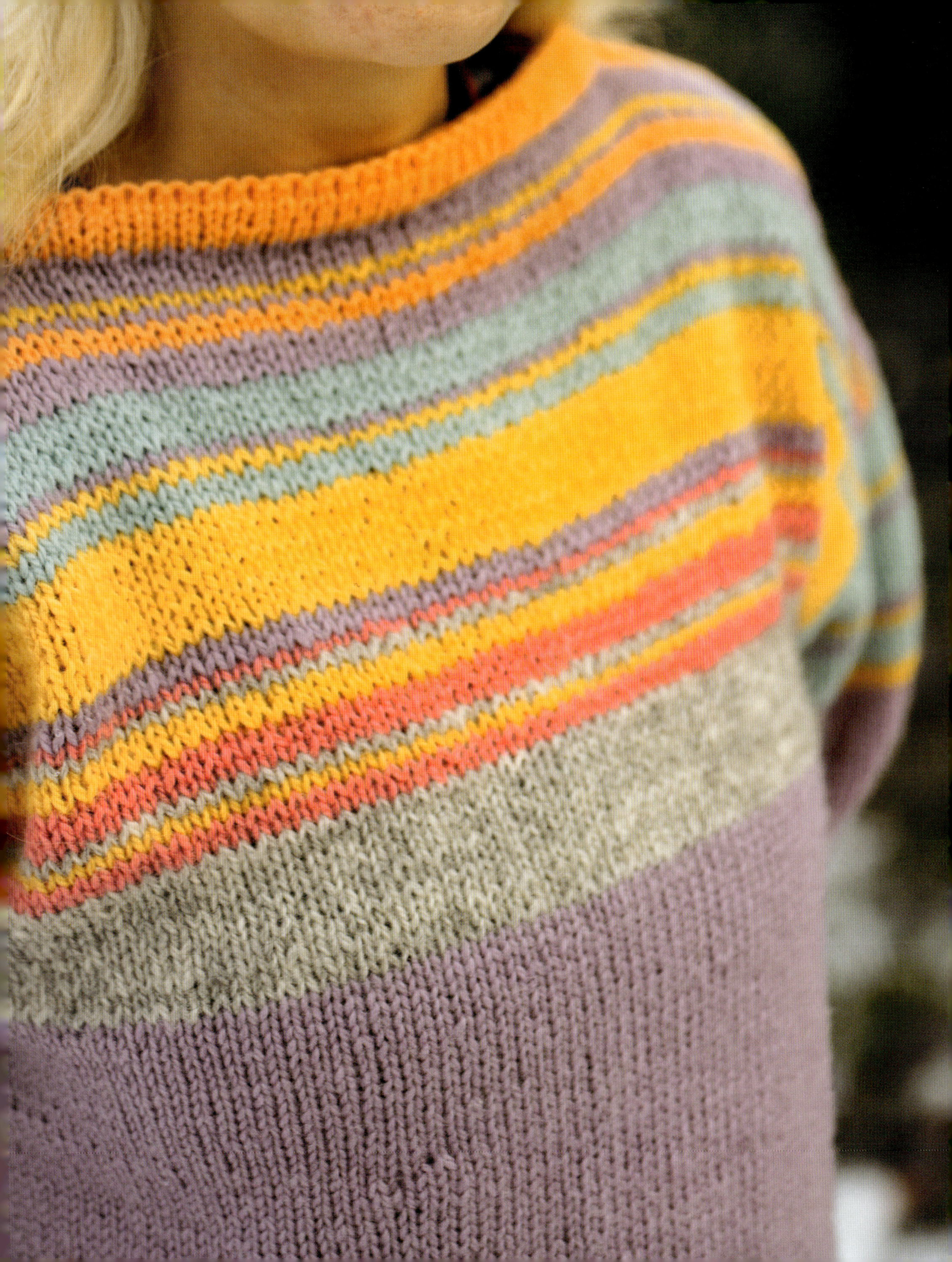

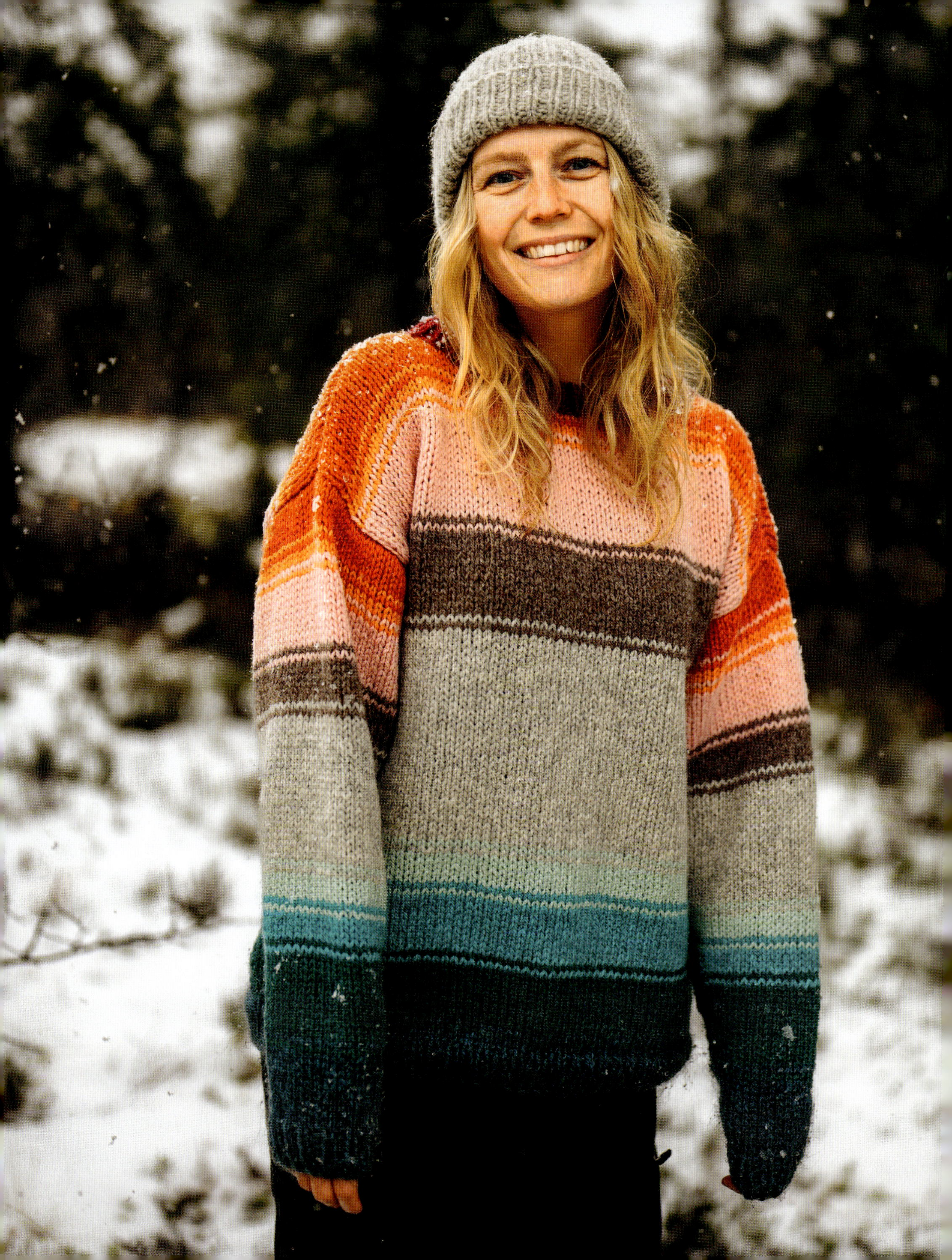

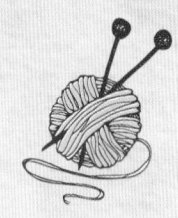

Bulky-Weight Scrap Sweater

Sizes
XXS, XS (S, M, L, XL) (2XL, 3XL, 4XL, 5XL)

Garment Measurements
This sweater is is designed to be worn with 6" of positive ease.
Bust: 37¾, 39¼ (41, 43¼, 45¼, 49½) (51½, 55½, 59, 61½)"
Total length: 22½, 22¾ (24, 24¾, 25½, 26½) (27, 27½, 28, 28¼)" or desired length
Sleeve length: 17, 17 (17¾, 18, 18½, 19¼) (19¾, 19¾, 20, 20)" or desired length
Note that the shoulder sits down on the arm and adds to the sleeve length.

Yarn
Use what you have of leftover yarn from Hillesvåg Blåne and Troll, and Rauma Vams. These are bulky- or chunky-weight yarns.

Total Yarn Amounts
Approx. 610, 630 (660, 690, 740, 780) (810, 860, 940, 1010) g

Needles
US size 9: 16" and 32" circular needles and set of double-pointed needles
US size 10: 16" and 32" circular needles and set of double-pointed needles
Adjust needle size as necessary to obtain gauge.

Gauge
14 stitches × 18 rows in stockinette = 4 × 4"

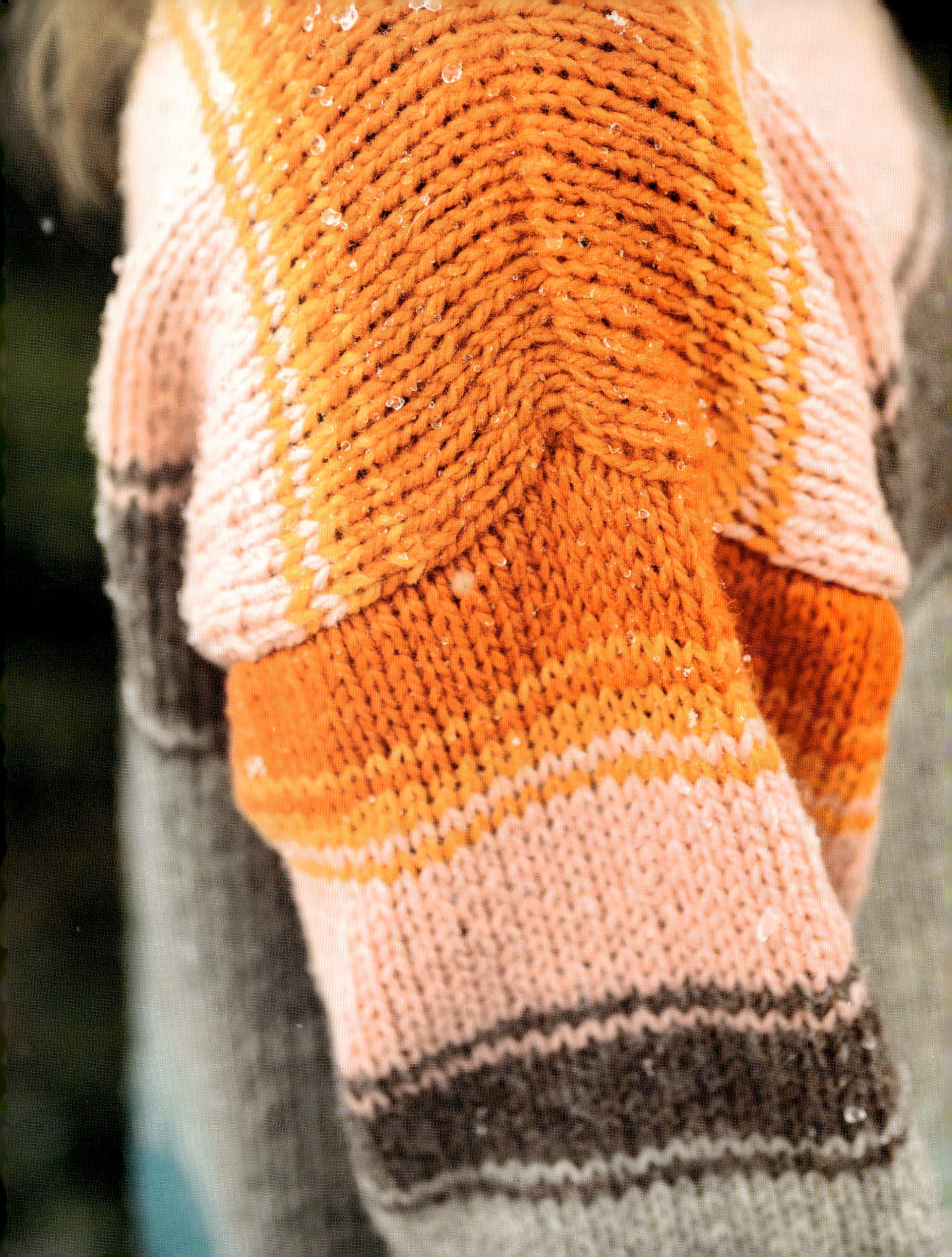

How to Knit this Sweater

You will knit this sweater in the round from the bottom up to the armholes. You will divide the stitches for front and back and finishing each part separately, knitting back and forth. Then, you'll knit the sleeves from the cuffs up to the armholes before you sew in the sleeves. The neckline is finished at the end.

No instructions are given for how to arrange the colors or the stripes. Change colors and knit your stripes in any way you please to make the best use of your collection of yarn leftovers.

Body

Cast on 134, 140 (146, 154, 162, 168) (176, 190, 204, 218) stitches on US size 9 circular needles. Place a marker to mark the beginning of the round. Work in knit 1, purl 1 ribbing in the round for 2½".

Switch to US size 10 needles and knit in stockinette stitch in the round until the piece measures 14¼, 14¼ (14½, 15¼, 15¾, 16) (16½, 16½, 16½, 16½)" or desired length to the armholes.

On the next round, divide the stitches for the front and back as follows: Knit 67, 70 (73, 77, 81, 84) (88, 95, 102, 109) stitches for the front and place these stitches on a stitch holder or a piece of scrap yarn. Continue knitting the remaining 67, 70 (73, 77, 81, 84) (88, 95, 102, 109) stitches to the end of the round for the back.

Back

Continue working back and forth in stockinette stitch over the back stitches until the piece measures 8¼, 8¾ (9, 9½, 9¾, 10¼) (10¾, 11, 11½, 11¾)" from the division. Bind off all stitches.

Front

Before knitting the front, you need to decide if you want a boat neck, a crew neck (as shown in the photos), or a turtleneck.

FOR A BOAT NECK:
Knit the front in the same way as the back. Omit the front neck shaping. Bind off all stitches when the front measures the same length as the back.

FOR CREW NECK OR TURTLENECK:
Continue back and forth in stockinette stitch over the front stitches until the piece measures 7, 7½ (7¾, 8¼, 8¾, 9) (9½, 10, 10¼, 10¾)" from the division.

On the next right-side row, bind off the center 19, 20 (21, 21, 23, 24) (24, 25, 26, 27) stitches for the neckline as follows: Knit the first 24, 25 (26, 28, 29, 30) (32, 35, 38, 41) stitches on the needle. Bind off the next 19, 20 (21, 21, 23, 24) (24, 25, 26, 27) stitches. Knit to the end of the row. Finish each side of the front separately as follows:

Right Front

Turn and purl the first wrong-side row back to the neckline. Turn and bind off the first 2 stitches on the right-side row, then knit to the end of the row. Repeat these 2 rows 1 more time.

On the next right-side row, bind off 1 stitch at the start of the row, then knit to the end of the row. You have now bound off 5 stitches, and the right front has 19, 20 (21, 23, 24, 25) (27, 30, 33, 36) stitches remaining. Turn and bind off all stitches with purl.

Left Front

Starting at the armhole edge with a right-side row, knit to the end of the row. Turn and bind off the first 2 stitches of the wrong-side row, then purl to the end of the row. Repeat these 2 rows 1 more time.

On the next wrong-side row, bind off 1 stitch at the start of the row, then purl to the end of the row. You have now bound off 5 stitches, and the left side of the front has 19, 20 (21, 23, 24, 25) (27, 30, 33, 36) stitches remaining. Turn and bind off all stitches with knit.

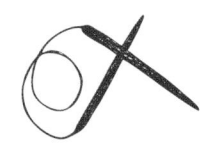

Sleeves

Cast on 24, 24 (26, 26, 28, 28) (30, 30, 32, 34) stitches on US size 9 double-pointed needles Place a marker to mark the beginning of the round. Work in knit 1, purl 1 ribbing in the round for 2".

On the next round, switch to US size 10 needles. Knit 1 row, while increasing 6 stitches evenly as follows: *Knit 4, 4 (4, 4, 4, 4) (5, 5, 5, 5) stitches, increase 1 stitch*. Repeat from * to * 5 more times. Finish by knitting 0, 0 (2, 2, 4, 4) (0, 0, 2, 4) stitches. You now have 30, 30 (32, 32, 34, 34) (36, 36, 38, 40) stitches.

Continue in stockinette stitch in the round. When you have knitted 1, 1 (1, 1, 1, ¾) (¾, ¾, ¾, ¾)" after the ribbing, increase 2 stitches as follows: Knit the first stitch, pick up the strand between stitches from front to back with the left needle, and knit it through the back loop. Knit the pattern until 1 stitch remains, pick up the strand between stitches from back to front with the left needle and knit it, then knit the last stitch. Increase in the same way every 1, 1 (1, 1, 1, ¾) (¾, ¾, ¾, ¾)" until you have 58, 62 (64, 66, 70, 72) (76, 78, 80, 84) stitches on the needle.

Continue in stockinette stitch without increasing until the sleeve measures 16¼, 16½ (17, 17¼, 17¾, 18¼) (18½, 19, 19¼, 19¾)" or desired length to the armhole. Knit 1 more round and then bind off all stitches. Knit another sleeve in the same way.

Finishing

Each shoulder on the front and back has 19, 20 (21, 23, 24, 25) (27, 30, 33, 36) stitches. Sew the shoulder stitches of the front to the corresponding stitches on the back (see page 169). Sew in the sleeves (see page 175).

Neck Edging or Collar

BOAT NECK:
You have knitted the front piece to the same length as the back piece. Using a 16" US size 10 circular needle, pick up and knit 58, 60 (62, 64, 64, 66) (68, 68, 70, 74) stitches evenly around the neckline. Purl 1 round. This is the turning ridge. Knit 4 rounds, then bind off all stitches. Fold the neck edging to the wrong side at the turning ridge and sew it down with loose stitches.

CREW NECK:
Using a 16" US size 9 circular needle, pick up and knit 60, 62, 64, 66, 68, 70) (72, 74, 76, 78) stitches evenly around the neckline. Place a marker to mark the beginning of the round. Work in knit 1, purl 1 ribbing in the round for 2½". Bind off all stitches in ribbing. Fold the collar to the wrong side and sew the bound-off edge to the first round of the collar with loose stitches.

TURTLENECK:
Using a 16" US size 9 circular needle, pick up and knit 60, 62 (64, 66, 68, 70) (72, 74, 76, 78) stitches evenly around the neckline. Place a marker to mark the beginning of the round. Work in knit 1, purl 1 ribbing in the round for 8" or to the desired length. Bind off all stitches in ribbing. Fold the collar to the right side.

Weave in all loose ends. Steam or wet block the sweater for a more even result.

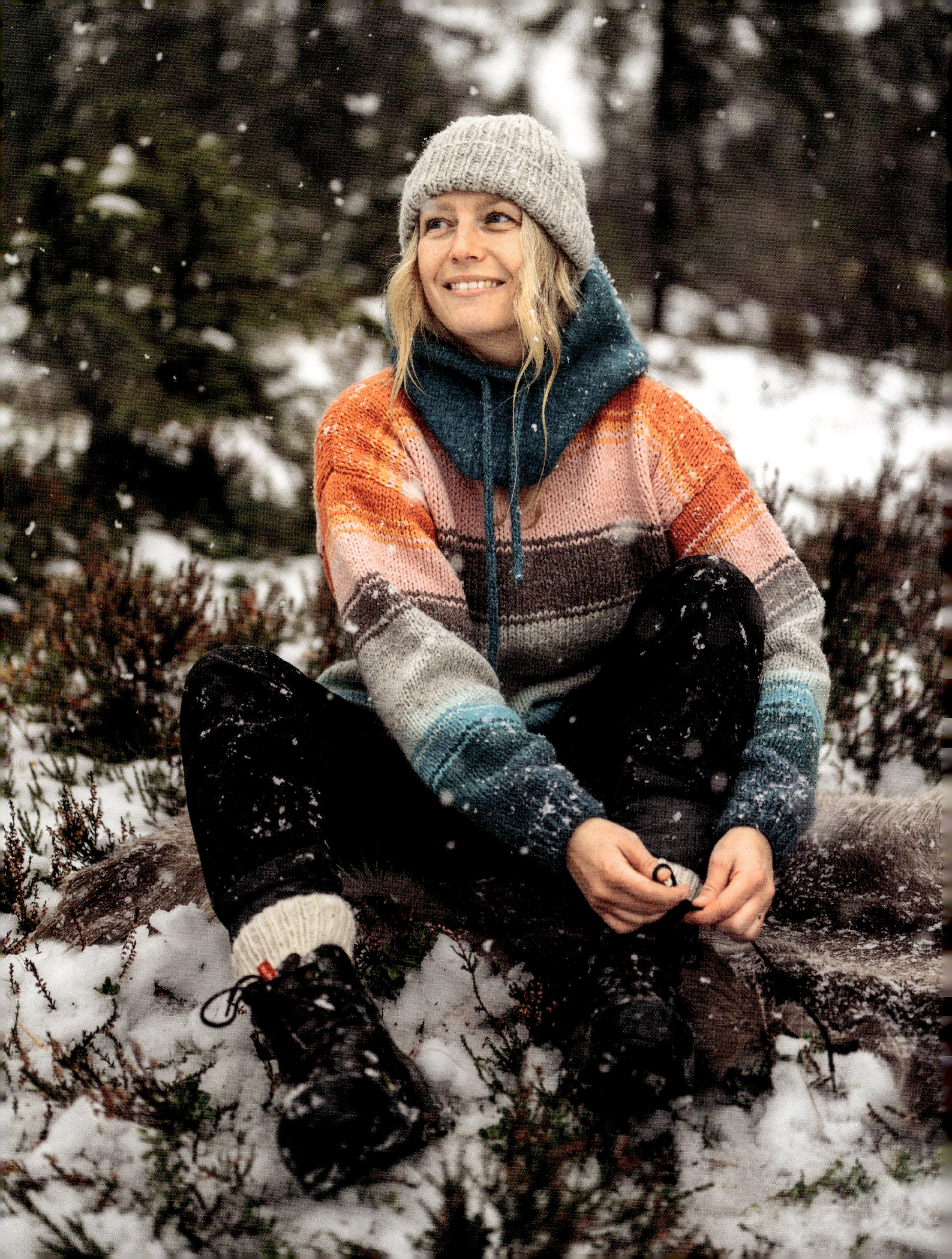

Troll, gray mélange 703
Troll, unbleached white 702
Blåne, burgundy 2104
Troll, dark brown mélange 707

Huv Hat

Did you know that the word for a knit hat in Trøndelag is *huv*? For a long time, I was looking for a hat that was warm, looked nice, and could be knit in 100% wool yarn. But I never found anything that was exactly what I wanted. That's how Huv came to be. You only need 100 grams of yarn. Play around with changing colors if you like and make it your own!

Sizes
S/M (M/L)
Fits head circumference of 19¾–22 (22–24½)"

Yarn
Hillesvåg Troll (100% Norwegian wool: 125 y [114 m]/100 g) or Hillesvåg Blåne (100% Norwegian wool: 125 y [114 m]/100 g) or Rauma Vams (100% Norwegian wool: 91 yd [83 m]/50 g)

Actual Yarn Amounts
100 g all sizes

Needles
US size 7: 16" circular needles and set of double-pointed needles
Adjust needle size as necessary to obtain gauge.

Gauge
20 stitches ribbing = 4"

How to Knit this Hat

Cast on 72 (80) stitches on 16" US size 7 circular needle. Place a marker to indicate the start of the round. The first round is a wrong-side round. Slip the first stitch purlwise without knitting it. Purl 1, *knit 1, purl 1*, repeat from * to * to the end of the round. Knit the first stitch of the next round, then slip it back to the left needle. This aligns the round so that it connects seamlessly. Turn the work. You will now work in the round with the right side facing. Work in knit 1, purl 1 ribbing for 8¾" or to the desired length.

Now, you'll decrease for the top of the hat. Follow the chart for your size, decreasing as shown in the chart. You will repeat the chart 4 times for each round. Switch to double-pointed needles or your preferred needles/technique when the hat becomes too small for the circular needle. See page 173 for an explanation of the slip, slip, knit (SSK) decrease.

When the chart is complete, you'll have 8 stitches remaining on the needle. Cut the yarn, pull it through the stitches, and tighten. Weave in all loose ends. Fold up the lower edge of the hat to your desired length. You can wet block the hat for a softer finish.

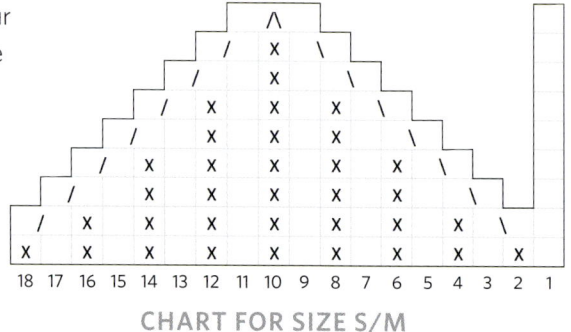

- ☐ Knit
- ☒ Purl
- \ Slip, slip, knit
- / Knit 2 together
- ∧ Slip the first stitch without knitting it, knit 2 together, slip the first stitch over the knit 2 together and off the needle = 2 stitches decreased.

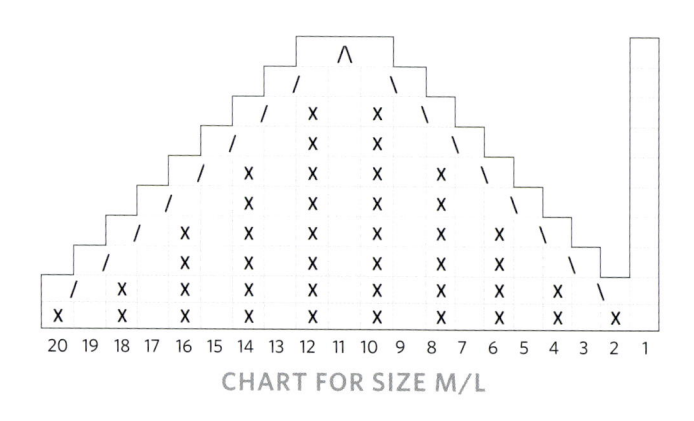

CHART FOR SIZE S/M

CHART FOR SIZE M/L

152

Color: Troll,
cotton candy 753

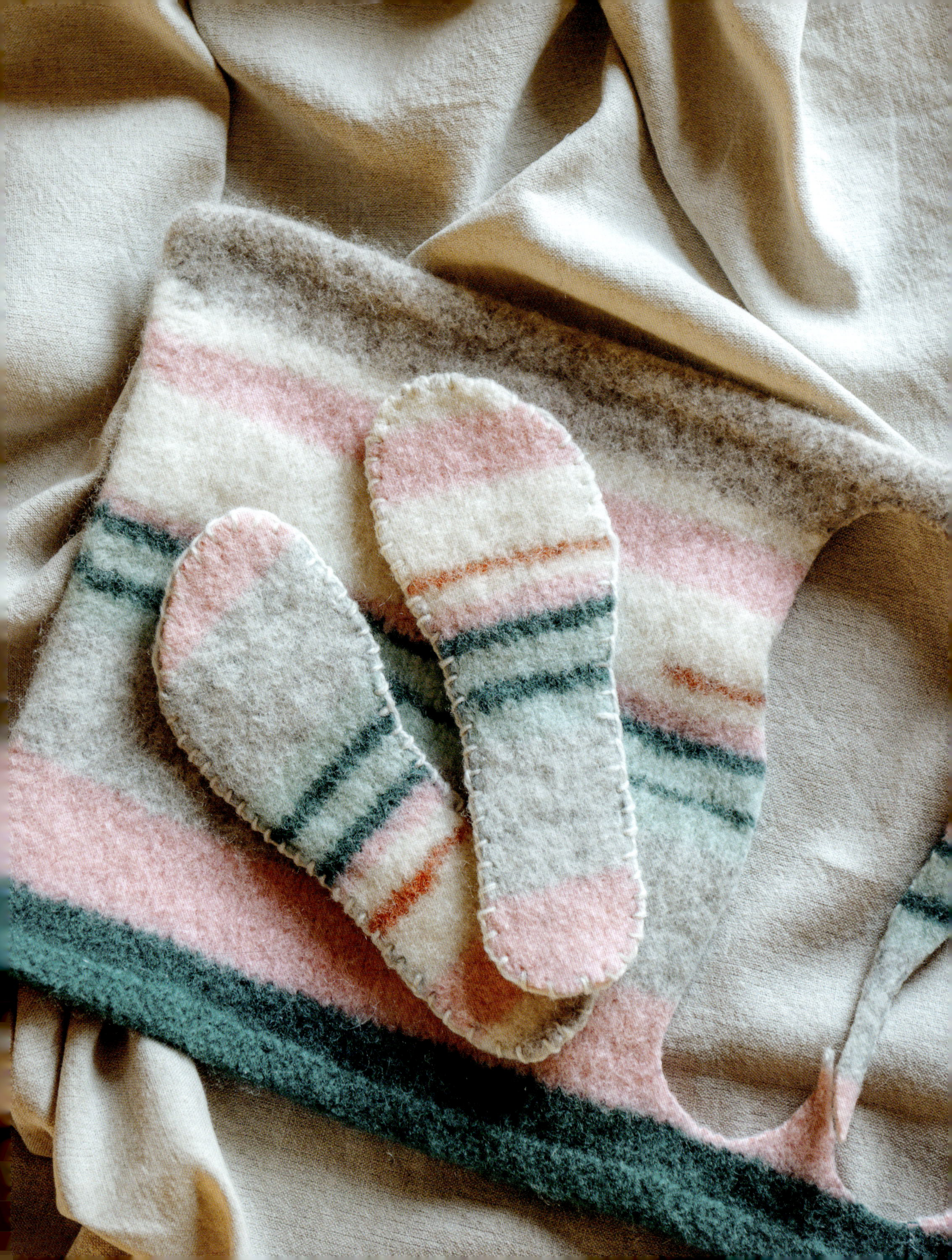

Felted Insoles

These soles are absolutely brilliant. For a long time, I've missed having good, warm insoles to put in my shoes when the weather gets colder. Making felted insoles from leftover yarn is creative, eco-friendly, and practical. They're the perfect gift for someone who always has cold feet in the winter.

Sizes
One size, the soles will be cut to size after felting

Measurements Before Felting
22½ × 18½"

Measurements After Felting
Approximately 17¾ × 12¼"

Yarn
Scraps of chunky-weight 100% wool.

Total Yarn Amount
Approx. 200 g

Needles
US size 10: 32" circular needles

Gauge
14 stitches × 18 rows = 4 × 4" (10 cm)

Tip: Different yarn styles or yarns from different manufacturers might felt differently, so it is a good idea to use the same yarn.

How to Knit these Insoles

The soles are knitted as a rectangle which is then felted in the washing machine. After felting, you will cut the soles to the desired size. You will finish by sewing blanket stitch around the edges.

No instructions are given for how to arrange the colors or the stripes. Change colors and knit your stripes in any way you please to make the best use of your collection of yarn leftovers.

Cast on 80 stitches. Knit 4 rows. Then repeat these 2 rows:

Row 1: Slip the first stitch purlwise, knit to the end of the row.
Row 2: Slip the first stitch purlwise, knit 2 stitches, purl until 3 stitches remain, then knit the last 3 stitches.

Repeat Rows 1 and 2 until the piece measures approximately 17 ¾", ending with Row 2. Knit 4 rows. Bind off all stitches and weave in any loose ends.

Felt the piece in a washing machine or by hand. See the felting guide on page 179. The piece must be felted firmly to create a dense fabric. Compare your piece to the approximate measurements after felting to determine when it is adequately felted. Dry the piece flat.

Cut out the soles to your desired size.

Tip:
Use the insoles from your shoes as a template. If you position your insoles to minimize waste, you may be able to get four insoles from your felted wool fabric.

Color:
Varde, burgundy
2104

Neck Warmer

On days when it's just a little cold outside, a neck warmer is perfect. It also works well for covering the face as an extra layer under the Bitter Cold Balaclava.

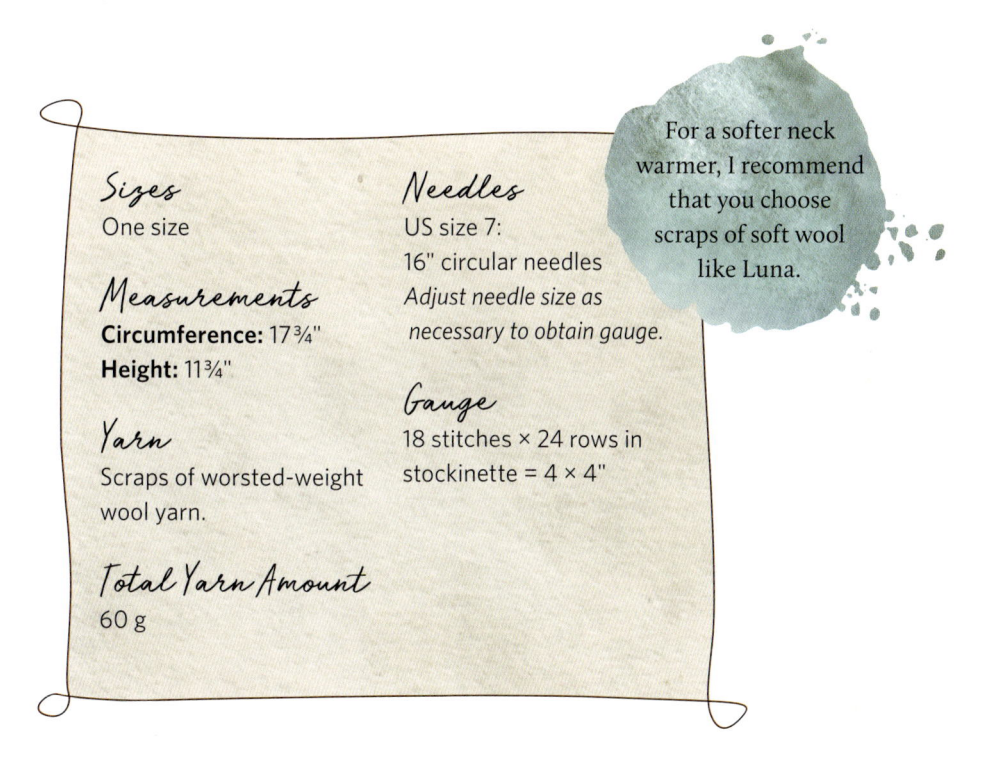

Sizes
One size

Measurements
Circumference: 17¾"
Height: 11¾"

Yarn
Scraps of worsted-weight wool yarn.

Total Yarn Amount
60 g

Needles
US size 7:
16" circular needles
Adjust needle size as necessary to obtain gauge.

Gauge
18 stitches × 24 rows in stockinette = 4 × 4"

For a softer neck warmer, I recommend that you choose scraps of soft wool like Luna.

How to Knit this Neck Warmer

Cast on 80 stitches. Place a marker to mark the beginning of the round. Work in knit 1, purl 1 ribbing in the round for ¾".

Continue in stockinette stitch in the round until the piece measures 10¼" or to the desired length.

Work in knit 1, purl 1 ribbing in the round for ¾". Bind off all stitches in ribbing.

Weave in all loose ends. You can wet block the neck warmer for a softer finish.

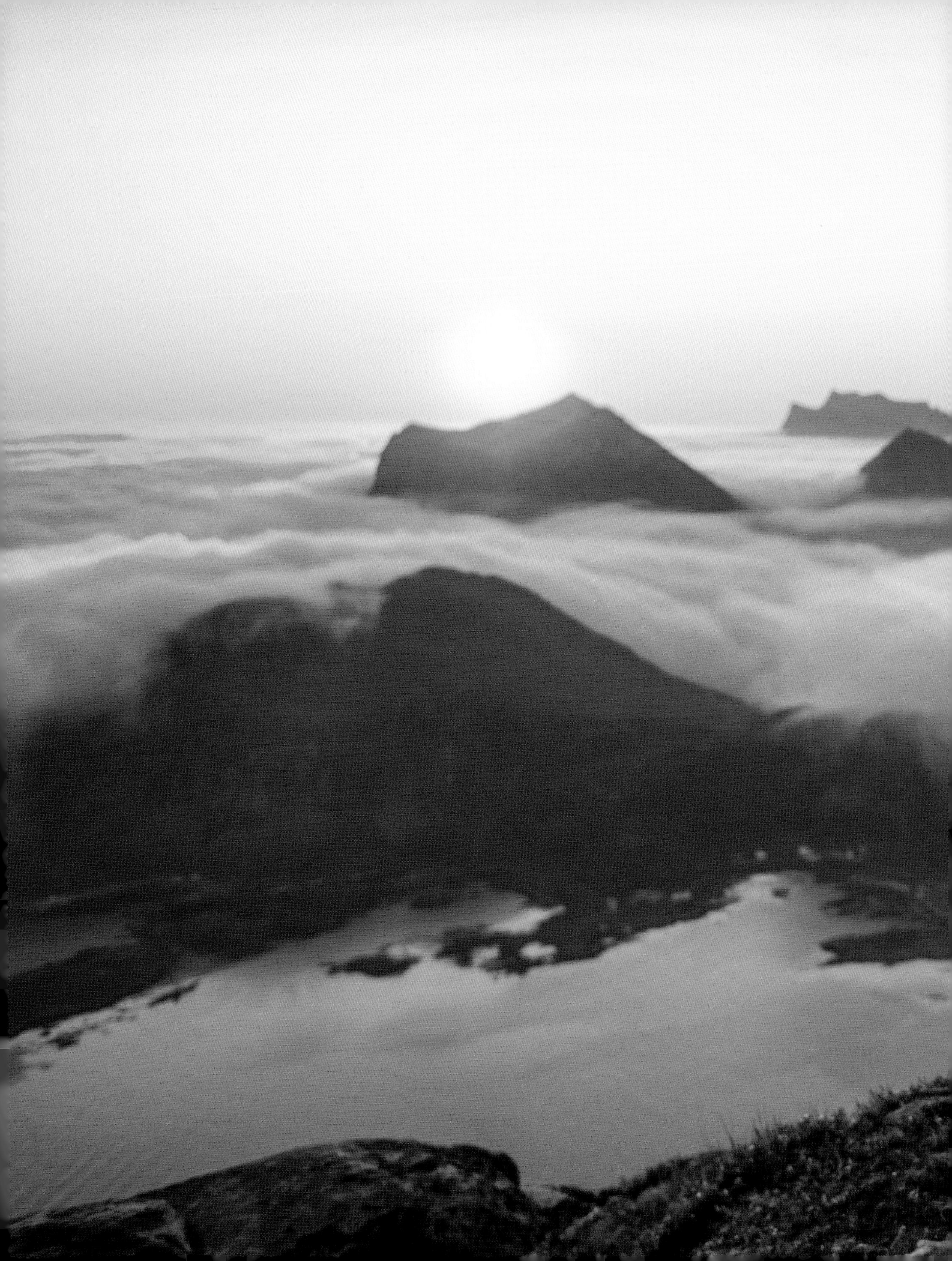

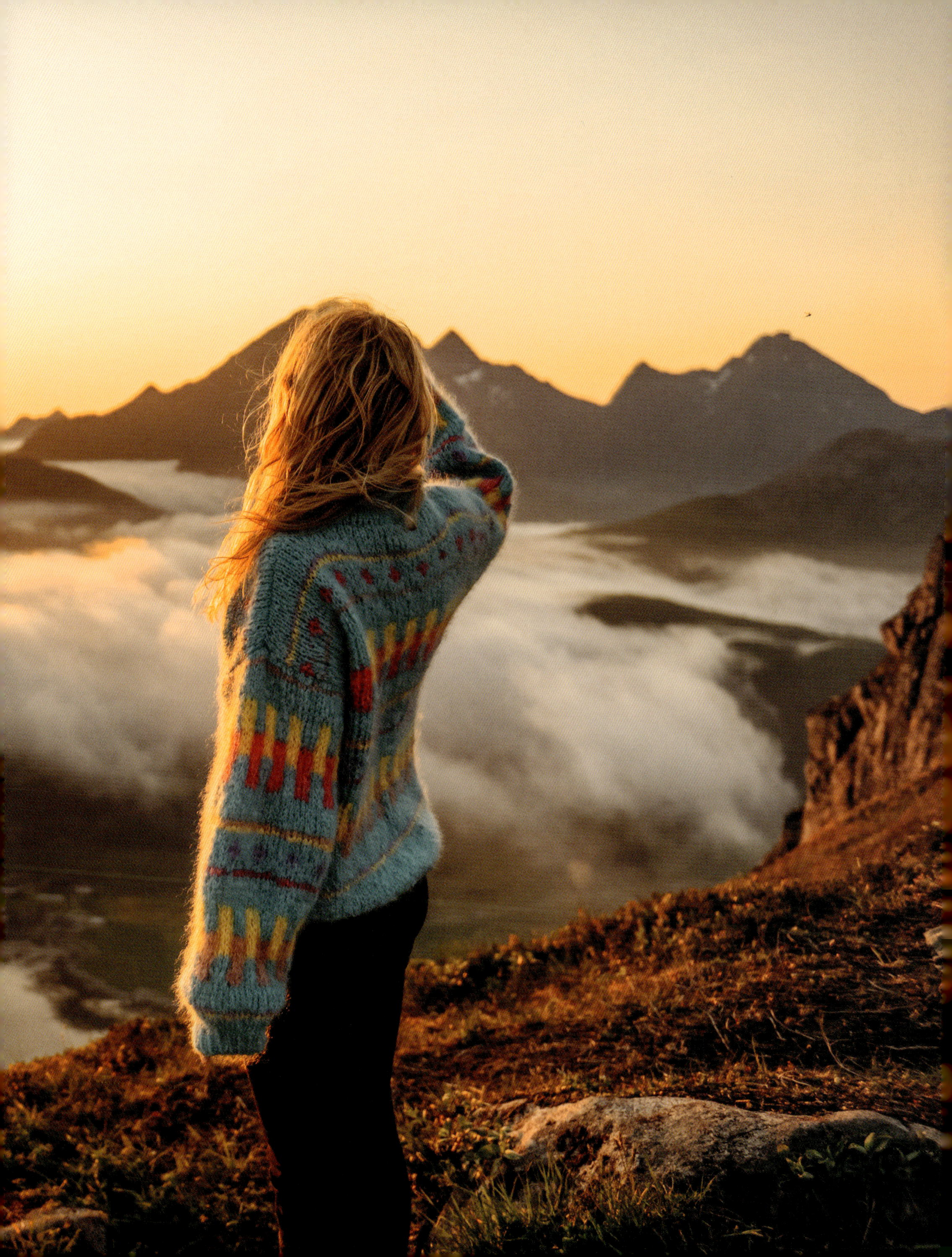

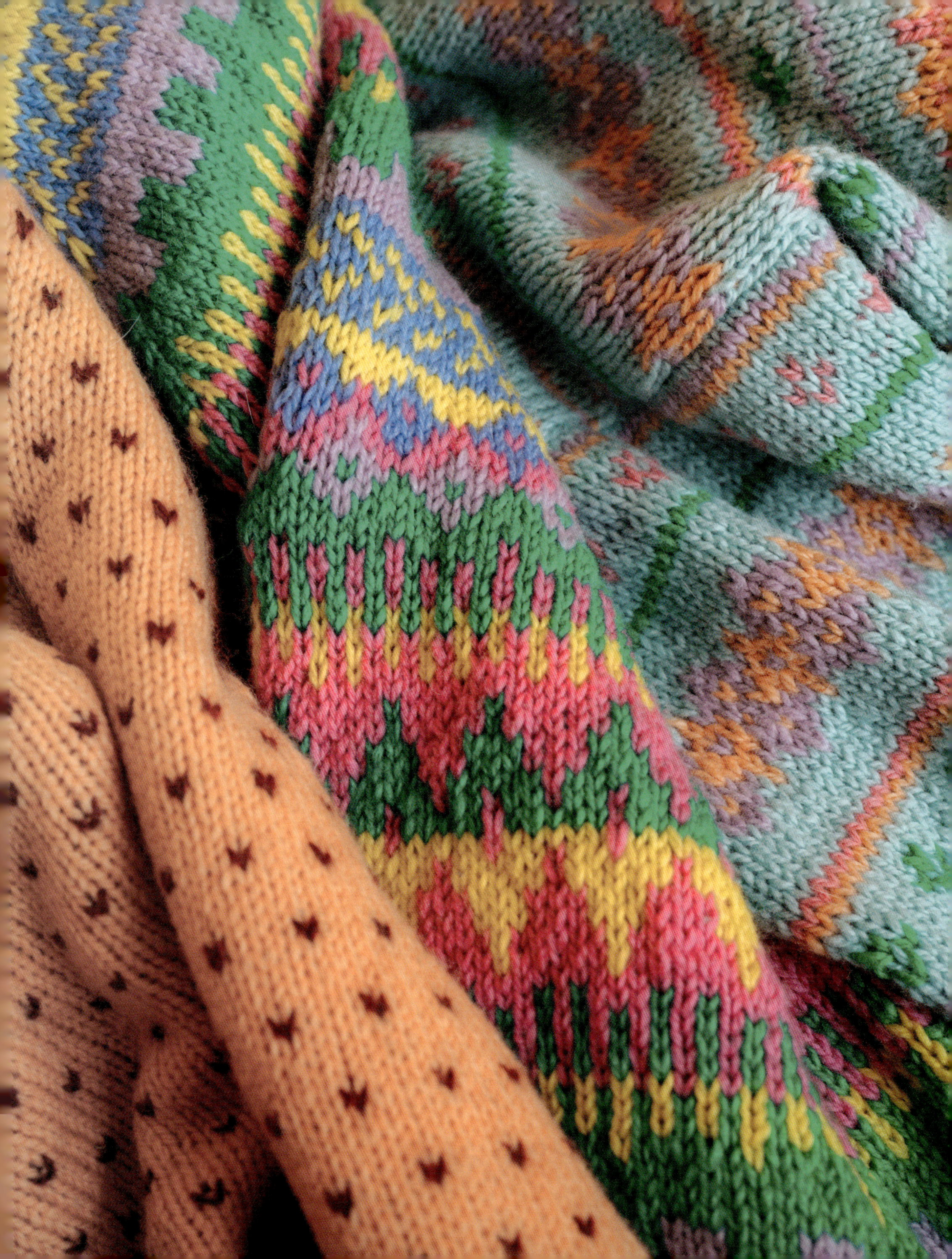

TECHNIQUES

In this final section, you'll get answers to various questions that may come up while knitting. Use these pages as a reference whenever needed. If you are a beginner, it can be helpful to read through the part on gauge before starting the patterns. I've made plenty of mistakes over the years in terms of gauge, assembly, and maintenance, so I find these technical pages invaluable for achieving the best results. I'm lucky to have had my sister Stine, who has worked as a knitting designer for many years, share her knowledge in this chapter.

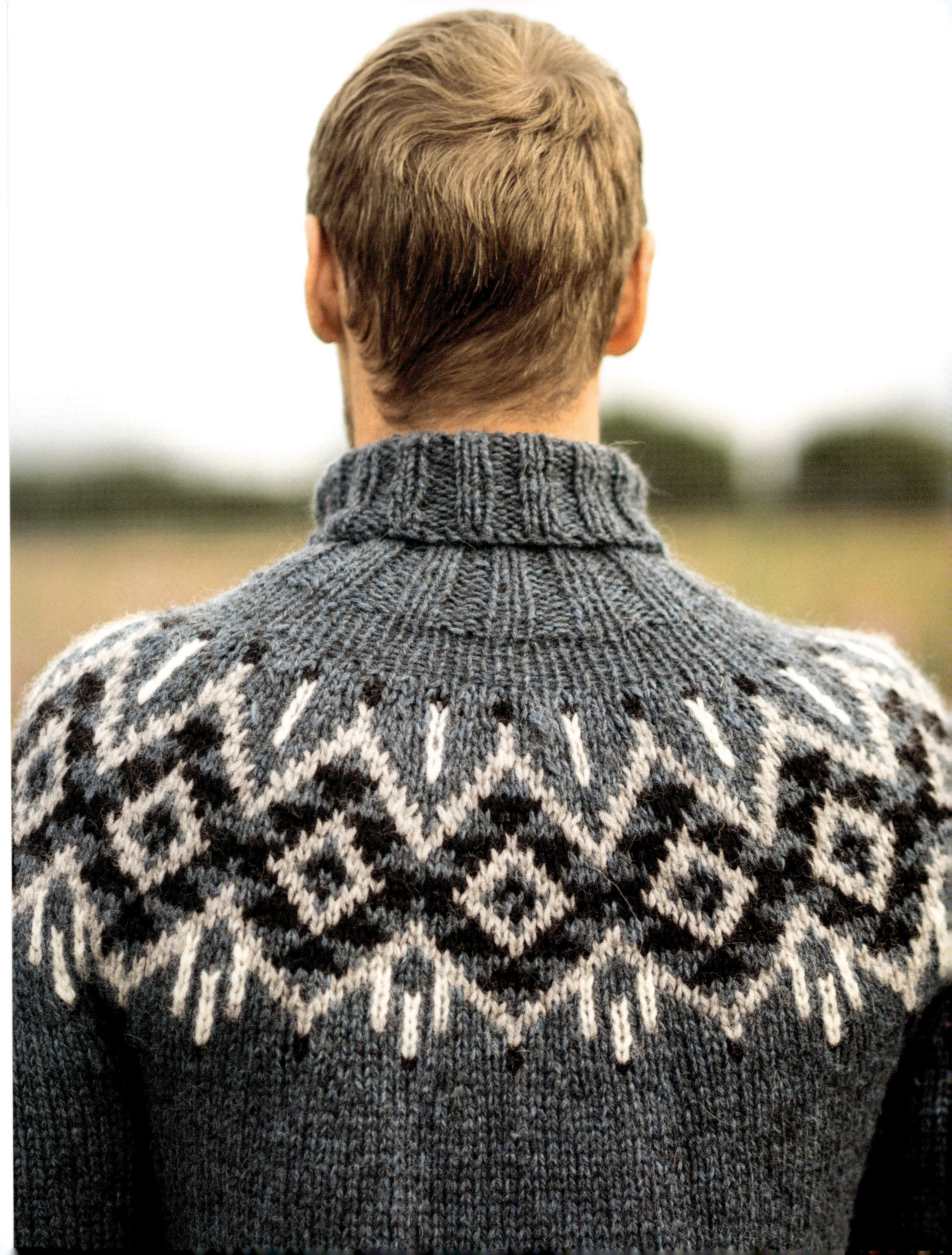

Colorwork Tips

Often, your gauge will change when you go from single-color stockinette to multicolored pattern knitting. Typically, people knit tighter when doing color work, though some may knit looser. If you find you're knitting too tightly or too loosely, try adjusting your needle size for this section. Go up a size if it's too tight, and down a size if it's too loose.

Another tip is to spread apart the stitches on the right-hand needle to ensure a longer float on the back, preventing tightness in the pattern section.

When your pattern has you stranding yarn behind many stitches on the wrong side, it's helpful to twist the yarns together to avoid long strands (or floats) on the inside of your garment. To do this, wrap the main color with the pattern color after a set number of stitches. A long float can be 5 stitches or more, but this varies by knitter. Ultimately, it's up to you to decide when and if to twist the yarn on the back.

Example: You have 21 stitches in the main color before switching to the pattern color again. Knit 5 stitches with the main color, then twist the pattern color on the back. This keeps the pattern color secure on the back and avoids a long, loose strand. Repeat the twist every 5 stitches, more or less.

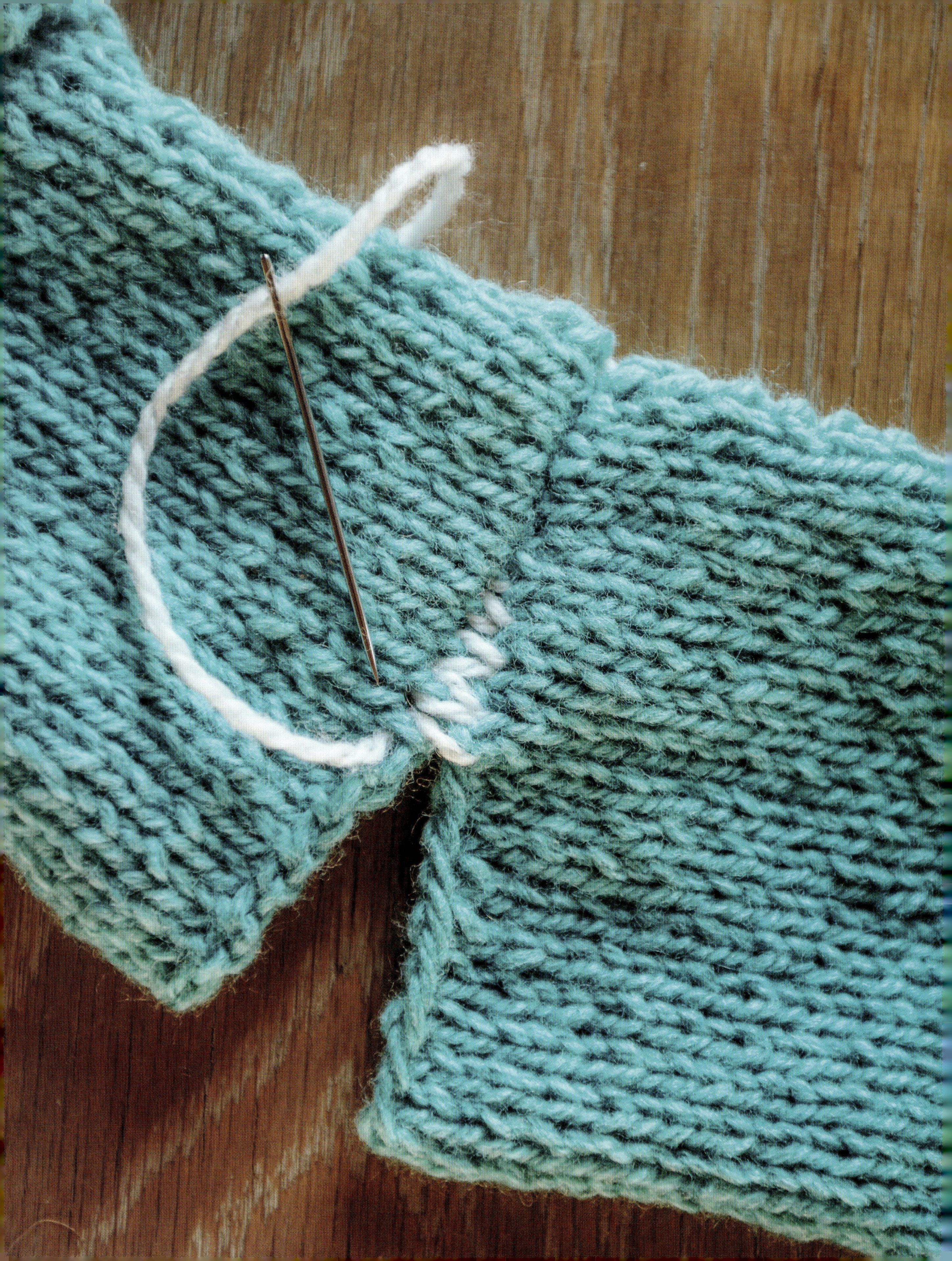

Stitches

◀ *Mattress Stitch*
Used in the assembly of sweaters. Insert the needle down into the bottom stitch on one piece and up into the next stitch. Then, move over to the other piece and insert the needle down into the bottom stitch and up into the next. Go back to the first piece and insert the needle down into the same stitch you just came up from, then up into the next stitch. Move over to the other piece and insert the needle down into the same stitch you just came up from, then up again into the next stitch. Continue this way, going back and forth from one piece to the other and advancing one stitch at a time on each side.

Whipstitch ▶
Whipstitches are another way to sew two pieces together. Place the pieces edge to edge. Work from right to left, stitch by stitch. The needle is inserted from the same side each time. You can choose to sew into both or one of the bars of each stitch. Be consistent with your choice.

Insert the needle down through the stitch on the piece closest to you. Come up through the corresponding stitch on the other piece. Bring the needle back over both pieces and insert the needle down into the next stitch on the first piece. Continue into the corresponding stitch on the second piece. Imagine that you are encircling the stitches along the way. Continue this way until all the stitches are sewn together.

Grafting

HOW TO GRAFT STITCHES TOGETHER INVISIBLY:
Place the stitches from each piece on a separate knitting needle and hold them together so both needles point in the same direction. Thread your sewing yarn on a blunt tapestry needle.

Make sure the needle tips are pointing to the right. When grafting the pieces together, do not turn the work; keep it in the same position, with the same needle closest to you. You will work from right to left.

> I'll refer to needle 1 and needle 2, where needle 1 is closest to you, and needle 2 is farthest from you.

Begin by inserting the tapestry needle into the first stitch on needle 1 as if to purl. Bring the yarn under the needle and to the first stitch on needle 2. Insert the needle into the stitch as if to knit. Pull the yarn through the stitch.

From here, repeat these 4 steps:

Step 1: Insert the needle into the first stitch on needle 1 as if to knit. Slip the stitch off the needle.

Step 2: Insert the needle into the next stitch on needle 1 as if to purl. Leave the stitch on the needle.

Step 3: Insert the needle into the first stitch on needle 2 as if to purl. Slip the stitch off the needle.

Step 4: Insert the needle into the next stitch on needle 2 as if to knit. Leave the stitch on the needle.

Repeat steps 1–4 until all stitches have been slipped off the needles. Be careful not to tighten the grafted stitches too much. They should ideally be the same size as the knitted stitches. The grafted stitches form a new row of stitches and create a seamless transition.

Blanket stitches are used to create a nice finish along an edge or around buttonholes. In this book, the blanket stitches are used to finish the edges of the Felted Insoles (page 155). To anchor the thread invisibly, start by sewing the thread into the sole itself so that the end is hidden in the felt, then bring the needle out where you want to start. You choose how close to the edge and how far apart each stitch should be; we recommend ¼" from the edge and about ¼" between each stitch.

Insert the needle into the piece from bottom to top. Pull the thread almost all the way through. The thread will now form a loop, and you will *pass the needle through this loop from right to left. Tighten so the thread lies snugly along the edge. Next, insert the needle down into the piece where you want the next stitch, from the top down. Pull the thread almost all the way through and repeat the steps above from *. Continue this way, all the way around the edge.

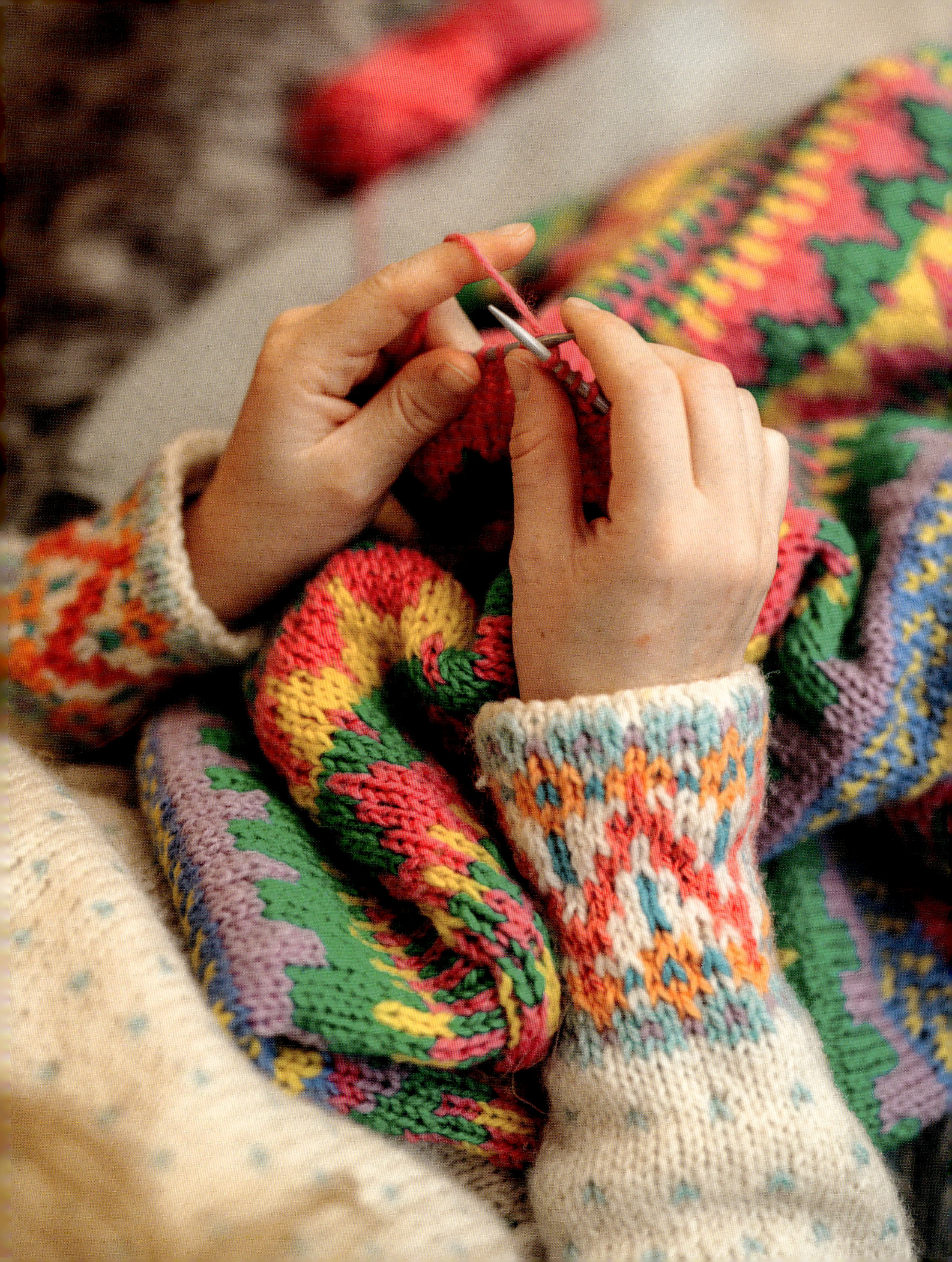

Decreasing Technique

Slip, Slip, Knit (SSK)

When you are decreasing a stitch, the technique you use will determine whether the decrease leans left or right. Knitting 2 stitches together will create a right-leaning decrease. If you want the decrease to lean left, you can use techniques like "knit two together through the back loop." In this book, we use a left-leaning decrease called "slip, slip, knit" (SSK). We think it looks especially nice.

Here's how to do slip, slip, knit: Slip the first stitch to the needle as if to knit, and do the same with the next stitch. Insert the left needle back into the front of these two stitches on the right needle, positioning the needle as if to knit through the back loop. Knit the two stitches together through the back loop.

Bind-Off Technique

Binding off is usually done from the right side. You knit the first two stitches, then, using your left needle, lift the second stitch on the right needle up and over the stitch that you've just knit. One stitch is bound off. Repeat this, knitting one stitch then binding off one stitch until all stitches are bound off. When a pattern just tells you to bind off all stitches, this is the method to use.

Assembling

Steeks

Some of the sweater patterns in this book require cutting steeks for armholes. Here's how to do it by first sewing with a machine and then, cutting the steek.

In these patterns, you'll cast on five extra stitches on each side of the sweater for the armholes. The center stitch column of this group of five is where you'll cut to create the armhole. Start by marking where you will sew. Do this by hand sewing a basting thread on each side of the center column of stitches from the top of the sweater down to where you cast on the new stitches. You'll recognize this spot by a small gap in the sweater. Aim for about ¼–1" between the basting thread marks. You can also use pins as markers.

Sew inside your marked lines. Sew two to three seams back and forth, alternating between one straight stitch seam and two zigzag seams. Make sure the stitching extends the full length of the steek stitches.

After sewing on both sides of the center column of stitches, you only need to cut open the armhole between the two lines of machine stitching. Use sharp scissors and take care not to cut into the machine stitching. If there's too much fabric between the machine stitching and the cut edge, trim it down with scissors to prevent a bulky seam. Aim to leave about ¼–½" of fabric beyond the patterned knitting.

The next step is to sew the shoulders together (see page 169) and then sew in the sleeves.

Sewing in Sleeves

1. Start by turning the body inside out, so the wrong side is facing out, while the sleeve remains right side out. Insert the sleeve into the sweater, with the right side of the sleeve facing the right side of the sweater.

2. Position the sleeve so it's aligned correctly, with the underside of the sleeve matching the underside of the armhole. This is at the start of the round on the sleeve and where you divided for the front and back sections on the body, or where you cast on steek stitches for the sweater.

3. Now you will sew the outer edge of the sleeve to the outer stitches around the armhole of the sweater. If you've sewn and steeked, sew between the last column of pattern stitches and the first column of steek stitches. Use your main color and stitch around using mattress stitches (see page 169).

> **Note:**
> You'll likely need to skip some stitches here and there, either on the sleeve or the sweater body, to fine-tune the fit. Even with careful stitching, there may be a slight difference in the width of the sleeve versus the width of the armhole.

Size Guide

How to read the sizes in the patterns:

Size: Each pattern indicates the size of the garment. This is the actual size of the finished garment, if your knitting matches the gauge specified in the pattern.

Ease: Each garment has an indicated ease. This is how many inches/centimeters larger than your actual body measurements the sweater is intended to be. In this book, all the sweaters are designed to be worn with positive ease, meaning they are larger than your actual body measurements.

Example: The Blossom sweater has approximately 6" of ease. Your bust measurement is 37½". Add 6" to your measurement. 37½" + 6" = 43½". Size Small is 43½" so this is the size that would give you a fit similar to what you see in the photographs. You can, of course, choose to knit a smaller or larger size to produce a tighter or looser fit, according to your preference.

How to take your own measurements:

Bust: Measure around the fullest part of your torso, often around the chest or stomach.

Total Length: Measure from the middle of the back of your neck down to where you want the sweater to end.

Sleeve Length: Measure from the middle of your underarm down to where you want the sleeve to end on your wrist.

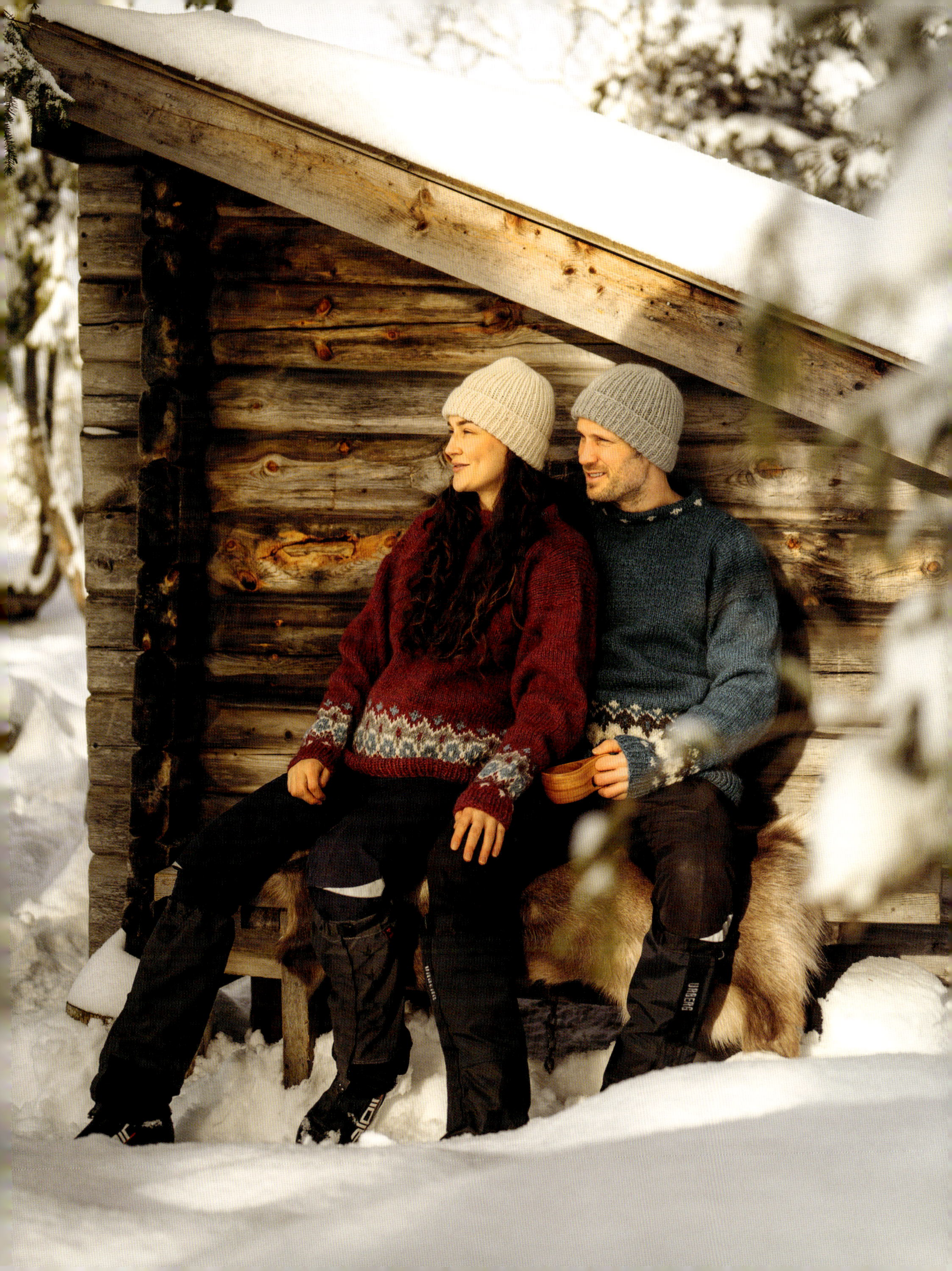

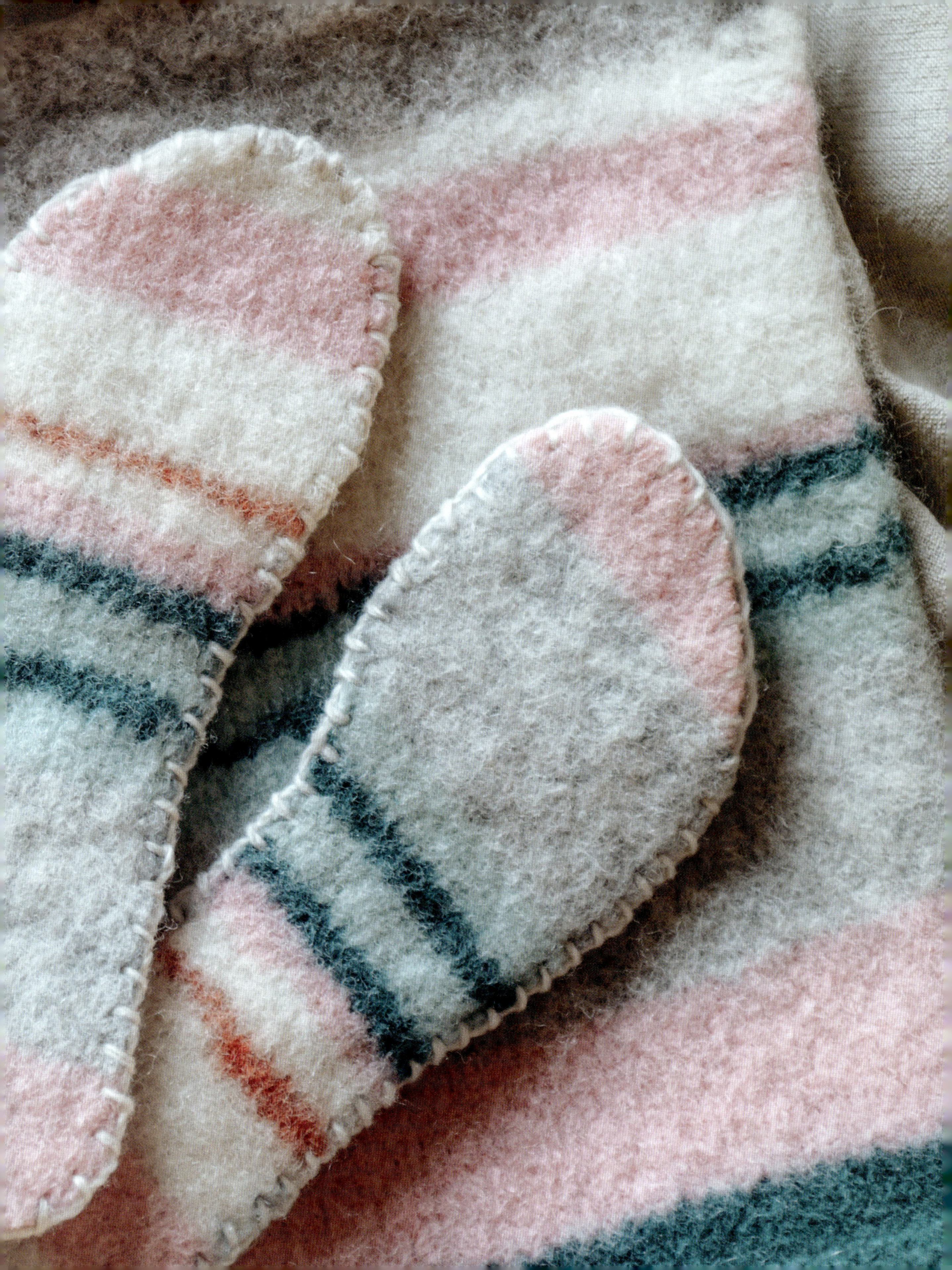

Felting Guide

Felting is genius because it creates robust, warm garments that are more water- and wind-resistant than regular knits, making them perfect for outdoor use.

Many find felting a bit unpredictable because they have less control over the outcome when felting in the washing machine. No two machines are alike, so it's important to get to know how your machine behaves with felting. If you felt by hand, you have more control over the final result. A good approach is to felt carefully over several cycles in the washing machine rather than starting with high temperatures or too much agitation.

Here's an introduction to felting to help make the process feel safer.

How Felting Happens

- Felting occurs when the wool is wet and in motion, ideally between warm (90° F) and hot (130°F).
- The more agitation there is, the more the fabric will felt.
- High spin speeds result in less movement of the garment, as it remains relatively stationary even though the drum is spinning at high speed.
- Soap encourages the felting process, as well as cleaning the wool.
- There are three ways to felt: by hand, in a dryer, or in a washing machine.

Felting By Hand

- Get a basin or something you can fill with water.
- Fill it with enough warm water to soak the garment and add a good amount of mild dish soap. The soap helps the water permeate the wool.
- Soak the knitted piece and rub away. You can either use your hands or rub the fabric against a surface. You'll notice the texture gradually changing, with the fabric becoming firmer as you continue to rub. Take care to felt all parts of the garment evenly.
- When you're happy with the felting, rinse the garment thoroughly to remove all soap.
- Shape the garment as desired and let it dry flat, ideally on a towel in a warm place.

Felting in the Washing Machine

- Place the garment in the washing machine with other items, such as a towel or old jeans, to create movement and friction that aids felting.

- The fuller the machine, the more movement, and the more the garment will felt.

- You can felt without soap, or you can use a wool-safe detergent. Don't use dishwashing soap, which can be harsh on the machine and isn't necessary for machine felting.

- Set the water temperature to HOT.

- The choice of washing cycle depends on how heavily you want to felt your garment. You need to get to know your machine, as machines felt differently. I recommend starting with a test swatch first. Alternatively, starting with a sitting pad (page 110) can be helpful, as it doesn't need to be perfect in size.

- In general, follow the instructions in your knitting pattern. If in doubt, start with a short cycle, and gradually increase the duration and intensity if needed.

After Machine Felting

If the garment is perfect:
Hooray! Shape it as desired and let it dry flat.

If the garment is too big:
There are several things you can do.

- You can run it through another machine cycle, with either the same or at a longer/stronger setting.

- You can felt it further in the dryer (see explanation on the right).

- You can continue felting by hand if only a little more shrinkage is needed.

If the garment is too small:
This is the biggest fear with felting, because it might be impossible to reverse. However, there are some things you can try.

- Stretch and pull the garment while it's still wet. You can usually stretch and shape it a bit before the felt dries.

- Soak it in a basin with water and a generous dollop of hair conditioner. Stretch it gently.

- Try Unshrink It (a product available in some yarn shops and online).

- If the options above don't work: Accept that this battle is lost.

If your adult sweater now fits a 5-year-old, unfortunately, there isn't much you can do.

Felting in the Dryer

Felting in the dryer is similar to machine felting but with even more control.

- Soak the knitted piece thoroughly.

- Place it in the dryer, ideally with a wet towel or pair of jeans to increase friction.

- Set the drying program. You can stop the cycle whenever you wish to check the progress, giving you excellent control over the felting process. At first, check frequently to monitor the change.

- When you are satisfied with the felting, remove the garment from the dryer, shape it as desired, and let it finish drying flat, ideally on a towel in a warm place.

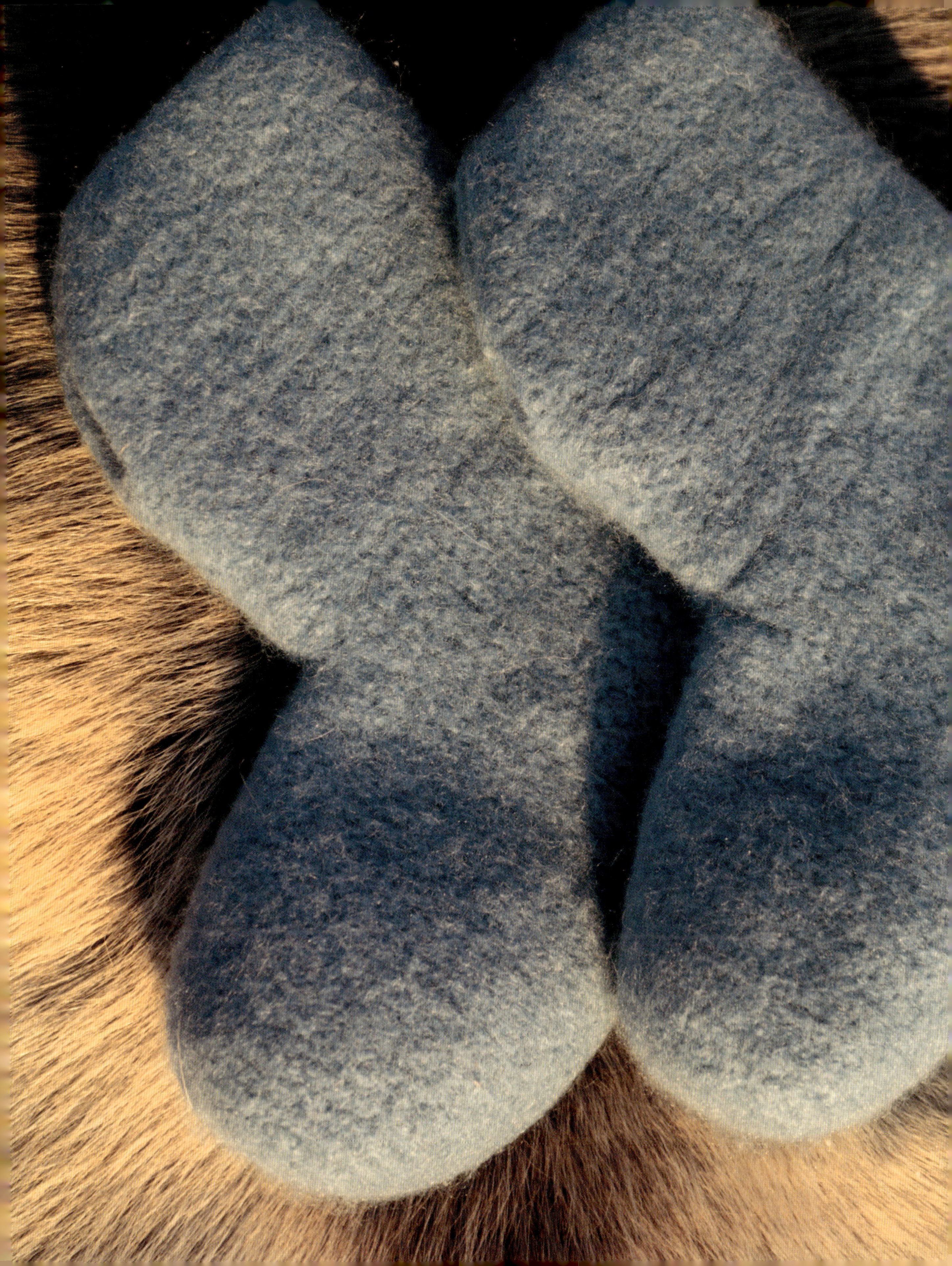

Washing and Maintenance

Washing

Wool doesn't need frequent washing. Often, simply airing it out or placing it in snow during winter is enough to remove any odors. Overwashing can shorten the life of the garment. However, if you do want to give your garment a wash, follow these steps:

MACHINE WASHING

Follow the washing instructions for the yarn used. If it indicates hand washing, you can still wash it in the machine if you have a handwash cycle. This is not the same as a wool cycle, which is often harsher and can felt the garment. It's important to be comfortable with your machine's cycle settings before washing your favorite sweater this way. Ideally, trying washing a sample swatch first.

If your yarn label specifies machine washing, follow the instructions for water temperature and cycle duration/intensity.

You can also wash the sweater by hand, then use the spin cycle of your machine to effectively remove excess water. Set the spin speed to maximum so that the garment remains still in the spinning drum.

Dry the garment flat. Hanging it while wet will cause it to stretch and lose its shape.

HAND WASHING

Soak the garment in cold water with wool-safe soap. Handle it gently while rubbing out any stains. The more you rub the wool, the greater the chance of felting. Be sure to rinse out all soap residue.

Press out excess water between two towels. Dry the garment flat.

Tip:
Before I wear my knitted sweaters, I soak the garment well in cold water, then run it through a high-speed spin cycle and dry it flat. This makes the wool softer.

Maintenance

- If you take good care of your knitted garment, you will be rewarded with a piece that can last for many years, even for generations. Air it out regularly and remove stains as described on the previous page.

- If the garment develops a hole, I encourage you to give it some extra love and attention. That way, your favorite sweater can stay with you for a few more years.

- For small holes, use a needle and thread to mend the hole. Be sure to secure any loose threads so they don't unravel further.

- For larger holes, you can either knit a patch with the same or similar yarn and sew it over the hole, or you can pick up stitches around the hole and knit a piece to cover it. You can also purchase ready-made patches to sew over the hole. Just make sure to secure any loose threads to prevent further unraveling.

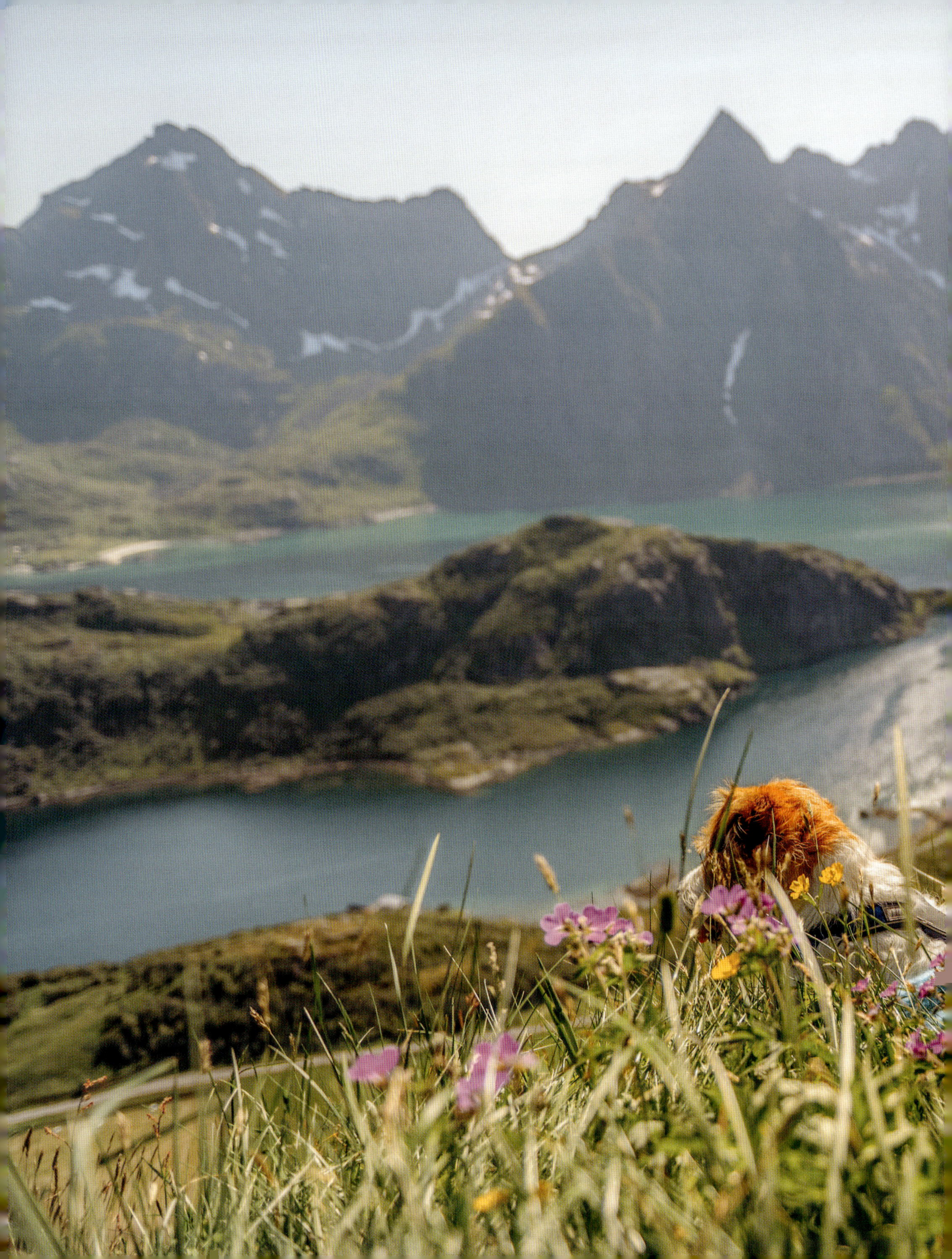

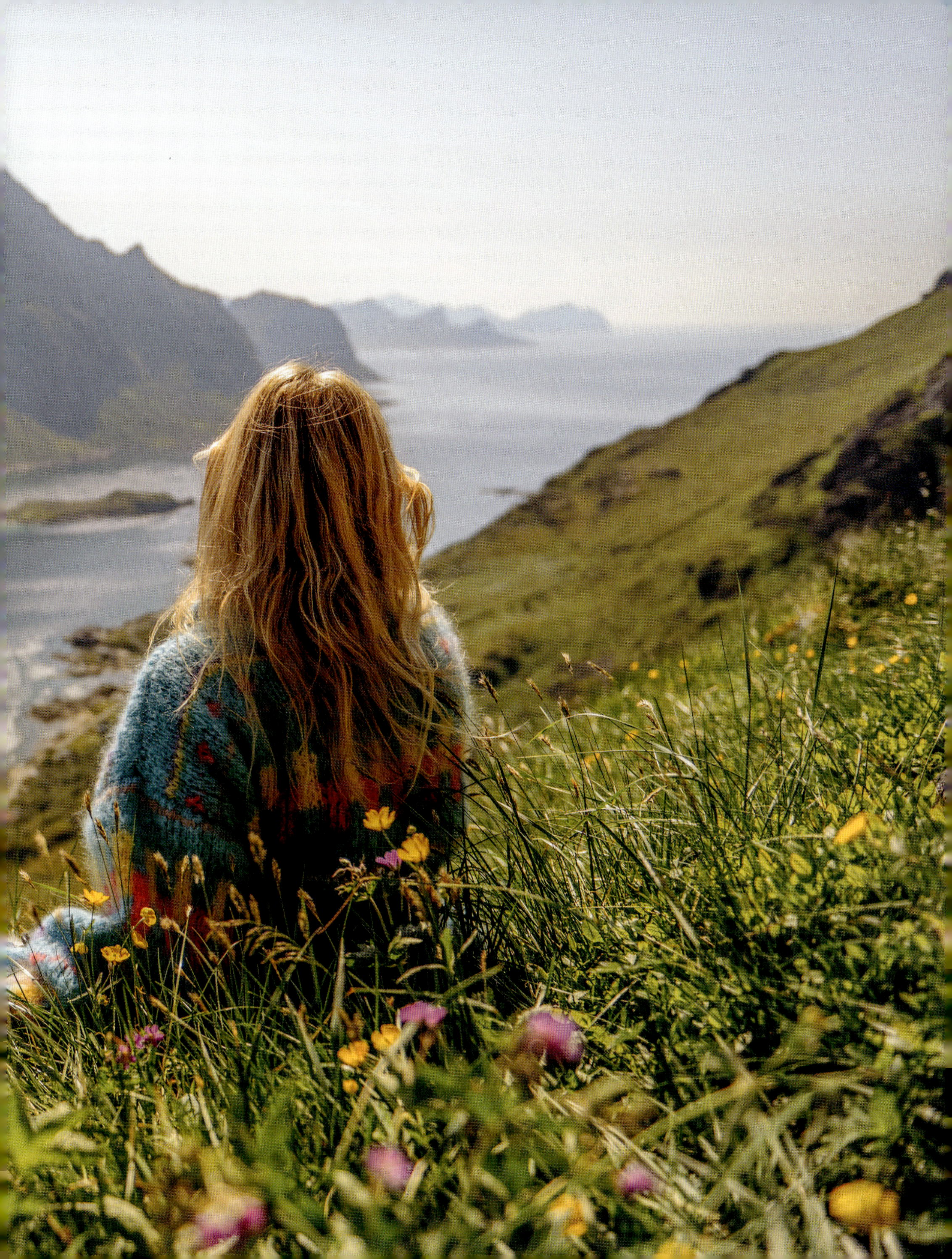

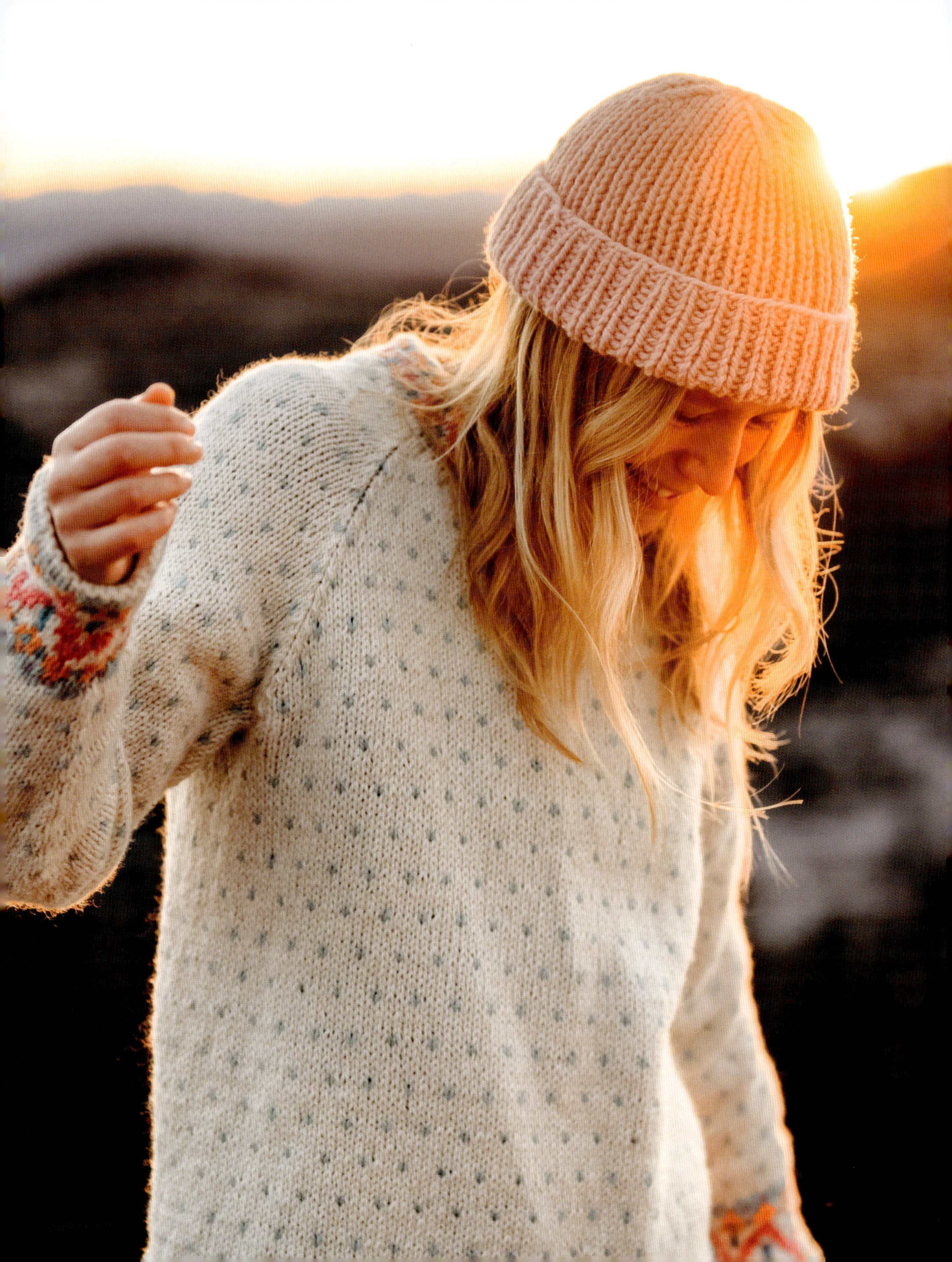

Afterword

Thank you so very much for joining me on my journey through this book. I hope you're inspired to be kind to yourself and to do things that bring you satisfaction and joy, despite life's ups and downs. I also hope you've been encouraged to explore nature more, preferably in handmade outdoor knitwear in wonderful colors that energize you and keep you warm.

For me, knitting has been essential on my mentally gray days. It has given me a sense of accomplishment and joy, even when my body hasn't been cooperating. It's truly yarn therapy that lets me deepen my love for the outdoors and gives me a creative breather in daily life.

Finally, I'd like to share a message I posted on Instagram, which I think captures my journey and what I've learned . . .

A little reminder for you who need it today:

You are allowed to put yourself first.

You are allowed to spend the day on the couch if you need it.

You are allowed to say no.

You are allowed to do nothing.

You are allowed to take a break from everything.

You don't have to be so extremely perfect.

But you must take care of yourself. You are the most important person in your life.
If you don't take care of yourself, you can't take care of others either.

So, log off. Breathe out. Do what you need to do.

Prioritize yourself.

I'm cheering you on. Feel free to send me a message or tag me on Instagram with your knitting journey or the pieces you create, if you'd like to share.

Une Cecilie

Acknowledgments

Stine, thank you for throwing yourself wholeheartedly into this enormous project we've been working on together over the past couple of years. I am endlessly impressed by everything you've managed to accomplish: two small children, a job, your own business, home, and this book project. Thank you for being such a steady pillar when I am a creative whirlwind. I've lost count of how many ideas, thoughts, and pattern charts I've sent your way, so that you could calculate and create patterns that bring my creative designs to life as real garments. This would never have been possible without you, and I am so grateful and proud of you.

Harald, thank you for your unwavering support and presence. For all the trips over the past year and the countless photo shoots around the country, capturing beautiful moments for the book, day and night. I am so grateful that you, my favorite photographer and dear partner, were willing to take the photos for the book. They turned out beautiful, and the book would never have been this good without you.

To Grandma Margot, Grandma Randi, and Great-grandma Hallfrid, who taught both Stine and me to knit in the 1990s. I am so thankful to have grown up with a great-grandmother and grandmothers who showed us the value of craftsmanship and inspired us to carry on the tradition in our lives.

Thank you, Agathe, for believing in me and wanting to support my book project. I would never have dared to self-publish my patterns if I hadn't had you by my side.

To Hanne, for having fun with the book design and creating the knitting book I've always dreamed of!

Thank you so much to Turi, Thov, Iven, and Harald for being so kind and volunteering as wonderful models for the book. It has been a joy to take photos with you, and I am so grateful to have such great friends in my life.

Thank you to everyone who helped knit the samples! Without you, I could never have completed this project: my mom Hanne Iren Stenstvedt Lian, Aunt Eva Rita von Werden, Maren Stenstvedt Koren, Aunt Vigdis Stenstvedt Meisler, Frida Haugum, Eirin Engan Tronsmo, Marnie Vikan, Randi Sandnes Holum, Grete Holden, Eva Kristin Hannasvik, and Miriam Rosøy Wathne.

To everyone following me on @unececilie. To those who have always supported, cheered, and spread love, and who continue to do so. It's hard to find a better group of people.

Index

A
anxiety, 8, 15, 23, 24, 31, 100
armholes, cutting steeks for, 174
assembling, 174-75

B
Balaclava, Bitter Cold, 83, 84-89
bind-off technique, 173
Bitter Cold Collection, 83
    Bitter Cold Balaclava, 83, 84-89
    Bitter Cold Headband, 83, 91, 94-95
    Bitter Cold Mittens, 83, 96-97
    Bitter Cold Neck Warmer, 83, 91, 92-93
blanket stitches, 171
Blossom Sweater, 23-29
Bulky-Weight Scrap Sweater, 144-49

C
childhood memories, 15, 59, 74
Chronic Fatigue Syndrome (CFS), 113-14, 123
colorwork tips, 167

D
decreasing technique, 173

F
Felted Insoles, 155-57
felted projects, 91
    Bitter Cold Balaclava, 84-89
    Bitter Cold Headband, 94-95
    Bitter Cold Mittens, 96-97
    Bitter Cold Neck Warmer, 92-93
    Felted Insoles, 155-57
    Frostbite Mittens, 41-43
    Lofoten Folk Sitting Pad, 110-11
    Sleeping Bag Slippers, 44-47
felting guide, 11, 179-80
felting prevention, 182
Frostbite Mittens, 41-43
Frostbite Sweater, 31-39

G
garment care, 11, 182-83
gauge, 11, 164-65
grafting, 170

H
hand washing, 182
Hat, Huv, 150-53
Headband, Bitter Cold, 83, 91, 94-95
hole repair, 183
Huv Hat, 150-53

I
Insoles, Felted, 155-57

K
knitting
    resources on, 7, 8
    as therapy, 8, 187

L
leftover yarn, 11, 135. *See also* zero-waste projects
Leif Sweater, 113-21
Lofoten Folk Sitting Pad, 110-11
Lofoten Folk Sweater, 99-109
Lucie Oversized Sweater, 48-57

M
machine washing, 182
Maddis Sweater, 74-81
maintenance, 183
mattress stitch, 168, 169
measurements, taking your own, 176
mental health, 7, 8, 15, 23, 24
mittens
    Bitter Cold Mittens, 83, 96-97
    Frostbite Mittens, 41-43
    Mountain Mittens, 69-73
Mountain Mittens, 69-73
Mountain Sweater, 59-67

N
nature
    mental health benefits of, 7, 8, 24, 31
    traveling to experience, 99-100
neck warmers
    Bitter Cold Neck Warmer, 83, 91, 92-93
    felted, 83
    Neck Warmer (from leftover yarn), 158, 159

O
outdoor clothing, 7, 8, 187
    patterns for, 11, 13
outdoor living
    adjusting to, 31, 44
    benefits of, 7, 31, 44
    camper van for, 112, 114, 120, 123
    camping gear for, 48

P
patterns, 11, 13
    reading sizes in, 176

R
Reading Socks, 131–33

S
scrap sweaters, 137
    Bulky-Weight Scrap Sweater, 144–49
    Worsted-Weight Scrap Sweater, 138–43
self-care reminder, 187
sibling relationships, 59, 74
Sitting Pad, Lofoten Folk, 110–11
size guide, 176
Sleeping Bag Slippers, 44–47
sleeves, sewing in, 175
slip, slip, knit (SSK), 173
Slippers, Sleeping Bag, 44–47
Socks, Reading, 131–33
steeks, 174
stitches
    blanket, 171
    decreasing, 173
    grafting, 170
    mattress, 168, 169
    whipstitch, 169
sweaters
    Blossom Sweater, 23–29
    Frostbite Sweater, 31–39
    Leif Sweater, 113–21
    Lofoten Folk Sweater, 99–109
    Lucie Oversized Sweater, 48–57
    Maddis Sweater, 74–81
    Mountain Sweater, 59–67
    Une Sweater, 123–29
    Yrjar Sweater, 15–21

T
techniques, 11, 163
    assembling, 174–75
    bind-off, 173
    blanket stitches, 171
    colorwork tips, 167
    decreasing, 173
    felting, 179–80
    gauge, 11, 164–65
    grafting, 170
    maintenance, 183
    mattress stitch, 168, 169
    for sizing, 176
    washing, 182
    whipstitch, 169

U
Une Sweater, 123–29

W
washing guidelines, 182
whipstitch, 169
Worsted-Weight Scrap Sweater, 138–43

Y
yarn remnants, 11, 135. *See also* zero-waste projects
Yrjar Sweater, 15–21

Z
zero-waste projects, 11, 135
    Bulky-Weight Scrap Sweater, 137, 145–49
    Felted Insoles, 155–57
    Frostbite Mittens, 40–43
    Huv Hat, 151–53
    Neck Warmer, 159
    Worsted-Weight Scrap Sweater, 137, 138–43